MOTHER TERESA

By the same author

Enid Bagnold: A Biography
Laura Ashley: A Life by Design
Battling for News: The Rise of the Woman Reporter

(For children)
Mother Teresa
Margot Fonteyn

MOTHER TERESA

BEYOND THE IMAGE

Anne Sebba

Weidenfeld & Nicolson
LONDON

First published in Great Britain in 1997
by Weidenfeld & Nicolson

© 1997 Anne Sebba

The moral right of Anne Sebba to be identified as the author of this work has been
asserted in accordance with the Copyright, Designs and Patents Act of 1988

A CIP catalogue record for this book is available from the British Library.

ISBN 0 297 81677 2

Typeset by Selwood Systems, Midsomer Norton

Printed in Great Britain by
Butler & Tanner Ltd, Frome and London

Weidenfeld & Nicolson

The Orion Publishing Group Ltd
Orion House
5 Upper Saint Martin's Lane
London, WC2H 9EA

ACKNOWLEDGEMENTS

There are many people across a broad spectrum who have made this book possible. Unfortunately, I cannot thank them all individually as some agreed to talk to me about Mother Teresa only on the basis of anonymity. I am grateful to everyone who took the time and trouble to share with me their experiences or thoughts, in particular:

Lesley Abdela, Pedro López Aguirrebengoa, Spanish Ambassador to the Holy See, Pjeter Arbnori, Speaker of the Albanian Parliament, G. V. Ashtekar, Nermin Basha, Director of the National Library of Albania, Radha Basu, Lord Bauer, Professor David and Mrs Angela Baum, Nicola Beauman, Marcelle Bernstein, Rev. Andrew de Berry, Neeta Bhandari, Dr Manorama Bhargava, Professor of Haematology, All India Institute of Medical Sciences, Tushar Bhattacharya, Oxfam, India, Rose Billington, Dr Vincenzo Bilotta, Rita Birma, Dr R. C. Biswas, Lionel Bloch, Vania del Borgo, Tom Bower, Jill Braithwaite, Sister Theresa Brittain, Alex Brummer, Bruce Buck, Helen Bullough, Gilly Burn, Sister Lavinia Byrne, Euan Cameron, Dr Penny Carson, The Catholic Media Office, Ruth Cathy, Peter Chafer, Dr Aroup Chatterjee, Aruna and Anjit Chatterjee, Miss S. Chatterjee, Principal, La Martiniere School for Girls, Calcutta, Nirad Chaudhuri, Navin Chawla, Anne Chisholm, Dr Nicholas Cohen, Tim Cook, Mary Cox, Des Cryan, Sister Maureen Cusick, Christopher Cviic, Chdananda Dasgupta, Monimoy Dasgupta, Rajeshree Dasgupta, Alan Davidson, Bejtullah Destani, Maheshewata Devi, Msgr Ivan Dias, Sister Frances Dominica, David and Carol Donnelly, Karla Ehrlich, Glyn Evans, Sister Elizabeth Farmer and the Community of the Little Company of Mary, Patricia Fernandes, Julian Filochowski, Dr Gillian Ford, Dr Robin Fox, Alexander Frater, Sir David Frost, Jean Gaffin, Gopal Gandhi, Marina Gandhi, Dharani Ghosh, Shobana Ghosh, Zerbanoo Gifford, Sister Ann Giles, Besnick Gjunkshi, my guide in Albania, Rumer Godden, Dr Germaine Greer, the Late Rabbi Hugo Gryn, Bunny Gupta, Shmuel Hadas, Israeli Ambassador to the Holy See, Paul Handley,

Marianne Haslegrave, Director, Commonwealth Medical Association, Himangshu Hazra, Vivianne Hewitt, Father Tedi Hochstatter, John Hodgeson, Beth Holgate, Joe Human, Rev. Oliver Hunkin, Fay Hutchinson, Msgr Jesus Irigoyen SJ, Peter James, Pat Jones, Ilir Kadija, Dr Sujit and Mona Kar, Sister Christina Kenworthy-Brown, Dr Sunil Khilnani, Glen and Linda Kielty, Ann King-Hall, Father Peter Knott SJ, Sunita and Naresh Kumar, Ravindra Kumar, Lee Langley, Sandra Lawrence, James Leek, Christine Leonard, Swami Lokeswaranandaji, Justine Long, Clifford Longley, Mary Loudon, Sean-Patrick Lovett, Norman Mackenzie, Nandini Madan, Ashok and Jessica Mahadevan, Diptosh Majumdar, Luan Malltezi, Director of the National Archive of Albania, Professor Peter Marshall, Milton McCann, Flora McDonnell, Frances Meigh, Ian Middleton, Senior Researcher, Reuters Library, Msgr Rok Mirdita, Aloka Mitra, Kate Moberley, Rekha Mody, Geoffrey Moorhouse, Colin Morris, Dr Biral Mullick, Meher Murshed, Bishop Vincent Nichols, Louise Nicholson, Nevile Nika, Head of Central Archives, Albania, Rosemary Noble, Michael Norton, Salome Parikh, Lord and Lady Paul, Primrose Peacock, James Pettifer, Padre Pittau, Marco Politi, Genc Pollo, The Poor Clare Community, Arundel, David Porter, Dr Jack Preger, Phil Pulella, Pavli Qesqu, Albanian Ambassador to the Court of St James's, Daphne Rae, Dr Kanti and Mrs Susan Rai, Usha Devi Rathore, Charles Raw, Peter Rawlins, Ashis Ray, Chris Oram Rayson, Peter Rennie, Jim Richards, Roger Riddell, Sister Gabriel Robin, Andrew Robinson, Msgr Franc Rode, Mrs Arax Roy, Lady Ryder of Warsaw, Sathya Saran, Dame Cicely Saunders, Frances Scott, Martin E. Segal, Rev. Noel Sen, Sister Margaret Shepherd and the Community of the Sisters of Sion, Msgr Milan Simcic, Nina Singh, Patwant Singh, Dr L. M. Singhvi, Indian Ambassador to the Court of St James's, Major and Mrs E. Somerset, Father Moreno de Souza SJ, Dr Teotonio de Souza, Kathryn Spink, Peter Stanford, Charles Stern, Sir Sigmund Sternberg, Professor Anthony Storr, David Sumberg, Nina Talukdar, Neil Taylor, Mrs Sudha Tewari, Trevor Thomas, Wendy Thomas, Gillian Tindall, Ihsan Toptani, Mark Tully, Paul Turley, Miranda Vickers, Mrs Avabai B. Wadia, President, Family Planning Association of India, Richard Walker, British Council, Delhi, Maureen Wallis, Desmond Wilcox, Edith Wilkins, David Willey, Meher Wilshaw, Mark Wood, Editor in Chief, Reuters, Isa Zymberi.

I must also thank Mother Teresa and the many Missionaries of Charity in several countries whom I have spoken to or watched at work. Both Ion Trewin and Rebecca Wilson at Weidenfeld & Nicolson, whose enthusiasm for this book has been unflagging, deserve a special thank-you as does Sandra Lawrence, who came with me to Calcutta, Dipankar Chakravarty, senior correspondent at Anandabazar Patrika, Gill Coleridge my friend and agent, and all my family for their love and much needed support over three years. In particular, I want to thank Rosalie Sebba for her vigilance in recording programmes as well as other grandmotherly duties, and my husband Mark for his constant encouragement and practical help in myriad ways.

Anne Sebba
London 1997

For Amy

CONTENTS

PREFACE

As you fly into Calcutta today, city of twelve million and growing, you are welcomed by a giant hoarding which announces this as the city of Tagore the poet, Ray the film maker and Teresa the nun. Extraordinary as it may seem, she has become a tourist attraction. Of the three, it is Teresa who is the best known internationally and it is she who has made Calcutta famous anew in the West. That the hoarding is sponsored by the United Bank of India should surprise no one; just one more contradiction in a truly fantastic story.

If the drama of the world is its paradoxical nature, nobody exemplifies this better than Mother Teresa, the diminutive, wrinkled nun of Albanian parentage. Universally praised for her humility and devotion, she is also adept at dealing with world leaders and financiers and has a canny instinct for publicity. How easily can these two aspects coexist in one person? The West has responded to her social work but what she is about is religion, specifically Jesus Christ, and this fact, so often overlooked, means that there is misunderstanding at the very core of her success. The work is not the vocation, Mother Teresa says over and over again, prayer is the vocation. At the same time, Mother Teresa is a skilled exponent of many late-twentieth-century marketing techniques from the brand management of her blue-bordered, white saris to the soundbite quotes she utters. And she is not afraid to negotiate; her sisters are taught how to bargain with travel agents before they learn any theological intricacies.

There are few living saints in our increasingly materialistic age yet Mother Teresa, as champion of the world's poor, has until recently been universally acclaimed as a rare example. She is, so transparently, someone who eschews the values of our age where success in life is measured by the number of trappings acquired and in so doing she offers us hope that spirituality, not materialism, will triumph; hope that there are higher standards we can aspire to; and hope that maybe one day all the children in the world will be fed.

Since 1990, however, the mood has been changing. In that year, following a near fatal heart attack, she tendered her resignation as leader of the Order, the Missionaries of Charity, that she founded forty years previously. But her sisters were unable to elect a successor. In spite of continuing ill health, she remained in charge, prompting criticisms that her Congregation is undemocratic, that she had failed to groom a strong candidate to take over and that she was being retained as a figurehead to ensure the continued flow of large donations.

The fiercest attack came in November 1994 from a Washington-based English journalist, Christopher Hitchens, in a television polemic that dubbed her 'Hell's Angel'. He accused her of personal hypocrisy, consorting with dictators, administering dubious medical treatment, courting the media and – perhaps most serious of all – blindly objecting to all forms of family planning. Abandoned babies and the terminally ill, society's most vulnerable and helpless, were there, he said, to supply the occasions for charity and the raw material for demonstrations of compassion in India. Hitchens later defended himself against the charge of bias by admitting that the programme set out to grab people's attention. He had, he said, just twenty-five minutes to set against twenty years of drenching sycophantic publicity. Mother Teresa was, he asserted, the least criticised human being on earth. He and the programme-makers could hardly have been surprised by the furious reaction to the programme and the vituperative nature of the criticism – some of it hitting far harder and wilder than that of the actual programme. The subsequent fall-out in the Indian and British media has rumbled on ever since as others joined in both the attack and the defence.

The unsympathetic television portrayal of Mother Teresa as a cantankerous harridan with a fondness for dictators may represent an extreme view, but the controversy it sparked also revealed that there is a growing body of moderate opinion which believes that uncritical defensiveness on the part of the Catholic hierarchy does Mother Teresa's cause no good. The subsequent debate is a clear indication that there is a demand for a study which, at the very least, is not afraid to give Mother Teresa's genuine spiritual imperatives a political, social and historical dimension. Surely this enhances rather than diminishes her considerable achievements?

As an article in the New York Times put it:

Although reviewing programmes that have little prospect of being shown in the United States does not ordinarily seem useful, *Hell's Angel* invites attention because there is so little prospect. In a season of complaints about the adversarial tendencies and the anti-religious slant of television it is still difficult to imagine an American network or cable station going after so esteemed a religious personage. If anybody is a television untouchable it is Mother Teresa.

Mr Hitchens' phrasings may be a touch sharp for a mass audience and he could be picking on Mother Teresa simply because he doesn't like her politics and her Church. All the more reason, now that such charges have been aired, for sending a crew to Calcutta to see whether he failed to give credit where it is due. How good or bad is the care? Where does the Mother Teresa Multinational obtain its money and on what is it spent? It could turn out that despite Mr Hitchens' animadversions the lady is a saint.[1]

I am no film crew, nor am I prepared to act as arbiter or referee. But I am full of questions and have put as many of these as I can to people qualified to answer them, including doctors, nuns, heads of charities, volunteers and former Missionaries of Charity. No synthesis is possible of such an enormous variety of views. But whatever else she may or may not have done she has inspired thousands of people from many backgrounds to see what difference they can make to the world and has provoked many others into examining their consciences, or at least discussing what ought to be done. I believe that it is almost always healthy to question and I hope this book will be read as a dialogue with as wide a range of experts as possible.

What follows is not a traditional biography. There are few facts known about her early life, her immediate family is dead – her brother died in July 1981 at the age of seventy-four – and such few records as might have shed some light on dates or facts were probably destroyed along with her childhood house in the Skopje earthquake of 1963. Biographically speaking, Mother Teresa's life is not interesting; there is the same straightforward religious faith that guides her in everything, and a list of awards won goes nowhere towards explaining either the inner motivation of my subject or the response of the rest of the world. Mother Teresa, it appears, has suffered from none of the inner conflict that give the best biographies their dramatic tension. Malcolm

Muggeridge went so far as to say that her life is biographically a non-event because 'to live for and in others, as she and the sisters of the Missionaries of Charity do, is to eliminate happenings which are a factor of the ego and the will. "Yet not I but Christ liveth in me," is one of her favourite sayings.'² Muggeridge may have made her name with his film and subsequent book, *Something Beautiful for God*, but he also set in train the criticism; she is not the saviour of humanity, what she does is symbolic.

In the first half of the book I have tried to tell her story chronologically, looking at how the phenomenon developed and why in 1947, at the time of Partition, when the two newly independent countries of India and Pakistan faltered on the brink of war, Sister Teresa (as she then was) responded to urgent human needs in a unique way. She knew then she must give up her relatively comfortable life educating the privileged few to work on the streets helping in any way she could the suffering masses. Although Mother Teresa encountered suspicion and distrust in some quarters in the 1950s, and one respected Calcutta charity worker told me there had always been two views of her in India – that which favoured welfare and that which recognised the need for developmental aid – nothing was openly voiced until very recently. In India she has been more or less consistently acclaimed, honoured and welcomed both by the national government and by the local government of West Bengal, which since 1967 has been Marxist. However unlikely this co-operation may seem on the surface, those who were concerned about the value of her work kept their criticisms muted. Calcutta was proud to possess a second Nobel Prize-winner (the first being the poet Rabindranath Tagore in 1913), and many world leaders came to pay their respects to her, hoping some of her saintly qualities would rub off on them if they got close enough in the inevitable photograph. Her contribution – and there is a danger of it being overshadowed in the recent controversy – was outstanding to a city repeatedly deluged by vast waves of refugees from the impoverished countryside or from neighbouring Bangladesh, but could never begin to solve a crisis of Calcutta's magnitude. Should the media be blamed for building Mother Teresa into something no individual could possibly ever be, or should we, the public the media feeds, take some of the blame in our constant search for heroes to make us feel better? God is a mystery. It is very hard for rational beings to believe in a just God when faced with daily destruction and misery. Yet here is someone apparently doing His work, doing things we could not possibly hope to do ourselves. It is comforting to believe that such good people exist and comforting to believe that such a person must have a direct link with God. But no individual is perfect, and by blacking out those aspects which make a fully rounded human being, the media and those who collude with them do her a disservice. Once any small weakness is observed people feel let down, cheated; eventually the person is exposed to attack.

The second half of the book is thematic and examines the criticisms of Mother Teresa in detail by means of a frank discussion of the compelling issues which arise from her work.

My own interest in Mother Teresa began some fifteen years ago when I wrote a short children's book about her. She agreed to it and put me in touch with the founder of her international Co-Workers, the friends and supporters of the Missionaries of Charity, who then lived not far from me in England. Ann Blaikie was a unique source of information and the book was duly written and illustrated. A few days before publication I received an urgent letter from Mother Teresa asking for publication to be stopped. There was already enough material about her on the market which was available for children, she wrote, adding: 'I have also today refused permission to Dominique Lapierre.' Lapierre, a French journalist, went on to write City of Joy, later filmed, about life in the Calcutta slums, a story in which Mother Teresa featured.

'I am so glad that Mother Teresa's letter came too late to cancel it,' Ann Blaikie wrote to me a few days later. The book was already printed and sitting in bookshops by the time the demand for cancellation arrived. Nothing more was ever said.

Why had Mother Teresa changed her mind? Of course, I understood the difficulties she faced in reconciling the greedy demands of a rapacious press, which had brought her both fame and the money she needed to do her work, and her stated aim to lead a simple life. Yet, as she has now come under criticism for the way that she spends the money raised – nobody knows precisely how much this is but Reuters International News Agency recently estimated it at about US $30 million annually – the real conundrum emerges: no doubt the money could be better spent, but if she were not there to raise it, the money would not be there in the first place.

What has intrigued me for nearly fifteen years is her very human response to a number of situations, indicated in this case by her desire to control who writes what about her. And yet, in so much else, Mother Teresa is driven by a deeply religious and spiritual urging. Finding the equilibrium has often proved elusive, even for her. Divine guidance and human imperatives are interesting bedfellows. The interaction between these two is what continues to fascinate me, and part of this book is an attempt to look at how this has worked in practice. Is it because many believe her to be divinely inspired that she has such a powerful effect on those who meet her? Or can her evident charisma belong to her alone? 'Did I come away glowing?' I have been asked many times of my own meetings with her, as if being in close proximity to such an icon would have a tangible consequence. Clearly, many people who have met her do believe their lives will never be the same after this, although not all go as far as one biographer who, commenting on the influence she had had on Malcolm Muggeridge, wrote: 'Through meeting Muggeridge, I sensed that I was meeting her and, at a sort of third hand, meeting the Lord Himself.'[3]

When I began researching this book in 1994 I was exercised by the problem of how to get information from Mother Teresa and the Missionaries of Charity themselves. I immediately encountered suspicion, which felt like an iron gate enclosing an already secretive organisation. 'I am sorry I sound so defensive,' one Catholic charity worker apologised. 'As Mother Teresa is suddenly a contentious figure I don't feel I can speak to you without being better acquainted with the facts,' a normally forthright commentator on Catholic affairs wrote. Another, a former sister with the Missionaries of Charity, wanted to talk to me, but only on the telephone, concerned that if we met face to face she might say more than she intended. Several others, whether fans or opponents, were prepared to see me only on the understanding that they would in no way be identified. More than one Catholic organisation expressed profound reservations about the work her institution was undertaking in this country, in India, in Romania, in Ethiopia and in Latin America but declined to be quoted by name since to criticise Mother Teresa in any way could jeopardise their own funds dramatically.

When I first visited the soup kitchens run by the Missionaries of Charity in Bravington Road, North London – and I had made an appointment – I was allowed to stay on condition that I did not ask any questions. 'The sisters are forbidden to give interviews to journalists,' I was told. I can only describe to you what I saw, therefore, without explanation and what I saw was a kindly, middle-aged Irishman unloading large amounts of food into a storeroom. 'The food just arrives,' I was told. 'We don't need to ask how, but simply trust in Divine Providence.' Divine Providence, however, is often given a helping human hand, as many Catholics believe it should be. But before the food was ladled out to some forty drifting and homeless men and women, there was half an hour of hymn singing and a sermon, delivered by Sister Theresina. No one should be in any doubt, and Mother Teresa has expressed herself very clearly on the point, the religious motivation is foremost.

It was obvious from my unpopular attempts to observe the soup-kitchen operation that knocking on doors without introductions was not going to work. Ann Blaikie, who had been so helpful fifteen years earlier with my children's book, was now seriously ill (and died while I was writing this book). One Co-Worker who did agree to see me was nonetheless visibly affronted when I asked to see a copy of the Order's constitution and told me my request was tantamount to asking for a document about the marriage settlement or divorce arrangements of one's friends; it was private, only for those who needed to live by it. And the Catholic Media Office, although extremely helpful through-out my work, could not assist me in gaining access to the Missionaries of Charity. Eventually I wrote to a young priest who was close to the Order.

After a preliminary session in which my views on religion (I am Jewish), feminism (I am in favour of it) and various matters worldly or otherworldly were scrutinised; after the religious background of my husband and the education of my children had all been laid out; and after I withheld, I believe, nothing about my motives for writing this book, explaining that I would be discussing contemporary criticisms as well as long-standing praise; that I found certainty in any religion difficult to accept and why I wanted his co-operation, the tennis-playing priest – I know that about him only because he conducted one of our meetings in his tennis gear – told me that he would pray for the right answer and God would decide. He would also need to consult the senior sisters in Calcutta, who would agree to co-operate only if they felt it would further their work. Several months later he wrote that he was prepared to help me, anonymously, with my research and I am most grateful to him for sparing the time to devote himself to what I suspect he did not find very enjoyable sessions.

There was much I wished to talk over with him. For example, can prayer ever be a substitute for social action or solve problems such as homelessness? Seeing Calcutta for myself made me redirect some of my enquiries but provoked others too. Mother Teresa is fond of telling journalists to pack away their notebooks and see the work; I did just that but fear my reactions at the Children's Home and the Home for the Dying were not always those she might have wished for. The Mother House, on the other hand, the nucleus of the operation, is an inspirational sort of place. A drab, concrete, four-storey building on a noisy street is what it appears from the outside. But inside I was aware of a palpable heartbeat as well as an extraordinarily soporific timelessness. The ritual of the passing of the buckets may be only symbolic but, for me, the chanting in English with lilting Indian accents was bewitching; the light, filtering through the brown window slats, painterly pretty and everything cool, calm and peaceful as the sari-clad women and girls rose one by one to take communion, forming as they did so a moving crucifix in a sort of highly stylised ballet. I could see why this communal time was so important in restoring energy and faith. I could begin to see why prayer made impossible tasks possible.

And then, just as I relaxed into another world of equanimity and tranquillity a modern, jarring note intruded and that was not simply because, with no microphones, the voices were almost overwhelmed by the deafening noise from the traffic. Above the roar, an American priest gave a sermon, following a reading from Jonah, which he based on the then current O. J. Simpson case. Whether or not Simpson was guilty was beside his point; O. J. Simpson was a frame of reference for us all to do something to deepen our spirituality and emerge a changed person, like Jonah. For a group of people who do not read newspapers, I could not help wondering how apposite the subject was.

There are some questions which clearly have no answers, but that does not mean one should not ask them. The one Mother Teresa herself sets out to answer is 'Who is my neighbour?' – to which she gives the resounding reply, 'Everyone.' However, succeeding generations and most religions have failed to offer a satisfactory solution to the eternal question of why there is suffering. Mother Teresa's response to this, with which many may disagree, poses some of the most profound problems of our age and there may not be answers to any of them. This book will, I hope, at least open up the debate.

PART ONE

CHAPTER ONE

ORIGINS

Nineteen-ten was a tumultuous year in Albania. It was a momentous year for the Bojaxhiu family too. On 26 August this Catholic Albanian family, one of the more prominent in the struggle for an autonomous Albania, was celebrating the birth of a healthy baby daughter. Agnes, the third child of Nikola and Dranafile, was born in Skopje, capital of the vilayet of Kosova, in Northern Macedonia. She had an elder sister Age, born in 1904, and elder brother Lazar, born in 1907.

These were heady times for Albanian nationalists who by the early twentieth century had a clearly developed sense of their own cultural identity but no independent state. For so long Albania had been used as a buffer between the interests of Austria–Hungary and those of the Slavs in the Balkans. None of the Balkan states wanted to see an independent Albania which, once the Ottoman Empire crumbled, would be harder to carve up among themselves. However, the Young Turks, who took over power in Istanbul in 1908, gave assurances that Albanians would be granted relative autonomy and, briefly, in the years before Agnes' birth, a new spirit of freedom flourished. The Albanians believed they were to be given a constitution, which would grant equal rights to all nationalities, Christian and Muslim alike, and for twelve days there was jubilant feasting and dancing. But the Young Turks soon reneged on their promises, declared that there was no such thing as Albanian nationality and looked for savage new ways to weaken the growing Albanian National Movement. They passed a number of laws to reinforce central authority and sent troops to crush

3

any resistance movements. In the spring of 1910, in the face of Young Turk insistence on the use of the traditional Arabic script, Albanians from north to south mounted huge popular gatherings in favour of adopting the much simpler and Western-leaning Latin alphabet. This was considered an important step towards claiming a new national identity.

The most serious uprising broke out in Pristina, in the north-east, in March 1910 after the population refused to pay new and severe taxes levied from Istanbul on imported goods. The revolt soon spread throughout Kosova before it was brutally suppressed by a 20,000-strong army. However, the severity with which the rebellion was crushed – whole villages were razed to the ground and the punishments meted out to Albanian leaders included public floggings – did little to dampen incipient nationalism and served only to strengthen demands for autonomy. By August the Ottoman forces had regained control of the area but only after many refugees had fled, and a new reign of terror throughout Albania had begun. By 1911, following the devastation of war, thousands of Albanian families faced illness and destitution.

Nikola Bojaxhiu, a prosperous building contractor and wholesale-food importer, travelled frequently in the region and was thus able to keep in touch with political realities and with his friends among the rather loose-knit nationalist leadership. He even went as far as Egypt, where there was an important Albanian colony supplying money and arms to the Nationalists. Over the next two turbulent years leading up to the First Balkan War of 1912, he was in close contact with several of the nationalist leaders, and politics was frequently discussed at home.

Spring 1912 was a season of shifting allegiances as the Balkan states formed an alliance to divide the European Ottoman possessions between themselves. Landlocked Serbia was hoping to prevent the rise of a new and independent Albania and to annex Kosova and Northern Albania. By the summer of that year, the Albanians were no longer able to remain neutral and found themselves fighting on the side of the disintegrating Ottoman Empire against the Balkan armies. Within months, however, once the Serbs were occupying Skopje, the outlook appeared very grim for the national aspirations of the Albanians. It was only the realisation by Austria that an independent Albania was vital if Serbia's expansionist aims of gaining a port and stretching to the

Adriatic were to be blocked that led to the proclamation, on 28 November 1912 at the Congress of Vlore, of the independent state of Albania. Here the black double-headed eagle on a red background, emblem of Skanderbeg, the fifteenth-century Albanian Christian hero who fought against the Ottoman invaders, was finally raised in triumph.

But the future of this fledgling country was far from secure when it was further discussed at the Conference of Ambassadors in London a month later. The pragmatism of some of the elderly statesmen present, including Sir Edward Grey of Britain, forced the ambassadors to recognise that the new country had been designed not for the good of its own inhabitants but to appease the interests of the Great Powers. More than half the Albanian population, including the Bojaxhius in Skopje and their cousins in Kosova, was left outside the borders of the new Albanian state.

As the leaders talked, Serbian atrocities, particularly against Albanian Catholics, redoubled. Serb hatred of Albanians was long-standing but these massacres were fuelled by rumours that the Great Powers intended to assign to Albania all districts where the Albanians had a 75 per cent majority. 'It is locally supposed that the Serbians wish to adjust the population to conform with their claim to have a majority in the district. These massacres are taking place for statistical purposes,' the British Vice Consul in Skopje wrote in 1913. 'I am beginning to suspect', he added, 'that much of the Albanian population is being murdered in cold blood.'

The Vice Consul, W. D. Peckham, went on to explain to the British Ambassador in Belgrade, Sir Ralph Paget, that he now believed that a prima facie case had been made for the Albanian claim that the Serbian military was responsible for deliberately throwing wounded Albanians into the river Vardar to die. 'A statement which I heard at the time, that "the Albanian wounded are healing with remarkable rapidity" takes, in the light of this story, a new and sinister significance,' he commented dryly. Peckham then elaborated for his superior in Belgrade the root cause of the problem. 'A remark I heard some time ago from a Serbian throws light on the mental attitude of the Serb to the Albanian. This gentleman, a person of some education, who spoke fluent French, arranged the first steps of the ladder of life as first, man; second, gorilla; third, Albanian. A peasant would probably put the Albanian lower down, along with the insect pests.'[1]

5

Vice Consul Peckham had been kept well informed of the atrocities by the Catholic curate of Skopje, who had paid him an urgent visit on 27 February 1913 along with his colleague, the curate of Ferisovich. Even allowing for the fact that both priests were Catholic and Albanian and 'have therefore a double motive for exaggerations to the detriment of the orthodox Serb', Peckham was still disturbed. He had heard from the two priests details of thousands of horrific deaths and hundreds of cases of torture since the Serbian occupation began. He learnt of Serbian soldiers entering the house of an Albanian family in Skopje, raping the wife and beating the husband until he told where his two daughters aged fourteen and sixteen were and then raping them too. In a nearby village rampaging soldiers fired into houses to drive out inhabitants who were hidden in the roofs. As the women came out they were shot; to save powder the children were bayoneted. There were stories of soldiers and officers robbing peasants of their money as they came back from market, of men being hung from trees by the arms until they died, of parties of poor Albanians going out to collect firewood only to find themselves surrounded by soldiers and shot. In some cases men were imprisoned simply for speaking to the Catholic priest. Not only would the Bojaxhiu family have known of these events, they would probably have been directly involved. One of the hospitals to which the wounded were sent was staffed by Catholic nursing sisters and the family was closely involved in the small Catholic community.

Occasionally Albanians did the killing – as in Dibra, when they attacked looting Serbian soldiers. But then Serbian revenge was swift, on this occasion twenty-four entire villages were burnt down. At Pristina on or about 23 October 1912, on the admission of a Serbian military doctor, some 5,000 Albanians were killed. They were tied together and mowed down by machine-gun fire. Vice Consul Peckham was able to corroborate this particular allegation as he had heard independent confirmation of extensive Albanian massacres at Pristina from an Albanian army doctor, who stated that the Albanians were placed between hurdles and then machine-gunned.

As the First Balkan War resolved almost nothing, few were surprised when the Second Balkan War erupted, which resolved little more. The statesmen and intellectuals of Europe laboured under the belief that nationalism was a good thing and the watchword of progress. They hoped and believed that, in the fragmentation of old empires, a separate national existence for each race was to be the key to a lasting European peace. They failed to foresee either the strengthening of Germany or that their plans largely ignored such important national needs as economic organisation. To an extent the new frontiers became barriers in a negative sense: peoples who had previously been in economic or political contact with each other became cut off.

In June 1913, Ottoman troops left Albania after 500 years of occupation and in November the Powers selected a German prince, William of Weid, as head of the new principality. But while the final settlement of the new state was postponed, Serbia continued to balk at the very creation of Albania, which it viewed as depriving it of an exit to the sea, continued to despise the Albanian people and continued to ignore international ultimata to leave Albanian territory. In addition, Italy began to intrigue against the new and inexperienced Prince and found a number of ambitious Albanians who were only too ready to collaborate. William of Weid lasted six months, but the Serb atrocities persisted until the outbreak of the First World War in 1914, which gave Albania's old enemies, particularly Bulgaria, a fresh opportunity to move in for whatever land they thought they could grab.

The Skopje into which Agnes Bojaxhiu was born was, therefore, a violent and brutal place, with brigandage on the road, vendettas in the mountains, unstable leadership and an unsettled future. But there was another side. Early-twentieth-century Skopje had evolved from an ancient civilisation and had been continuously inhabited from pre-Christian times. In the thirteenth century it had been captured by the Serbs before it fell to the Turks a century later. A bridge over the river Vardar was said to have been rebuilt in the fifteenth century on the foundations of a bridge constructed when the area was a Roman province. In fact Christianity spread into Albania along the route of the Via Egnatia, replacing the pantheistic religions of the Illyrian tribes. But, after the conquest of the Ottoman Turks, Islam soon became the majority religion, although Christianity proved tenacious in the mountainous regions, especially in the north.

Skopje, or Uskub as it was then called, was described by one traveller in the early part of the century as a quiet and sober town, 'nestled in a valley of death. Tombstones are always the prominent feature of a Turkish town but Uskub resembles an oasis in a desert of dead. Acres of them in general disorder, a few erect but mostly toppling or fallen surround the town and stretch long arms into it; they flank the main road and dot the side streets and far out into the country. Lone deserted stones stand where no man's hand has been for ages. The sight is gruesome and one's mind is wont to picture the many massacres that have made this sea of silent slabs.'[2]

Because Catholic Albanians were such a small part of the Albanian population – estimated at about one-tenth of the total – they clung tenaciously to their faith, which the Austrians, for their own reasons, were keen to protect. This gave them a right to advance rival claims in the region against Russian support for the Serbs. One of the most important events in the calendar for Skopje's Roman Catholic community was the service for the feast of Corpus Christi held at the big church which was very close to the Bojaxhiu home. An American journalist who happened to be passing through a few years before Agnes was born was struck by the colourful nature of the festivities. 'It was a dusty summer day and the church was decorated with garlands of mountain flowers and many flags. A vast Mohammedan banner floated from one side of the Christian belfry and an equally large emblem of the Dual Monarchy from the other and strings of bunting, alternately Turkish or Austro-Hungarian, streamed away from the tower to the high mud walls about the churchyard. Over the door, where only the Catholics entered and could see, hung a large print of Francis Joseph much bemedalled.'

Hundreds of Albanians were converging on the place from all directions. The American who slipped in with them described:

> the darkened church aglow with many candles around the crucified Christ and the fourteen stations of the cross set like little chapels about the courtyard contained life-sized pictures of the saviour's labour to the crucifixion. During the indoor service the Albanian women, veiled like their Mohammedan sisters, occupied one side of the church and the men the other. In the pew of honour sat the Austrian reformajis in full feather.
>
> At the conclusion of the indoor service on Corpus Christi day, priests and people left the church chanting, each carrying a lighted candle and made a tour of the stations kneeling and praying a few moments at each. Little flower girls, dressed in gayest shalvas, preceded the pro-

cession scattering rose leaves. Two proud Albanian boys swung the incense lamps and four others bore a panoply of silk over the heads of the priests. First behind the priests came the Count and Christian Vali and then followed the Austrian consul and other Austrian officers and the people. The ordeal of kneeling in the grass was trying to the trousers of the Count and painful to the rheumatic limbs of the venerable Christian Vali, whom the Count was required to assist to his feet on each occasion.

It was a windy day and the candles borne gingerly at arm's length sputtered and spattered the gorgeous uniform and frock coat. The delegates at their divine duties wore on their faces, I must say, most unholy expressions and at the conclusion of the ceremony the poor old Christian with the fez presented the appearance of having eaten his supper without stuffing the end of a napkin in his collar. Religion and politics make an unhappy mixture; they war within one like custard and cucumbers.

This same American described another aspect of religious life in Skopje. The Christian burial ground was behind the Turkish one and to the side of the Hotel Turati.

The Christians do not carry their dead on their shoulders but convey the corpse on a litter to lower it into a wooden coffin in the grave. Priests precede the funeral parade on foot in all vestments chanting as they march and friends follow the body, one carrying the coffin lid. A strange sacrifice for the dead takes place quarterly. The peasants gather from far and near bringing cakes and pans of boiled wheat of the best they can afford and place them on the graves of the dead. Candles are stuck about the food and tinsel paper cut in fine shreds arranged over it. Priests pass from grave to grave praying with the peasants for the souls of the departed and sons of the priests [sic] who serve as acolytes swing censers. At the conclusion of the ceremony the sacrificial food is distributed to the poor – or rather the poorer – and lazy gypsies gather with many naked babies at the border of the cemetery.[3]

In spite of the ubiquitous beggars, gypsies and 'naked urchins', Skopje was an attractive town in the early part of the century. There was a covered bazaar at one end but craftsmen displayed their pottery, usually jugs and urns, at various street corners. Many of the shops, situated on wide pavements either side of the cobbled streets, sported large awnings and balconies.

It is not known exactly when Nikola and Dranafile came to Skopje, as the Bojaxhiu family originated from the Kosova town of Prizren, to the north of Skopje. It was here in 1878 that Albanian Nationalist leaders came together to form the Prizren League, vowing to fight for autonomy for Albania. Prizren was an important trading city in medieval times which ultimately became part of Yugoslavia and was known for its silver filigree jewellery, carpets and fine embroidery. In the middle of the nineteenth century it was hit by a cholera outbreak and some of the Bojaxhiu family may have moved away at that time. According to Lazar in a later interview with an Italian newspaper, some went to Scutari, where there was in 1930 a Bojaxhiu Street. The Bojaxhius have been described as a large, long-established, merchant-trading family with wide-ranging business interests. One biographer of Mother Teresa has suggested that the family may once have traded in paints, as boja means colour. However the standard translation of the Albanian word bojaxhiu is whitewasher, or house painter.

For centuries the Albanian people had been divided into two distinct groups, Ghegs and Tosks, with different dialects and great variations in social structures. The Bojaxhius were Ghegs, the group which lived in the mountainous region of the north and who were organised along tightly knit tribal lines. The Tosks lived in the lowlands and plains of the south and were largely made up of landless or subsistence-level peasantry. Some tribes in the inaccessible mountain regions lived by laws known as the Kanun of Lek, dating from the fifteenth century or before. The Kanun was a highly complex legal code which attempted to regulate the blood feuds or vendettas that even today Albanian rulers have not managed to stamp out. Countless young men, often from Catholic families, were wiped out in these revenge killings, which could be perpetuated for generations.

It is probable that Nikola, who spoke Turkish, French and Italian in addition to his native Albanian and Serbo-Croat, was recruited to the Nationalist cause while he lived in Prizren. According to some accounts it was there that he met his future wife, Dranafile Bernaj (or Bernai), whose family apparently owned estates in Serbia. Others, including the authorised biography of Mother Teresa by Eileen Egan, describe the mother of Age, Lazar and Agnes as having come from the Venetian region. Egan says the couple were married in a Catholic ceremony in Prizren. Lazar has pointed out that his mother's Italian origins did not mean she was not Albanian. In fact her given name, generally shortened to Drana, meant Rose in Albanian. It is this name, spelled Roza, which appears today on her gravestone in Tirana, Albania.

Most accounts of Agnes' childhood describe it as comfortable and prosperous. It appears that Nikola was extremely successful and owned several houses. The home they lived in was a large one with a pleasant garden and flowers and fruit trees, on the same street as the Church of the Sacred Heart. Young Agnes was 'plump, round and tidy' and soon acquired the nickname Gonxha, meaning flowerbud, by which she is still known in Albania. Lazar would say in later years that she was always sensible and a little too serious for her age, the one who did not steal the jam when he did. If Agnes ever discovered him helping himself on the quiet she would reprimand her elder brother reminding him that he was not to touch food after midnight if they were going to mass and communion with their mother in the morning. But she never told tales on him.

Nikola, known as Kole, was a good-looking man with a bushy moustache who lived a very full life. He became a member (the only Catholic) of the Skopje town council, regularly played in a Skopje brass band and loved to sing. 'He was full of life and liked to be with people. Our house was full of visitors while he was alive,' said Lazar. He vividly recalled the family's celebration in 1912, when he was only four, of Albania's first taste of independence. Some of the most famous names in the fight for Albania such as Barjram Curri (who now has a town named after him), Hassan Prishtina and Sabri Qytezi visited the Bojaxhiu household, singing rowdy songs to the accompaniment of a mandolin and talking long into the night. The image that remained for ever in Lazar's mind was of a mountain of matchboxes piled on the floor by his father and friends and then set alight.

Kole had a keen entrepreneurial eye for an opportunity. At first he went into partnership running a pharmacy with a Dr Suskalović, who had a reputation as one of the best doctors in Skopje, but he also joined forces with a building contractor and was responsible for building the Skopje theatre overlooking the river. Soon he joined a third enterprise, this time in partnership with Signor Morten, an Italian, and the pair traded in luxury goods and foods including oil, sugar, cloth and leather. Whenever he returned from a business trip the children remembered the excitement with which they would greet him and the many parcels he brought back for them all. He may have been stern and a disciplinarian, but he regularly regaled his family with funny accounts of his travels abroad.

Kole was known as a generous local benefactor and encouraged his children to be generous and compassionate to those less fortunate than themselves; this was as important as working hard at school. 'Never forget whose children you are and from what background you come,' he told them. He had high expectations of their educational possibilities and was considered by contemporaries to be somewhat progressive in this field since he was prepared to send not just his son but also two daughters to school. However, Drana was obviously the more religious of the parents. She took the children to morning mass most days and when not working in the house or helping others was always saying the rosary. Kole, when he travelled, would leave enough money with her so that she could feed anyone in need who came to their door. Sometimes she went out, often accompanied by Agnes, who was growing up into a studious, book-loving girl, to deliver parcels of food and money to the poor.

The three children went at first to an elementary school within the Sacred Heart Church, where lessons were in Albanian and then, after some years, in Serbo-Croat. But although they subsequently attended state schools, Gymnasia, indicating the importance their father placed on education, life for all three of them was bound up in the parish of the Sacred Heart. Since the Catholics were a minority, the church was an important focal point for the Bojaxhiu family and gave them a clear sense of cultural and religious identity.

Because Skopje was not on any borders, it was spared the sort of street butchery suffered by other Balkan towns during the Great War. But, enveloped by the fighting, it obviously could not avoid all strife. In 1918, however, as the end of the war led to still more debate over the new Balkan border, the prosperous childhood years of the Bojaxhiu family were brought suddenly to an end. Nikola recognised that the struggle for Albanian nationalism was far from over and he joined a movement which sought to have the disputed province of Kosova, inhabited chiefly by Albanians, joined to a Greater Albania. In fact the new federation of Serbs, Croats and Slovenes, known after 1929 as

Yugoslavia, was given much of Northern Albania, including Kosova, leading to a sense of fear, anger and betrayal among the Albanian villages within the vilayet. According to one petition presented to the League of Nations by Kosovars in 1921, the Serbs had been responsible for killing 12,371 people, with a further 22,000 imprisoned. They begged for reunion with Albania, a situation which almost everyone else involved in deciding Albania's future was trying to prevent. Small autonomous fiefdoms, with direct allegiance to Belgrade, were more to the liking of the Serbs, the Austrians, the Great Powers and even one or two Albanian leaders themselves.

Kole clearly felt strongly about the issue, for he travelled 160 miles to Belgrade to attend a political dinner on the subject. But his support for a Greater Albania would have made him many enemies, and when he staggered home in the early evening some days later, driven in a carriage by the Italian consul, the family saw that he was dying. They did not immediately know the cause, which was probably poisoning.* Drana sent Agnes to fetch the parish priest, but when she could not find him she went for some reason to the Skopje railway station, where she found another priest unknown to the family. She persuaded him to accompany her home, where he administered the last rites to Nikola. The family then rushed him, haemorrhaging badly, to hospital where the next morning he underwent emergency surgery. But he died the following day. The funeral of Nikola Bojaxhiu was an important event in Skopje. Large crowds attended, including official delegates from the city council and representatives of other religions. On the day of the funeral every jeweller's shop in the city was closed; the pupils in all the city's schools received commemorative handkerchiefs. The number of handkerchiefs given away was, traditionally, an indication of the wealth of the person who had died.

Mother Teresa herself has consistently refused to talk about her childhood. She dismisses it as unimportant, though she will say that she came from an exceptionally happy family background. 'I remember my mother, my father and the rest of us praying together each evening. I hope our Albanian families have remained faithful to this practice. It

---

* Poisoning as a method of eradicating a political enemy is almost unknown in Balkan history, because the emphasis placed on honour usually demands use of a gun or a knife. Death by poison was not only considered unmanly but it was also unnecessary as almost everyone at the time carried a weapon.

is God's greatest gift to the family. It maintains family unity. The family that does not pray together does not stay together.' The anonymous priest I consulted for help explained this attitude to me when I asked him for more details about her early days: 'Her work is to spread the Gospel and to answer the call of Christ. Any personal details which don't enhance that are irrelevant ... intrusive.'

The accounts in English which carry most about her childhood years are Egan's biography, published in 1985, and David Porter's Mother Teresa: The Early Years, published in 1986 and largely based on an Albanian book, also authorised, by Dr Lush Gjergi, Mother Teresa's cousin who still lives in Kosova, where he combines the occupations of both journalist and priest. However, both books are tantalisingly short on dates for those early years. And there are discrepancies. For example, Egan says Nikola Bojaxhiu died in 1919, aged forty-five. Porter does not give a date but implies 1918. In 1982 Lazar, then living in Italy, said in an interview: 'The suffering of our family started when the Yugoslavs and Albanians were fighting for Kosova and the other provinces of Albania in which was the City of Skopje. Our father ... was very active in politics and the Albanian National question. He tried very hard to obtain the national rights of Albanians, with all his heart he tried to keep the Albanian territories in Yugoslavia together with Albania. When Yugoslavia took over the territories the family was persecuted and my father poisoned.'[4]

When I visited Tirana in 1995 I went to see the mixed-religion cemetery where Mother Teresa's mother and sister Age are buried. After a short bus ride, I walked for a mile or so down a dusty road alongside an enormous but disused Soviet-built textile factory. Like so much else in the country, it now lies inert, a prey to looters and other criminals, but the nearby electricity plant, once so crucial to the factory, still belches out its black smoke. To reach the cemetery I crossed the main road and walked up a short hill. The ubiquitous, derelict concrete bunkers on either side of the road remind one that only a few years previously this country was hostage to one of the most ruthless dictatorships in the world. Enver Hoxha, who ruled from 1944 until 1985, installed 600,000 of these pillbox bunkers the breadth and length of the country at vast human and financial cost, to combat aerial attacks from an imagined foreign enemy.

At the entrance to the cemetery itself, the foreign visitor, instantly marked out by dress and mien, is greeted by begging mothers and ragged boys. They offered to show me, for a price, what they assumed I had come to see: the grave of the former dictator himself. He was, briefly, buried in a polished red granite tombstone in the Cemetery of Martyrs, alongside the statue of Mother Albania. But eventually Hoxha was discredited and the red granite reused as a memorial to forty-three British soldiers killed in Albania during the Second World War. His remains were disinterred and today lie in the same crowded cemetery as thousands of his subjects, just a few feet away from Drana and Age Bojaxhiu.

According to the women's simple marble gravestones, Drana, or Roza as it says, lived from 1889 to 1972. This would mean that she was just fifteen when she gave birth to her first child – perhaps fourteen at the moment of conception – and was some fifteen years younger than her more worldly husband. This would not have been particularly unusual for the time and the place. Many Albanian girls were betrothed in infancy. Betrothal was such an important element of Albanian society that often, as soon as a female child was born, a part of her purchase price was immediately paid by the family of her prospective husband. But Age's gravestone gives her dates as 1913–73, clearly a nonsense as all the accounts – and there is photographic evidence too – are agreed that she was six years older, not three years younger, than Agnes.

I have puzzled over this. Perhaps the marble-carvers in Tirana are not concerned about accuracy. Perhaps Drana's birth date as carved is as wrong as her daughter's. But, if so, why has Mother Teresa, who has visited these graves in recent years and has approved the crosses now placed over them by her Missionaries of Charity, not had such inaccuracies rectified? In 1991 she had one of the graves resited so that both were closer in the same cemetery. Three years later she attended an informal ceremony to bless the graves with the American Albanian Archbishop of Durrës, Rok Mirdita. 'We prayed there together for some time and she was very happy,' he told me. Is it possible that someone, and not necessarily Mother Teresa herself, thought it best not to advertise to the world that Mother Teresa's mother had conceived at such a tender age and therefore deliberately falsified the dates? And suppose this were the case, might one not therefore praise Mother Teresa as a dutiful daughter for going along with the deception in order to protect her mother's memory? Both tombstones were originally organised by the Albanian Catholic opera singer, Maria Krja, who was honoured by the communist state as an Artist of the People, which gave her some slight privileges. Krja became friendly with Age and her mother in Tirana from the 1930s onwards. She looked on Age as a sister. When Age died, one year after her mother, it fell to Maria Krja to organise the inscriptions and photograph on Age's tomb. 'I was afraid of the system,' she explained, 'as the communists were still in control and so I could not put my own name but inscribed the message: "In fond memory from Lazar and Gonxha."' The dates, she insists, were the same as those she found on Age's identity card.[5]

The life of the Bojaxhiu children changed dramatically after their father's death. The young widow soon found that her husband's business partners wanted nothing more to do with the family and they were left with only their house. At the same time, Drana believed she was entitled to family property in Novi Selo, but as there were no documents establishing her rights she was unable to insist on her share of the disputed estates, or of the income. For a short while Drana appeared a broken woman and it was Age who shouldered much of the burden at this time. Then Drana set up a business of hand-crafted embroidery and textiles. With Lazar's help, negotiating at textile factories, the business soon expanded to include the locally crafted carpets for which Skopje was famous.

The family also consolidated its faith. Whereas politics and the future of Albania had been the dominating topic in family conversations, church liturgy and discussions of missionary activity in distant lands took over in this predominantly female household. Although now poor themselves, they continued to offer hospitality to those who were poorer. In later life Mother Teresa recalled how she thought at the time that the others regularly sharing mealtimes were relatives, but she realised later her mother was often feeding and clothing complete strangers. Among the many, Agnes particularly remembered helping her mother to wash an alcoholic woman who was covered in sores, and visiting a mother of six in her dying days.

One of the regular parish functions which Agnes particularly loved was an annual pilgrimage to the shrine of the Virgin Mary at Letnice in the mountainous region of Montenegro. Most families went for just a short time but the Bojaxhius, usually travelling in a horse-drawn carriage, stayed longer in the hope that it might restore Agnes' health. She had suffered from malaria and whooping cough as well as a club foot, and for her sake the family often spent holidays at the famous spa town of Vrnjačka Banja. They were put up at a house in Letnice owned by a local man, who lent it to them in gratitude to their late father. They spent the days going for walks or playing games and the evenings sitting around the fireside telling stories.

Christianity, therefore, became an increasingly important anchor for Agnes. Not just at home, where the family gathered in the living room every evening to say the rosary, but at the festivals which she especially loved as times when she came together with many other young people. According to photographs Agnes enjoyed many picnics and outings with her friends in the countryside around Skopje during the years after the First World War. She was also an avid singer, a soprano, while her sister was a contralto, not just in the local church choir, but in the Albanian Catholic Choir too. The two sisters performed at charity concerts that took place almost every month, usually organised by the young Catholics. Agnes was punctual, cheerful and keen to learn. A local musician and relative taught her to play the mandolin and commented later that she was quick to learn and became a good player.

There were two particularly important figures within the local church at this time: Monsignor Janez Gnidovec, Bishop of Skopje 1924–39, a charismatic figure who came to know Agnes' family well; and a Jesuit priest, Father Franjo Jambreković, who became Pastor of the Sacred Heart in 1925. Father Jambreković established a parish library for young people, and set up a youth group called the Sodality of the Blessed Virgin Mary. While Agnes was still at the state Gymnasium, Age, always considered a very bright pupil, went to study economics at a commercial college and Lazar was awarded the Sabri Qytezi Prize, which entitled him to a one-year scholarship to study in Austria. The following year he won a place at the Military Academy of Tirana in Albania. The two priests thus became the dominant male figures in Agnes' life.

Agnes had been moving in a religious direction for some time – she often acted as interpreter from Serbo-Croat to Albanian for the parish priest and had started teaching young children the rudiments of the Catholic faith. She said in later years that from the age of twelve she was conscious of a desire to devote her life to God. She was influenced in this partly by her mother who, at a time of adversity, managed not only to support her family but to devote more of her time and energies to helping and consoling those less fortunate than herself. But she was especially receptive to Father Jambreković and his enthusiasm for the work of the missions. When her cousin refused to accept payment from Agnes and her friends for the mandolin lessons she rebuked him and said he should take the money and give it back to her to send to India to support the mission work. Jambreković was especially welcomed by the young people of Skopje, who had found his predecessor harsh to the point of cruelty. This man, Father Zadrima, demanded order and good behaviour and enforced his demands with a thick and threatening walking stick. Not surprisingly, Lazar and his friends did not like Father Zadrima. But his younger sister Agnes admonished him: 'It is your duty to love him and give him respect. He is Christ's priest.' Her unquestioning acceptance of authority, especially ecclesiastical authority, was instilled from an early age. It was to be her rule both for herself and others throughout her life.

Jambreković galvanised the small community in Skopje. He clearly had a gift for communicating with young people and made his stories both exotic and romantic and full of adventure. He organised prayers as well as collections of money to help support the work of missionaries; he distributed some of the plentiful Catholic magazines and newspapers full of exciting accounts of their progress. One magazine in particular, Catholic Missions, published by the Association for the Propagation of the Faith, with its vivid eye-witness reports of Croatian and Slovene missionaries working in India, caught Agnes' imagination. The magazines, well endowed with photographs, were full of moving calls to 'assist in the education of future Apostles . . . and share in their reward'. There was also a keen element of competition with the hard-working Protestant missionaries involved. Agnes now began working closely with the priest to help inspire others.

Father Jambreković it was who first taught the girls of the Sodality about the Jesuits, the Militia of Christ founded by St Ignatius Loyola in 1534 to combat Christian reformers – it was Jesuit priests who went on missionary duties from Yugoslavia to Bengal in 1924. He challenged his students to think of the words of St Ignatius in his Spiritual Exercises: 'What have I done for Christ, what am I doing for Christ and what will I do for Christ?' As she pondered this, Agnes started to feel the stirring of a call, but she admitted to friends it was hard to know how to respond. How could a teenage girl with such limited experience of the world be expected to disentangle the romantic overlay from a genuine and heartfelt desire to help others?

If she stayed in Skopje, what was the future for her? Although she was not short of friends, contemporaries describe her as shy with boys. She loved teaching but as a member of a double minority was she not bound to suffer discrimination in this career, with virtually no schools for the Albanian minority in Yugoslavia? After 1918, the situation for Albanians in Kosova and Skopje began to deteriorate as the Yugoslav government tried to colonise the area with Serbs and exerted pressure on the native Albanian population either to emigrate or be assimilated. Albanians were denied the right to use the Albanian language for official matters, all schooling was conducted in Serbo-Croat and Albanian surnames had to be altered to include a Serbian suffix such -vić or -vć. Under new laws on the Colonisation of the Southern Regions, advantages for Serb settlers included gifts of up to 50 hectares of land, the right of free transport up to the place of settlement, free use of state or communal forests and exemption from any taxation for three years. As Serb persecution intensified, the memories of Serb atrocities committed during her childhood could not be easily erased. Another reason compelling the clear-sighted teenager to leave was her despair over blood feuds, which continued unabated.

In the two years before she decided to become a nun Agnes spent longer periods on retreat at the shrine of Cërnagore and she sought guidance from her Father Confessor. He told her: 'If the thought that God may be calling you to serve him and your neighbour makes you happy, then that may be the very best proof of the genuineness of your vocation. Joy that comes from the depths of your being is like a compass by which you can tell what direction your life should follow. That is the case even when the road you must take is a difficult one.'

Choosing to become a nun is not to be confused with choosing a profession, be it teacher or social worker, any more than a vocation to become a nun can be compared with a vocation to write or act, for example. Agnes would have been brought up to believe that a vocation is a sign of God's will, and if the call to serve God was insistent enough one dare not ignore it even though that involved not just leaving home but choosing celibacy and denying the very essence of herself as a young woman. Aged seventeen, she was able to take the decision because she had been well taught that chastity, for those to whom it is given, is a special grace; it is pure grace. This was a defining moment for Agnes. She chose a life of self-sacrifice. But, although she could not possibly have known that she would find huge freedom in travelling the world and in meeting world leaders as equals, there was a secular element in her choice. Choosing the convent was a well-trodden route for women seeking education and Agnes wished to educate others, but in a language that was not Serbo-Croat. More than sixty years later young women still need to hear the voice of God within them before committing to religious life. As one English nun explained: 'Somebody says, "How do you know you have a vocation?" and you just know. You can't put it into words. No way of describing what you feel ... It's just total conviction that you've done the right thing, and you're in the right place.'[6] Yet most nuns today would say that you need 90 per cent idealism and 10 per cent realism. 'You can't do it in the first place without the idealism and the belief in God but as you grow up and mature it's the other 10 per cent that keeps you on course.'[7]

It cannot have been a great surprise for Drana when her younger daughter told her she had decided to become a missionary in India. She went to her room, closed the door and did not re-emerge for twenty-four hours, so the story goes. When she did so she told her daughter: 'Put your Hand in His – in His hand – and walk all the way with Him.'

Lazar was less encouraging. He was a sporty, good-looking youth who spent much of his time before he joined the army outside the house with his friends. How could she do such a thing? he exploded in reply to her letter telling him of her decision and congratulating him on being made a lieutenant. On 1 September 1928 Albania, minus Kosova, became a monarchy under King Zog I, and Lieutenant Bojaxhiu was to become an equerry of the new King. 'You will serve a king of two million people. I shall serve the king of the whole world,' Agnes replied.

CHAPTER TWO

MISSIONARIES

A few days before Agnes' departure for Zagreb, at the beginning of her journey to India in September 1928, a farewell concert was held in her honour. She also had a photograph taken which she later sent to her aunt 'to remember me'. The picture shows her dark, deep-set eyes and serious intent. By this time, Agnes had assiduously studied as much as she could about the history of the missionary movement in India, especially in its most recent, expansive phase. She would have known that attempts to Christianise the country had been made repeatedly for almost 400 years.

In Kerala, South India, there was a long-established but small community of Syrian Christians who trace their foundation to the Apostle Thomas. Doubting Thomas reached the Malabar Coast (modern Kerala) in AD 52 and was martyred twenty years later near Madras. But the Portuguese, from 1500 onwards, were the first foreigners who set out to convert the country, and initially the Syrian Christians warmly welcomed them as allies in the fight against local tyranny. Soon, however, especially when it became clear that the Indians had never heard of the Pope, theological difficulties arose. The Portuguese naturally deemed it impossible for any community of Christians to exist independently from the Bishop of Rome and, with the arrival of a forceful new archbishop in Goa, Alexio da Menezes, the Portuguese were able to stamp their authority on the ancient church.

At the same time, one of the most significant events in Roman Catholic missionary history, the foundation of the Society of Jesus, was to have an immediate and long-lasting effect in India. The Jesuits, bound to the Pope by a direct vow of personal obedience, were dedicated to seeking conversions to the Catholic faith. Their achievements in sixteenth-century India rest partly on the establishment of a seminary in South India which offered excellent instruction in both Syrian and Latin, but more especially in the work of Francis Xavier, a Basque, and one of the first followers of Loyola. Xavier, statesman as well as missionary, went to India in 1542 as the representative of the King of Portugal and, with extensive authority from the Pope, became one of the most famous of all Roman Catholic missionaries.

He went first to Goa, the centre of Portuguese dominion in India. By that time Goa was a flourishing city, boasting many churches and monasteries, but its inhabitants were only nominally Christian and, Xavier believed, greatly in need of moral reform. Many of the Europeans, flamboyantly flaunting their wealth, had taken Indian mistresses and produced children whom they then ignored. At the same time, many of the Hindu population had converted under extreme pressure but had little inclination towards Christian practices. After a short while, Xavier moved south to the Coromandel Coast, to give succour to thousands of poor fisherfolk who had been baptised *en masse* some years earlier and then abandoned. These illiterates knew nothing of Christianity, but had agreed to convert in return for Portuguese protection from Muslim raiders. 'Xavier arrived to find an untutored mob, he left behind him a church in being,' wrote the Anglican Bishop Stephen Neill, the twentieth-century historian of the Christian missions. Today, the body of St Francis Xavier is venerated in Goa, but his arms, 'which had baptised thousands and thousands of infidels', were taken to Rome at the beginning of the seventeenth century. There, in Rome's baroque masterpiece, the Jesu Church, they rest today guarded in magnificent oval urns, forming part of an altar, a clear statement of Europe's determination to impose its own set of values on a foreign culture.

Following Xavier came a number of other well-known Catholic missionaries to India. Many suffered breakdowns either because of the climate or because of the nature of the work and lack of support in depth. The voyage from Europe to India still took about six months and a further month, at least, might be involved in travelling across land from one city to another. Another major stumbling-block from the eighteenth century on was Rome's insistence on suppressing practices which local Jesuits might have tolerated but which Rome regarded as too nearly allied to Hindu superstitions. Only Roman practice, as it was conducted in Rome, was to govern the missions.

In 1773, following accusations of arrogance and improper missionary methods, Pope Clement XIV suppressed the Jesuits. This was little short of a disaster for the Catholic Church as at least 3,000 missionaries were therefore withdrawn from their fields. The Coromandel Coast, where Xavier had worked so hard, was supplied with local Goanese priests whose behaviour came in for heavy criticism. As the Roman missions languished, so the Protestant missionaries stepped in, at first German Lutherans and Dutch Presbyterians. Their great advantage was that they did not insist on the use of Latin and quickly set about translating the Bible into various vernaculars.

It was not until 1793 that the first British missionaries in India, a group of Baptists led by William Carey, arrived via the Hooghly river and set to work. The delay arose partly because the East India Company, launched in 1599 to enjoy a 'quiet trade in the East', was never keen on encouraging missionaries. Although originally a commercial enterprise, the Company gradually took over more and more responsibilities of government. It was not that it was anti-Christian, but it feared that too much missionary activity would unsettle the native populations so vital for the development of commerce. The profits amassed by free-trading Englishmen could be enormous and Calcutta soon began to thrive on greed, rapacity, exploitation and corruption. Lord Wellesley (Governor General 1798–1805) initially expressly forbade missionaries until he discovered how useful the Serampore Baptists, who arrived in 1800, could be in spreading education in Bengal. In 1813, when the Company charter was renewed, Anglicans were permitted to function as missionaries, not just as chaplains to the British. But only in 1833, when the Company's charter was renewed again, was India opened up without restriction to missionary enterprise of all nationalities, and by then there was already plenty of it in Bengal. Twenty-five years later, the East India Company handed over power to the British government.

The great expansion of missionary activity came during the nineteenth century, coinciding with the spread of British colonial rule throughout India and with a variety of efforts by the other governments of Europe to turn India Christian. By the end of the century there were at least twenty-two different Protestant Missionary Societies with as many printing establishments to disseminate the vernacular Gospel. One of the most revolutionary changes, not without its opponents who forecast endless trouble, was that by mid-century all the missions, Protestant and Roman Catholic alike, started sending out single women. They soon outnumbered the men.

There is no doubt that, in the fight to deliver Christianity to the heathen, both Protestants and Catholics sent their best brains to India, rather than to Africa or China. This implied a recognition of the inherent spirituality of Hinduism, which demanded more than average sophistry and persuasion to win converts. There was a belief that India had a high degree of ancient civilisation which by the late eighteenth century, as the Moghul Empire was fading, had allowed decadence to seep in, offering Christianity the chance to fill the gap. As the thirty-eighth report to the Calcutta Auxiliary Bible Society made plain in 1851, India had been a great country. 'But its people are not happy ... the Hindus may be clever, acute, skilful to a certain point but their moral character as a native is debased in the extreme.' The missionaries were confident that the greatest need of early-twentieth-century India was 'the power of the spirit of the Lord. His people must bring themselves much more into subjection to his spirit.'[1] They rejoiced therefore at the number of mass conversions – sometimes as many as 8,000 adults were baptised within six months – particularly among the poor, the tribals, the outcasts and the lower castes, who saw becoming Christian as a method of social mobility. Yet the flaw in this type of missionary activity *en masse* was that it failed to eradicate the deeply ingrained values inherent in the caste system and many Christian converts found all that changed was the name of their faith and their method of worship, not their way of life. The problem of lower-caste (Dalit) Christians was one which, more than a hundred years later, defeated even Mother Teresa. The Roman Catholic Church today has recognised that any continuance of caste practices within Christianity is a scandal and is beginning to take steps to investigate this.

It was not for lack of trying that the missionaries failed, with one or two notable exceptions, to win adherents from the country's elite; nor was it simply that Christianity became tainted as a poor man's religion. In the nineteenth century Hinduism started to fight back.

Some notable thinkers urged Indians to reclaim their own traditions, which they saw Christianity threatening. The centre of this cultural ferment was Bengal.

The beginnings of the movement can be traced to Raja Rammohun Roy, today widely considered the greatest Indian intellectual of the century. The Bengal Renaissance, the name history has given to the movement which flourished largely after his death in London in 1833, rested on achievements such as his Bengali grammar and his tract denouncing suttee or widow-burning, a practice which the British eventually banned in 1829. In his aim to rid contemporary Hinduism of what he deemed inauthentic traditions he looked back to reinterpret the Vedas, Hinduism's earliest scriptures. Hardline Hindus rejected his ideas while some European Unitarian missionaries liked them sufficiently to claim him as one of them. The sect which he founded three years before his death appealed to anglicised Hindus, sceptical of extreme dogma, and became known as the Brahmo Samaj, the most influential rational movement of religious and social reform in nineteenth-century India.

Rammohun Roy had many spiritual heirs. There was a high point in 1893 when Swami Vivekenanda, a young Bengali at the Chicago World Fair, took the Parliament of Religions by storm as he pleaded for the mutual recognition of the spirituality of East and West; each had an important contribution to make and there should be fellowship between the two, but no attempts at proselytism. At the same time an eccentric Englishwoman, Annie Besant, proponent of the philosophy of Theosophy, gave many a lecture in which she aired her views that India was a victim of the mischief wrought by Christian missionaries. A friend of Vivekenanda, Mrs Besant was trying to lead Indians back to their own gods and arouse their sense of self-respect and pride in the greatness of their religions. Partly thanks to Annie Besant and her espousal of Theosophy, the British public was being exposed to the ideas of comparative religion almost for the first time and became aware of the words karma and reincarnation. Theosophy, which became briefly fashionable in Edwardian London, did not exclude Christianity or any other religion: it taught an adherent to live his own faith. Novels and travel writing of the period were also beginning to transform Western attitudes to non-Christian religions. Ignorance and suspicion were finally giving way in some enlightened quarters to sympathetic interest. Nowhere is the ambivalence between the values of East and West more vividly demonstrated than in Rabindranath Tagore, the Bengali writer of prose and poetry, musician, artist and religious reformer whose father was a devotee of the Brahmo Samaj and who had believed, like many other highly educated Bengalis, that British colonial rule was a force for the good and necessary for the reform of a degenerate society. But he also insisted on the importance of India's ancient spiritual values for contemporary India. Bengalis may have seen him as the product of Western influence but the West, which largely learnt about him from 1912 onwards, when he visited England for the first time, saw the bearded mystic as an embodiment of Indian spirituality. In 1913 he won the Nobel Prize for Literature, the first Asian writer to be thus honoured; the award confirmed both his status as a spiritual ambassador of India and his central role in Bengali literature.

However high-minded and devoted to the interests of the natives some of the individual missionaries may have been, their belief in colonial supremacy, at least until the end of the nineteenth century, underpinned the entire structure of their work. It was partly responsible for rumours in 1857, which may have fed the Indian Mutiny, that there were plans forcibly to convert the whole population to Christianity. It is most clearly seen in the failure to promote native bishops. By the end of the nineteenth century there were more than twenty Catholic bishops in India but every single one was a European, and this in spite of a Papacy, particularly under the vigorous Pope Leo XIII, that had been pressing for some years for the indigenous clergy to be given greater responsibility. It was not until well into the twentieth century that the number of Indian priests equalled and then surpassed that of foreigners.

Thus, towards the close of the nineteenth century, there were Indian voices calling for pride in Indian culture, gently gnawing at this colonial confidence. These voices were most fiercely expressed from mid-1905 onwards in the patriotic Swadeshi movement, which began in Bengal, but spread throughout India as opposition to the British grew. In the face of this new-found Indian pride, European missionaries began to display some uncertainty and even to question the purpose of their work for the first time. Conversely, the Roman Church at the end of the nineteenth century was staging something of an energetic comeback in India. The Jesuits had been re-established and many new orders and sisterhoods, some of them specifically established for missionary activity, found themselves with apparently inexhaustible supplies of recruits. The Protestant missionaries, whose churches were allied with the Raj and the empire-builders, were now seen as less trustworthy than the Catholics, whose convent schools, especially in Calcutta, were a great success in teaching and in building a rapport with the country's elite. It was this late-nineteenth-, early-twentieth-century resurgence which fired Agnes Bojaxhiu in Skopje.

However, even if, from the sixteenth century onwards, those selected for missionary activity were among the more intelligent of European society, their intelligence rarely stretched to an understanding of native traditions of worship. Jesuit annual reports, when referring to any opposition to missionary activity, frequently describe the 'devil' at work. 'It implies a mentality that was closed to seeing God at work in the traditional native religions and their cultures ... There was a complete failure to analyse the cultural conflicts within a local context and no mental disposition on the part of most foreign missionaries to see anything good in the native cultures,' one modern commentator, a former Jesuit priest and director of the Xavier Centre for Historical Research in Goa, has explained. This man, whose Catholic family has been in Goa since the sixteenth century, is now appalled at the colonial mentality of a Church which allowed Hindu temples to be demolished and which has left a lasting legacy of resentment towards foreign missionaries. 'It was not just the architecture of the temples that mattered. The temples in the ancient Hindu culture were also the repositories of literature that was mainly of a religious nature and were centres of learning and teaching. The Portuguese missionaries introduced the first printing press in Goa, but they also sought to destroy the existing books on Hinduism in Goa,' wrote Dr Teotonio R. de Souza.[2]

And yet, considering both the time and the vast financial resources Christian Europe devoted to converting India over four centuries, Christianity is hardly a success story there. By the end of the millennium, merely 2 per cent of the population is estimated Christian compared with nearly 50 per cent in Africa. Nonetheless 20 per cent of Indians are educated by Catholics, and those 20 per cent comprise a much larger percentage of the country's opinion formers.

Thousands of missionaries may have followed in St Xavier's colonial footsteps but in the latter half of the twentieth century there are concerns whether missionary activity, with conversion as a goal, can be defended as a moral activity at all. Of course the missions, both Catholic and Protestant, have from the first provided valuable educational institutions – not just training institutes for priests but excellent schooling from the youngest age – many of which, in improved form, are still in operation today. By the end of the century, there were a large number of mission schools, often government-aided, teaching (in the main) the poorest classes. As a result, in what was still for the most part an illiterate country, the Christians were second to the Parsis in terms of literacy. 'The European powers found the peoples divided, poor and barbarous and left them united, prosperous and well on their way to taking their place in the councils of the nations of the world,' Bishop Neill concluded in 1964.[3] On the other hand, there is no doubt that societies are destabilised as people are torn away from their roots. The final breakdown of colonial rule led to deep self-reflection for many missionaries who had, inevitably, often allied themselves with the imperial powers. By the middle of the twentieth century, they wished to stand more clearly with the casualties of colonialism.

'Go therefore and make disciples of all nations: Baptise them ... and teach them everything I have commanded you.'[4] These words, spoken in the Bible by the resurrected Christ, stand at the heart of Christian mission. From the first, the followers of Jesus Christ recognised it as their holy duty to pass on their faith to all. Mother Teresa herself has said, 'A missionary is a person who has to go and spread the good news.'[5] However, by studying other religions and seeing how they have enriched their communities, many modern theologians conclude that there is not only one route to God and that perhaps the limit of missionary activity should be to set an example by doing good, practical work. The key word seems to be inculturation, or learning, by dialogue with other religious traditions, how to live alongside other cultures without either losing or imposing one's own. 'The Church no longer sees itself as the perfect society, over against and independent of the world.'[6] But as Cardinal Joseph Ratzinger of the Sacred Congregation for the Doctrine of the Faith pointed out in March 1995, it is not a straightforward process applicable in all circumstances. 'The operation can only have sense if Christian faith and the other religion, together with the culture which lives from it, do not stand in utter difference to each other ... Inculturation therefore presupposes the potential universality of each culture.'[7]

I went to visit one of the senior lecturers at the Missionary Institute in North London. 'Mission today is enabling others to find God, or the divine element, and facilitating others in the discovery of their own truth,' the Catholic sister told me. 'The young men and women I teach will be involved in helping to find the divine element in themselves and in others. Of course there will be older men and women operating the old model who are still into the numbers game – how many baptisms have we had this week? – but we certainly don't say we must save you any more.'

The future missionaries studying here on a four-year course come from many countries and backgrounds. They have all made a commitment and will take the three vows of poverty, chastity and obedience. 'But the meaning of obedience has changed and no longer means just doing what you are told, but taking responsibility for listening to what do we need in this area. The modern missionary does not want to go abroad to a less well-developed country in order to do good, but to be a presence and work alongside the people. They may do good, but that is a spin-off, and then they might move out. A missionary today will be taught how to get in touch with the culture and myth of the religion he is working among ... to search for the divine spark within themselves and others and perhaps even find this through such a simple experience as a child being awestruck by flowers. They are trained to help people find the transcendant as translated by their own culture.'[8]

Agnes wanted to be sent to serve in India. Barely eighteen when she took the decision, she had chosen with characteristic determination to join a specific religious order in Ireland because she had been well advised that that was the route most likely to fulfil her ambition, once she had grasped some basic English. She can have been under little illusion that entry into this Order would probably mean never again seeing her family or home town, since religious life of the era did not allow for holidays at home. Her choice of the Loreto Sisters, the Irish branch of one of the top women's orders, the Institute of the Blessed Virgin Mary (IBVM), was perhaps more significant than she realised, although it is highly unlikely that she knew much, if anything about, Mary Ward, foundress of the Order she was joining. Mary Ward is, today, recognised for carving out a new role for women in the Church in defiance of the male hierarchy in Rome. Nor would she have known much about earlier women missionaries in the field, because they were until recently rarely written about.

When Agnes arrived at Loreto Abbey, Rathfarnham, in 1928, Mary Ward was newly rediscovered. But for more than two centuries her sisters had been forbidden to mention their pioneering foundress who had, quite literally, been cut out of their history. Mary Ward was born in 1585 into a well-to-do English recusant family in York. When she first decided to be a nun she had to go abroad and joined a community of Poor Clares in St-Omer, in Northern France. However, by the age of twenty-four, she realised that 'some other thing' was required of her by God and she returned home with high hopes of being a new kind of nun. She gathered around her a small group of like-minded women and went abroad again to run girls' schools, which met, not surprisingly, with fierce opposition from the Church hierarchy. Over the next years as she pleaded for recognition of her Institute from Rome, she developed three main requirements; the first and most essential was not to be enclosed. Secondly she required government by a woman as general superior, which, by implying that God can speak directly to women and that a cardinal is not required in the background, was equally offensive to the male dominance. The third demand was for no rigidity in the hours of prayer. She was determined that her sisters would not face tension between attending prayers at set times and ministering to those in need. She looked to a spirituality that would give 'the freedom to refer all to God, seeking and finding him in all things'.

However, Mary Ward was making huge and visionary demands on the seventeenth-century Church, for which she suffered enormously in her lifetime. She was even, in 1630, imprisoned in a convent in Munich and Pope Urban VIII compared her Institution to 'a weed in a cornfield' to be uprooted. At the time of her death in 1645 her sisters were still living under a Papal cloud without validation of the Institute. Only in 1713 did Pope Benedict XIII agree to give the Order orthodoxy, allowing it to take the name of the Institute of the Blessed Virgin Mary – but on condition that there was no mention of Mary Ward as founder.

And so Mary Ward's sisters continued to pray and to teach, setting up new centres in Europe, often unaware of the original vision. One of the centres was the Bar Convent at York and it was here, in 1812, that Frances Teresa Ball, a judge's sister, was sent by the Archbishop of Dublin to make her noviceship. She then returned to Ireland and, with the Archbishop's help, founded a new convent in 1822 at Rathfarnham House, three miles outside Dublin. This became known as the Irish branch of the IBVM, although as Frances Teresa Ball lost contact with the sisters in York she in effect founded a new community, to be called Loreto Abbey. Loreto was a shrine in Italy to which Mary Ward was especially devoted, so it would seem likely that Frances Teresa Ball was well aware of Mary Ward's importance. The Loreto sisters soon moved out to Australia, Kenya, South Africa and India, establishing a foundation in Calcutta in 1841 along with their reputation as educators of girls – middle-class girls who went to nice schools, unashamedly elitist. Finally, in 1909, the vindication of Mary Ward began in earnest when Mother Catherine Chambers, a former Anglican sister who joined IBVM, started researching Ward's life, a project which resulted in a two-volume biography. In 1953 the Vatican spoke of Mary Ward as 'this incomparable woman whom England gave to the Church'. She has yet to be canonised, but she is recognised today as a pioneer of the active, unenclosed congregations for women whose spiritual message is of timeless importance.

Rathfarnham still exists. It is a magnificent building set at the end of a long driveway bordered by trees. In the front hall hangs an imposing full-length portrait of Mother Frances Teresa Ball in black from head to toe and, in the words of one IBVM sister, 'quite luscious'. Agnes stayed at Rathfarnham for several months, mostly studying English but also learning something of the history of the Institute, which by this time was again fairly monastic and traditional. She would probably have been given a doctored version of Mary Ward's life as someone with a vision for educating girls but not as someone who opposed the Church. She would also have learned of the twelve young pioneers who bravely went to Calcutta in 1841 when a request came for the nuns to teach there. India already had some resonance in Irish homes as a place where many sons died as soldiers, leaving Catholic children as orphans. At first Mother Teresa Ball felt she could not spare any of her sisters from Loreto schools in Ireland; after all, Dublin had slums too. But eventually she agreed and then there was no shortage of volunteers ready to go to India, swayed by tales of wild pagan children who would otherwise be lost to the faith.

The party of twelve, some of whom were as young as sixteen, were a sombre-looking group in their black serge habits with black cashmere veils over their eyes, starched tippet linen caps and the heavy underwear that was both customary and necessary in Ireland. They allowed themselves no fans and no ice. After four months aboard the *Scotia* they were met with a formal reception in Calcutta and soon found a splendid three-storeyed mansion in the city as their convent. Number 5 Middleton Row, with two and a half acres and full of choice trees, was the oldest house in Calcutta, formerly the country residence of the Governor, and was considered equal in stature to Rathfarnham. By January 1842 the nuns had the first sixty pupils of Loreto House and within three years they had established three boarding schools, two orphanages and three day schools in and around Calcutta.

Some seventy years later, on 1 December 1928, when Sister Teresa, as Agnes now was, and her travelling companion from Yugoslavia, Sister Mary Magdalene, were deemed ready to leave for India aboard the sailing ship *Marchait*, little had changed. Their voyage out was a mere five weeks but the seas were heavy and, as there was no Catholic priest on board, although there were three Franciscan missionaries, they were unable to attend mass until the ship reached Port Said.

CHAPTER THREE

ARRIVAL

The young novice from Skopje now wrote long and enthusiastic letters to *Catholic Missions* herself. She described landing in Colombo at the end of December: 'We observed the life in the streets with strange feelings. It was easy to pick out the Europeans' elegant garments among the multi-coloured garments of the dark-skinned people. Most of the Indians were half-naked, their skin and hair glistening in the hot sun. Clearly there was great poverty among them.' She and her friends were appalled at the idea of being pulled by an emaciated rickshaw man, but when she found herself having to travel thus, she decided the only answer was to pray that her weight was light enough not to cause the man to suffer too much.

When the group re-embarked, she was relieved and delighted to find that a Catholic priest had joined them, so they could now have daily mass. 'Thanks be to God we began the New Year well with a sung mass, which seemed a little more majestic to us than low mass.' They sailed on to Madras, where Teresa and the other novice 'were shocked to the depths of our beings by [the] indescribable poverty. Many families live in the streets, along the city walls, even in places thronged with people. Day and night they live in the open on mats they have made from large palm leaves – or often on the bare ground. They are all virtually naked, wearing at best a ragged loin cloth. On their arms and legs they wear very thin bracelets and ornaments in their noses and ears.' After describing another 'horrifying sight' she concluded: 'If our people could only see all this they would stop grumbling about their own misfortunes and offer up thanks to God for blessing them with such abundance.'[1]

On 6 January 1929, they moved up the Hooghly to Bengal. A group of Indian sisters were waiting on the docks to greet them. 'With a joy which I cannot describe,' wrote the young Teresa, 'we touched the soil of Bengal for the first time. In the convent church we first of all offered up our thanks to the Redeemer for allowing us to arrive safely at our destination. Pray for us a great deal that we may become good and courageous missionaries.' During the journey out the girls had confided to each other what sort of life they thought lay ahead. According to Sister Francis Michael Lyne, who trained with Mother Teresa in Calcutta, Agnes had intimated to another novice 'that she realised that there was a future for her which was different for most of us'.[2]

Sister Teresa and her friend from Yugoslavia stayed just a week in Calcutta and were then sent to Darjeeling in Assam for the rest of their two-year noviciate. Darjeeling, at 7,000 feet in the foothills of the Himalayas, was the fashionable summer headquarters for the British, who escaped there annually when the heat of Calcutta became unbearable. Here, the wealthy expatriates led a life of luxury and leisure, parading around the town or indulging in resort activities. For the next two years Sister Teresa was trained here in prayer, the scriptures, theology and the spirituality and history of her Order. She started to learn Hindi and Bengali and to improve her English. The Novice Mistress undertook all the training herself and there were weekly visits to the confessor.

In addition, for two hours in the mornings the novices taught young boys and girls in a local school. Sister Teresa also worked occasionally in a small medical station and wrote an emotional account of her time in the hospital for *Catholic Missions*: 'In the hospital pharmacy hangs a picture of the Redeemer surrounded by a throng of suffering people, on whose faces the torments of their lives have been engraved. Each morning, before I start work, I look at this picture. In it is concentrated everything that I feel. I think, "Jesus, it is for you and for these souls!" Then I open the door. The tiny veranda is always full of the sick, wretched and the miserable. All eyes are fixed, full of hope.' Recognising that many of the patients had undertaken appallingly long journeys simply to attend the hospital, she explained: 'I tell them to bring those children whom their doctor is unable to help, that I have wonderful medicine for them. They promise and do as they say. I am happy to be able to give them the best medicine of all: holy baptism, eternal blessedness.'

On 24 May 1931, Agnes took her first vows of poverty, chastity and obedience as a sister of Loreto. During the ceremony, Agnes would have prostrated herself, lying prone for some time with her face to the floor. This was a symbolic death, as the sister was leaving behind all worldly desires. The dramatic nature of the action, undertaken by all nuns at that period, was to emphasise the solemnity of the decision and the difficulty of undoing it at any time in the future.

Agnes chose as her name in religious life that of St Thérèse of Lisieux, although she omitted the 'h' in order to avoid confusion with another sister in the congregation. St Thérèse, the French Carmelite nun who died in 1897 of tuberculosis aged twenty-four, had led an utterly simple convent existence devoted to prayer for the missions and missionary priests. Although her life was totally lacking in activity, her autobiography, Story of a Soul, became a bestseller in many languages. She was canonised in 1925. Significantly, this was the role model Mother Teresa took for herself, not the other St Teresa of Avila, the Carmelite nun of sixteenth-century Spain, renowned for her writings on spiritual life and on the importance of spiritual growth for the sisters in her care and declared, in 1970, a doctor of the Church, the first woman to be so named.

Soon after her first vows, Sister Teresa went to Calcutta to begin her teaching career. The Loreto sisters were by now famous throughout India for the high quality of their teaching in the 'English medium'. Many Hindu, Parsee and Anglo-Indian families, who might otherwise be critical of the Catholic Church, nonetheless sent their children to Loreto schools; women educated at Loreto schools and colleges have assumed some of the highest positions in post-Independence India. Sister Teresa was despatched to Loreto, Entally, in the eastern, industrial district of the city, one of the least exclusive of the six Loreto schools in Calcutta. This was one of a group of schools in an extensive compound behind a solid wall, broken only by an impressive entrance erected in the classical style with two columns on either side. The main school had about 500 pupils, most of whom were boarders, from wealthy families who could afford the fees. In the same compound was another establishment, St Mary's, attended by some 200 pupils who came from a variety of backgrounds, poor and middle class, many of whom were orphans who paid no fees and were taught in Bengali. The Daughters of St Anne, a diocesan congregation of Indian women, who wore saris rather than nuns' habits, did much of the teaching at St Mary's.

For the next nineteen years, Sister Teresa lived the life of a Loreto nun and educator of girls in a form of semi-enclosure. Her chief subject was geography, until she became headmistress. According to the strict rules, no Loreto sister was ever to go outside the convent walls except for the yearly retreat to Darjeeling or in an emergency, such as a hospital visit. But even then the sister would be shielded from the rest of the world as a private car would be sent and she would always travel with another sister as companion. Sister Francis Michael recalls Sister Teresa standing out in those days 'in a sense that she was so very virtuous and good and anxious to do the right thing. She was very, very much as it were in love with Almighty God and any of the sidelines of friendship or enjoyment that would have distracted her from that, I would say, she never really went in for. Even when she did go for a holiday ... she would have enjoyed it and would have been very nice with people but not the type of person that put any kind of pressure before her tremendous work for God.'[3]

On 14 May 1937, also in Darjeeling, Sister Teresa repeated her three vows for life and shortly afterwards also became headmistress of the school.

But neither the sheltered atmosphere of Darjeeling nor the protected life of a convent compound can have been quite what Agnes Bojaxhiu had hoped to find in India when, as a teenager in Skopje, she dreamt of her future life. The stories in *Catholic Missions* had been of sisters so poor that they lived in thatched huts with wild animals rampaging through the encampments and hardly enough money for food and clothes. Other sisters regularly had to tramp through rice fields and running streams, and one issue told how a Mother Superior was saved by her orphans from a snake poised to bite her, another of a lucky escape from a tiger.

In addition, Sister Teresa had seen for herself that there was desperate need in Calcutta. In 1935, she had been asked to teach at the school of St Teresa, which involved her in a short but significant walk through the city. Immediately as she emerged from the compound, directly on the other side of the wall from St Mary's, throbbed the impoverished life of a typical Calcutta slum or bustee. It was, like the many other slum areas in Calcutta, rapidly expanding both in numbers and in space. This one was called, picturesquely, Moti Jhil or Pearl Lake, a name derived from the pond of discoloured sump water at its centre. There was nothing picturesque about it for the number of poor who managed to exist there in the sparsely covered hovels which they made themselves as best they could from a mixture of corrugated iron, old cans, plastic and rags or whatever could be found. Families had to pay rent for the right to remain there, even though conditions were unhealthy and unsanitary in the extreme; there was little money left for food.

Many of the older girls at St Mary's, Entally, including several who were Hindus, belonged to the Sodality of the Blessed Virgin Mary, a group very similar to the one which had so influenced Agnes. At the study club attached to the Sodality they discussed the ties binding those who have with those who have less, and the girls were eager to become more actively involved by visiting families who lived in the slums or poor patients in the large Nilratan Sarkar Hospital. Sister Teresa could reinforce the yearnings of the sensitive young by telling the girls that there was joy in transcending self to serve others. But, however much she wanted, she could not accompany them because of the strict rule of enclosure.

Calcutta in the 1930s wore its former imperial splendour with difficulty. This was a city founded on marshy swampland purely for the trading opportunities it offered. The seventeenth-century village became first a flourishing town and then an imperial capital. It was the second city in the British Empire and the Victorian seat of the British Raj, until superseded by Delhi on 1 April 1912. But its reputation had always gone before it. Clive of India described it as 'One of the most wicked Places in the Universe. Corruption, Licentiousness and a want of principle seem to have possessed the Minds of all the civil servants, by frequent bad examples they have grown callous, Rapacious and Luxurious beyond conception...'[4]

In 1905 the British partitioned Bengal, creating two separate administrative provinces and huge animosity on the part of educated Bengalis in Calcutta. The division separated Calcutta from its hinterland, cutting off both supply and demand routes, and stirred Muslim–Hindu rivalries in a dramatic foretelling of 1946. Yet still Calcutta remained the second city of the Commonwealth, after London, and fourth city in the world. 'In a sense,' wrote Geoffrey Moorhouse, the historian of Calcutta, 'the story of Calcutta is the story of India and the story of the third world in miniature. It is the story of how and why Empire was created and what happened when Empire finished.' For the City of Palaces, in spite of its unhealthy climate, ubiquitous lepers and beggars, smelly slums and, today, thousands of international charity workers, has never completely lost its palatial air nor its reputation for vice. It was thought of then, as now, more often as being the location of the Black Hole, in which between 123 and 146 (the exact number is disputed) whites died in foul circumstances than as a city of thriving culture, which it is. There were dramatic changes in the aftermath of the First World War as a number of younger men, juniors in their firms, came out from England and appeared to flout many of the traditions of older Calcutta society. These fast young men, searching for novelty and excitement, centred their way of life on the newly opened Firpo's Restaurant. Firpo's, with its jazz band, advanced lighting and modern furniture, was an immediate success and symbolised the louche way of life taking over. It was sometimes difficult to know whether Calcutta's Old Guard felt more threatened by the fashion for cocktail parties or by the constant political disorders. At all events, by the mid-1930s it was clear that fortunes were harder to make, servants' wages were going up and both the imperial and commercial splendour were decaying; Europeans were both concerned and critical of the decline but essentially inactive.

When Kipling famously described Calcutta as the City of Dreadful Night, what had particularly appalled him were the activities of the Eurasian (Anglo-Indian) whores in the city's back streets. Several residents of 1930s Calcutta remember a city embarking on a downward moral spiral. Rumer Godden, the writer, who lived there from the mid-1920s until 1939, was one of the few Britons who made it her business to understand the seamy side of the city – the Calcutta which Mother Teresa was just beginning to witness.

In 1930 Godden opened up a dancing school, where she taught not only English girls but also Anglo-Indians, an unheard-of idea for which she was ostracised by the British community. Then, when she married and did not want to live the life of other British women of her class who would visit clubs and gossip all day long, she reinforced her social isolation and ability to observe with her sharp, writer's eye. Superficially, Calcutta could still give the appearance of being a well-kept city. 'People would go out in the evenings in their buggies for a drive – cars came into fashion very slowly – Chowringhee was the main street, a wide boulevard which used to have the most beautiful palatial buildings such as the Bengal Club, the Army and Navy Stores and the Grand Hotel and the Maidan [open space] all edged with flowering trees. In spring this was an absolute sight of jacarandas and acacias, then there was football and cricket,' Godden remembered.

'But at the same time Calcutta has always been a dreadful city; there is a legend that if you put a bag of Calcutta dust under a virtuous woman's bed she'll become unvirtuous immediately and there was, when I was there, a tremendous number of exchanges of wives among European society and all sorts of scandals and corruption.' Godden, who had started her mixed ballet school 'as an act of defiance', later took to prowling around the back streets of Calcutta to research her novels. 'When I married, I couldn't put up with the life of clubs and parties and I used to walk alone behind Chowringhee. You come to the New Market, a big conglomeration of food shops together, where I would wander for hours. It was a festering labyrinth of little narrow streets and I learnt so much about those back streets ... people living on pavements, whole Eurasian families in two rooms with very little furniture, and a naked light bulb. The meat safe was usually on a shady wall to keep all the food in. It was very squalid. The streets were crowded with lepers, begging all amongst the people, smallpox was rampant and you did see babies in dustbins. What was horrifying then was that no one did anything about it,'[5] Godden recalled sixty years on.

The brutality of life in Calcutta, the snobbery of the clubs and the total lack of conscience was witnessed by others too. Roy Nissen, who went out to Calcutta in 1924 to work on the East India Railway, quickly became acquainted with the detailed rules of behaviour. 'On Saturday nights, the girls would go out only with a covenanted wallah, i.e. one of the direct recruits from Britain, not a domiciled wallah. The covenanted wallahs would take the Eurasian girls, who were very pretty, around the Maidan in their cars for some canoodling in the back of the car, hoping not to see their bosses, as part of the rule of covenant was that they were not allowed to get married for three years. But these relationships were never going to end in marriage.' According to Nissen, even the liaisons between covenanted wallahs and domiciled European girls – still a notch down from English-born English girls – rarely resulted in marriage but often in pregnancy. 'However, this was a simple matter in Calcutta at the time; there were many Bengali doctors who were very good at that sort of thing – it cost between 200 and 300 rupees to arrange an abortion. Parents were to blame as they were always hoping they would entangle a covenanted wallah eventually and therefore encouraged the relationships.'[6]

Malcolm Muggeridge, the British journalist whose role was to be so central in the Mother Teresa story, acquired his first taste of Calcutta life in the 1930s and pretty hedonistic it was too. Leaving his wife Kitty and three small children behind in England, he lost little time in indulging in an obsessive relationship with a local girl which nearly cost him his marriage. As a journalist working on the *Calcutta Statesman*, whose offices were in Chowringhee, he could have immersed himself in Indian life. Yet as a sahib with a car and driver, who rode his horse in the early morning along the Maidan, he was easily able to isolate himself from the life and people of the city. 'On one occasion I did get involved and then too nearly for my taste,' Muggeridge wrote in his journals. He was being driven to a dinner party for which he was rather late when his driver ran over a man. As the threatening crowd drew closer and there was no sign of an ambulance, the driver picked up the apparently lifeless body and drove him to a hospital. Muggeridge, feeling rather absurd in his dinner jacket, went with the injured man to the hospital, offered money for treatment, and was relieved when it appeared that the victim was no more than badly shaken. After witnessing several more sprawling bodies in the hospital, including one with his neck slashed and blood pouring, Muggeridge repaired to his dinner party even later. Here the guests spent the evening calmly discussing how such things came to pass in Calcutta.

Yet there were some people who not only saw the enormity of the problem but were prepared to do something about it. The Rev. and Mrs Arfon Roberts, for example, first went out to the Mission Hospital in West Bengal in 1926 because they had heard stories of such desperate need. Mrs Roberts, a trained nurse, found it difficult to make her patients accept any Western treatment; they often left it too late to ask for any help and died. Because the Mission House was near some shady trees, beggars, waifs and strays would often sit all day on the pavement and sometimes just lie down there to die. Mrs Roberts particularly remembered a madwoman, a Hindu, who was sometimes completely naked, just shouting and screaming outside the house. 'In Hinduism, I saw no compassion. A beggar would come to the door and their religion would make them give alms: a coin, a handful of rice, but if that beggar, through want of food or illness, collapsed on the doorstep they would do nothing, they wouldn't touch them, their religion would forbid them to. They would give alms because that was an insurance for them for the future life, but never the helping hand.

'I saw so much of it in midwifery, the terrible hardship of life for women. They were absolutely bound hand and foot.' She felt the worst burdens were borne by a childless wife, many of whom she knew committed suicide. 'If they can't give their husband a son they were worth nothing at all. I had so many come to me whose life was absolute hell because the other village women taunted the husband. Then there were so many occasions when girl babies were mysteriously killed in the night with no police inquiries.' Arfon Roberts and his wife were among a group of missionaries working among lepers and the blind. 'It was social work of course, but that was the beginning. Before, hardly anything was done for blind people and work among the poor like Mother Teresa's work in Calcutta – all that is a direct result of the caring work of the Church.'

Calcutta in the 1930s was, therefore, already a deeply troubled city when British involvement in the Second World War further engulfed it. Few Indians felt that this was their war – indeed many, but not a majority, supported the Bengali hero Subhas Chandra Bose in his attempt to organise an Indian National Army, which led to him declaring war on the Allies in 1943. But Calcutta that year had its own problems as it faced one of the worst famines in a long line of famines and natural disasters. In 1943 the cause was partly that the Japanese occupation of Burma had cut off a vital outside supply of rice after Bengal had been producing indifferent harvests for several years, nothing like enough to feed the sixty million inhabitants of the province. In addition, 1942 had brought both a devastating flood and a cyclone which had destroyed the winter paddy harvest. Meanwhile official, largely British, incompetence aggravated by the inevitable profiteering and stockpiling made a natural disaster even worse.

It was not long before the number of beggars and destitutes roaming the city of Calcutta in a desperate search for food had dramatically increased. What started as a trickle became rampaging mobs, many of whom crowded for shelter into suburban railway stations or took up pavement space for want of anything better. The starving peasants, who had probably lost everything they possessed in the cyclone, now sold what little remained to undertake the journey to Calcutta because they had no other choice. Widows who had lived for years with brothers were now asked to leave. Husbands abandoned sick wives and wives forsook young children, all in a desperate attempt to forage for something to eat. A reporter describing what was quickly to become commonplace told the story of a family settling on Lower Circular Road, the husband lying as if dead while the mother cooked vegetable peelings for her three young children. She was so emaciated that the reporter said he could count her ribs from a distance of ten feet. 'She was not more than twenty-five years old yet there was no womanly breast. Only two nipples dangling from two parched sheets of skin, from which everything else seemed to be dried up...'[7]

As frantic children staggered from door to door begging for some tiny scrap or gruel, charitable institutions began to set up soup kitchens. There were reports of families so tortured by starvation that they tried to sell their children; others began to eat dogs (occasionally dogs were seen to eat human bodies too) or scramble among refuse heaps for scraps; people even threw themselves on the ground to eat food that had been dropped.

Exactly how many people died in the cataclysm is still at issue. The communists claim twelve million lost their lives while statisticians at Calcutta University in 1944 put the death toll at three and a half million. 'Whatever the truth of the catastrophe it scarred the soul of Calcutta in a way that partly explains some of its history since,' wrote Moorhouse.

The British were not exactly fiddling while Calcutta was burning. Nonetheless, the Secretary of State for India, L. S. Amery, felt confident enough of the situation to tell the House of Commons in London that 'there is no overall shortage of food grains. India has harvested a bumper crop of wheat this spring. There is, however, grave mal-distribution.' With the men mainly serving in the forces, it was the women who came in for most stick. The wives from England had, on the whole, never found it easy to adjust to such a male-dominated society. With servants to do the shopping, cooking and other chores, and ayahs to look after the children, there was little for them to do and the climate made many of them ill. Now there were accusations that, in a time of real crisis, many were still leading idle, highly social lives and contributing little to the war effort. Rumer Godden, who knew Bengal well, was invited in 1945 to investigate. The result, *Bengal Journey: A Story of the Part Played by Women in the Province, 1939–45*, mounted a good defence for the wives. Godden pointed out that they had learnt to manage in spite of the heat – Englishwomen had previously been sent to the hill stations in summer. Many of them had not been home for eight years, had had babies in India and had coped with dreadful illnesses uncomplainingly.

In 1940, the wife of the Governor of Bengal formed the Lady Mary Herbert Bengal Women's War Fund to finance the Red Cross, and the following year the Calcutta Women's War Committee published a pamphlet in which nearly twenty women's voluntary organisations gave an account of themselves. '1942 was a terrible year for India after the fall of Singapore because it was flooded with exhausted men, refugees, the wounded, sick, dying, lost and insane. The women often had their homes full of refugees while they were driving or nursing in the great heat with little food. They ran canteens and staffed hospitals in spite of much violence, panic and antiwar slogans.' Godden's brief was to write about British women undertaking predominantly Anglican-based initiatives but, increasingly, Bengali women were involving themselves in these crisis committees too.

With the Japanese armies threatening in nearby Burma, there were times when Calcutta appeared perpetually in smoke, either from bombing raids or from the burning ghats, constantly in use with so many deaths. For Sister Teresa the war must have been a severe frustration. In spite of worsening food shortages she continued to teach at Entally until 1942, when the entire compound was requisitioned for use as a British military hospital. Girls' dormitories became hospital wards and most pupils, including orphans, were evacuated to converted hotels miles away. Sister Teresa, however, remained in the city and, as headmistress of St Mary's and teacher-in-charge of the Daughters of St Anne, oversaw a difficult move to a building on Convent Road,

Calcutta. The enclosed nature of her Order demanded that she did not go outside and involve herself more actively in the crisis, but she soon found herself pressed into other roles such as teaching religion as well as geography and history. 'She taught it in such a wonderful way that everything came alive for us,' one of her pupils recalled later. It was at this time that she met Father Celeste Van Exem, a Belgian Jesuit who became her spiritual adviser as he came to celebrate mass and give sermons during the school's evacuation period.

Yet from about 1941, according to another Belgian priest, Father Julien Henry, she started to take girls from the Sodality with her into the slums and the hospitals, presumably recognising that the emergency conditions made a strict interpretation of the rules of enclosure no longer tenable. As she walked around the filth and squalor she would say to the girls: 'Would you give a helping hand if someone began a service to help these poor people?' When the girls naturally said yes she then asked: 'But supposing your parents objected.' After what they had just seen, few of the girls believed their parents possibly could. Mother Teresa inspired many girls in this way. 'She was testing our minds,' explained Sister Florence, a Bengali girl from a middle-class family and another former pupil from Entally.[8]

In August 1946 an even greater disaster compounded the famine and wartime dislocation and destruction of the city. Although the British emerged victorious from the war, they were far from a conquering nation. It had been clear for some time that British rule was almost over and, in the subsequent jockeying for political advantage, Bengal played a key role. The negotiations between Jawaharlal Nehru and Muhammad Ali Jinnah about a division of the country into Hindustan and Pakistan were further complicated by a threat to declare Bengal an independent state if the British eventually handed control of all India to a Hindu government. Mahatma Gandhi, who had shown the strength of his peaceful, non-violent approach during the salt march of 1930, intensified his passive resistance from 1939, but had little control over the escalating violence in Calcutta. As the negotiations deadlocked, Jinnah and the Muslim League declared Friday, 16 August a direct-action day and the Muslim leader of the Calcutta administration, H. S. Surawardy, declared the day a holiday, which ensured that everyone was free from work and on the streets.

In Calcutta itself, a city already tense from demonstration and counter-demonstration, strike and further strike, the trouble began as usual in the north with stabbings, lootings and soda-water bombs. But as Friday progressed – a day of 91 per cent humidity and a temperature of 88 degrees Fahrenheit – it quickly and savagely degenerated into a day of butchery with both Muslims and Hindus either burnt to death, hacked to death or beaten to death. The violence, looting and numerous gangs on the rampage increased until Saturday, when the military was called in to quell what was fast becoming a bloody massacre. With piles of bodies all over the town there were then fears of a cholera epidemic. Only after a further nine days of intimidation and slaughter did a peace of sorts emerge. At least 5,000 people had been killed, and although an estimated 110,000 had fled from Calcutta another 100,000 had been displaced within the city itself, and many thousands wounded.

In the face of such violence and killing, all deliveries of food and supplies were stopped. Sister Teresa, responsible for 300 girls in the boarding school with nothing to eat, eventually found herself forced to go outside the convent in a search for food. She told her friend and biographer, Eileen Egan: 'We were not supposed to go out into the streets, but I went anyway. Then I saw the bodies on the streets, stabbed, beaten, lying there in strange positions in their dried blood. We had been behind our safe walls. We knew that there had been rioting. People had been jumping over our walls, first a Hindu, then a Muslim. You see, our compound was between Moti Jhil, which was mainly Muslim then, and Tengra with the potteries and tanneries. That was Hindu. We took in each one and helped him to escape safely. When I went out on the street – only then I saw the death that was following them.'

That day, 16 August, Sister Teresa, a recognisable figure in her thick, black, street-length habit with voluminous folds, a white coif around her head and black veil reaching to the floor, managed to get hold of a large quantity of rice to feed the children. But what she had seen – butchery and hatred on an unimagined scale, known as the Day of Great Killing – was an image never to be erased. Although the immediate crisis passed, Muslim and Hindu killings continued sporadically.

Less than a month later, on 10 September 1946, Sister Teresa was able to leave the smouldering city as she set off for Darjeeling on her annual retreat. Throughout the train journey to the peaceful hill station, the gruesome images of the last few bloody weeks were still fresh in her mind. But for more than ten years now, whenever she had been exposed to the real city beyond the compound walls, she had seen indescribable misery and need and she knew she was failing to meet that need. She heard about the poverty and squalor from girls in her school who had joined a branch of the Sodality, very like the one which had influenced her in Skopje. These girls went regularly to visit patients in a local hospital and the poor in the Moti Jhil slums. Yet all she could do was encourage her pupils in work she had herself once hoped to be doing. In addition her mother, who had always been a strong influence in her life, had been writing to her regularly from Tirana, reminding her of her original purpose in going to India 'for the sake of the poor' and those who are alone in the world.[8] She had just had a birthday, her thirty-sixth, which she might reasonably have expected to be the mid-point in her life. She must have been reflecting: how could she make an impact on the lives of the poor if she spent her days teaching the children of the well-off? One alternative had been tried already. Her predecessor, Mother de Cénacle, had persuaded twenty girls from Moti Jhil to come to the convent in an attempt to educate them. But the convent life was such a stark contrast to their own that the experiment had not lasted. Mother Teresa's decision to reject a life of teaching is extremely significant. Meditating on these contradictions and the future direction of her life, she came to a decision. But she describes the process rather differently as 'a call within a call'.

'This is how it happened,' she told her spiritual director, Father Julien Henry. 'I was travelling to Darjeeling by train, when I heard the voice of God.' Father Henry then asked her how she had heard his voice above the noise of a rattling train and she had replied with a smile: 'I was sure it was God's voice. I was certain that He was calling me. The message was clear. I must leave the convent to help the poor by living among them. This was a command, something to be done, something definite. I knew where I had to be. But I did not know how to get there.'

Mother Teresa has said repeatedly, ever since, that her change of direction was 'God's doing, not mine'. Perhaps even more importantly she has insisted that it 'was the work of God, I knew that the world would benefit from it'.[10] In examining what has subsequently become the myth, this is of crucial significance. If Mother Teresa is, as she maintains, 'simply a pencil in God's hands', she is at once both more humble than an ordinary nun and yet also much more powerful than any world leader. Equally, it means that anyone who believes in the possibility of divine inspiration, and not necessarily from a Christian standpoint, must stop before questioning any aspect of Mother Teresa's work and ponder the legitimacy of doubting what is divinely ordered. Or does it? Is what Mother Teresa has achieved in any way diminished if it is seen fair and square as the work of a determined woman who had a clear vision of what needed to be done in her adopted home? Many good, not always religious, people feel moved to pursue a particular purpose in life without having had a direct communication with, or mystical experience of, God. This does not lessen their achievements.

Yet Sister Teresa, with her innate sense of discipline, was the first to recognise that the Church could not possibly easily agree to any nun going off and founding a new order whenever she felt merely inspired, or challenged to move in a new direction. She continued on to Darjeeling, prayed fervently during the retreat, and, on her return to Calcutta, spoke to one or two of the nuns who were closest to her about what she believed had happened.

She also approached Father Van Exem and explained to him about her 'call within a call', which she knew necessitated leaving her teaching Order and starting something new. She had a clear idea from the beginning that her new vocation was to offer care for the poor in the streets and that she and any helpers who might join her would be linked to the poor by a special vow. Van Exem was sympathetic to her idea. 'Mother was not an exceptional person. She was an ordinary Loreto nun, a very ordinary person but with great love for her Lord,' he recalled later.[10] He felt instinctively that her very ordinariness indicated the genuineness of her call, 'and subsequently, all that has happened is difficult to explain in a natural way'. He gave Sister Teresa two options: either she could write directly to Rome and ask the Congregation for the Propagation of the Faith to release her from Loreto or she could discuss the problem with the head of the Calcutta Archdiocese, Archbishop Perier, and seek his co-operation. Van Exem favoured the latter and Sister Teresa agreed.

However, Perier was not pleased when Van Exem eventually told him. 'The Archbishop became upset,' says Egan in the fullest account of how Mother Teresa eventually came to leave one order and set up another. 'He wondered about the effect on Loreto and did not relish the idea of a lone nun on Calcutta's streets.' He decided that no decision should be taken for at least a year. Shortly afterwards, when the Mother Superior had been informed, Sister Teresa was sent away to Asanol, a mining town about 130 miles north of Calcutta, where she was put in charge of the kitchen and garden and allowed also to teach some geography. It was a time of reflection and she wrote many letters to Father Van Exem, which he described as 'beautiful'.

This year of waiting, from 1 January 1947, when Sister Teresa was largely out of Calcutta, coincided with the first year of India's freedom. In August 1947, when the British finally quit India, the partition of the subcontinent between the newly created Muslim state of Pakistan and largely Hindu India caused yet further bloodshed and dislocation on a scale previously unwitnessed. The explosion of violence which followed the end of British rule resulted in at least a million deaths, with some of the worst violence in Bengal as the line of partition went right through its heart, slicing entire communities, even fields, down the middle. There followed one of the largest population shifts in history, with as many as sixteen million men, women and children displaced as Hindus and Sikhs fled into India and Muslims into either of the two sides of East or West Pakistan. At least four million refugees made their desperate way into West Bengal within a matter of weeks. As the wave of revenge killing spread first to neighbouring states, such as Bihar, there were eventually few areas of the subcontinent untouched by the slaughter.

Meanwhile, Archbishop Perier was having private consultations with some churchmen who knew Sister Teresa as well as with some who did not. One such was Father John Jansens, the head of the Jesuits in India, whose view was sought as to the viability of a nun living on the streets of Calcutta to help the poor. It was a highly volatile and dangerous time politically to be starting such a new venture and the reputation of the Church could be seriously put at risk. But at the end of the year he concluded that at least she might take it a stage further by writing to the Mother General of Loreto asking to be released from the Congregation. However, still not convinced that it was necessarily a wise course of action or that God was directing matters, Perier insisted that his own co-operation was dependent on his being allowed to vet such a letter. When he saw it he insisted on changing the word 'exclaustration' – being put outside the convent compound – to 'secularisation' – being returned to the secular world. This was no mere detail: such a momentous change would have meant that in her new life Teresa would no longer be a vowed nun but a laywoman. The modification was a severe blow to Teresa. Van Exem remonstrated with Perier on her behalf, pointing out that it would be extremely hard for her to attract other young women to join her if they were without vows. However, as Perier was immovable, saying that God would decide, Teresa agreed and rewrote the letter to Dublin asking simply for secularisation.

According to Van Exem, who recounted the story to Egan – no copies of the letters are available for release – the Mother General at Rathfarnham gave her permission immediately for Teresa to write to the Congregation at Rome, but told her to ask for the indult of exclaustration. Armed with this new letter, Teresa duly prepared a letter to the Pope, Pius XII, and the Congregation for the Propagation of the Faith, explaining that she believed God was calling her to give up everything and surrender herself to Him in the service of the poorest of the poor.

But once again, when the Archbishop read the new letter with the request for exclaustration, he refused to send it unless the word was changed to secularisation. Once again, Sister Teresa agreed and rephrased the letter; in February 1948, Perier sent it to the Apostolic Nuncio in Delhi for forwarding to Rome. In July 1948 Sister Teresa was informed that a one-year decree of exclaustration, which she had been praying for but had dared not ask for, had been granted. This came about apparently because the letter never even reached Rome, although it was not until 1971 that Mother Teresa discovered this. The Delhi nunciature, well aware of the appalling conditions in Calcutta and perhaps sensing Mother Teresa's deep desire to remain a nun, had agreed to the request, under conditions of exclaustration, on their own initiative without forwarding the letter to Rome. It is almost certain that, had the letter gone to Rome, it would have been dealt with 'in a routine manner'. In other words, according to Eileen Egan, 'if the request had been granted it would have been granted precisely as worded. Who in far-off Rome would have been minded to make a

word change in such a matter?' Luck, coincidence, human drive or
even God's will?

Eileen Egan comments that, perhaps by stretching the term somewhat, 'It was a sort of prevenient grace that prevented the request ...
reaching the Vatican.'[12] Prevenient grace, she describes as being the
sort of anticipatory grace often applied in reference to the Mother of
Jesus – Catholics believe she was preserved from original sin in
anticipation of the fact that the Messiah was to be born to her. Just as
likely, however, is that those in Delhi recognised the desperate need
for anyone who was prepared to offer themselves with any social or
humanitarian aid. It is also just possible that, since Delhi took seven
months to reply and then with a letter dated April, there was an
element of human bungling involved. Might the request and its reply,
amid the chaos of post-war independence, have been buried under a
mound of papers? At all events the myth received a further twist when
in 1969 Mother Teresa told Malcolm Muggeridge, 'I wrote to the Holy
Father and, by return post, I got the answer on 12 April.' Memory
plays strange tricks and for her, seven months of anguished waiting
had been compressed into 'by return post'.

At a distance of fifty years and 4,000 miles there is a danger that
by reducing Partition, one of history's most cataclysmic events, to a
few lines the impact is completely blurred. Yet the pain and severity
of the dislocation it caused cannot be underestimated. However, if
Sister Teresa had claimed that she wished to be released from the
convent in order to help alleviate the human misery on her doorstep
she would not have been allowed to do so, other than by leaving
religious life altogether. Because of her insistence not just on leaving
but on remaining vowed with the aspiration of setting up a new order
she had to prove the unprovable, that this was the will of God. It was
for this reason that Archbishop Perier tried to test Sister Teresa's
obedience. It would hardly be surprising if he were not also concerned
that letting a nun go off on her own might set a bad precedent and
possibly break down the authority of the established orders. In the
event he could not fault her and this led him to believe he was
witnessing the will of God.

As quickly as it could be arranged, Sister Teresa, now thirty-eight,
went to stay with the Medical Mission Sisters in Patna to learn some
basic nursing skills. She changed into the more practical, cheap white

cotton sari, similar to the one worn by the Daughters of St Anne, which was to become the uniform of her Order throughout the world. The Medical Mission sisters were mostly American and European women trained as doctors with specialities in obstetrics and surgery, nurses, laboratory technicians and nutritionists. At their nurses' training school they prepared many Indian girls in various branches of nursing skills, some of whom had been Loreto pupils.

Teresa arrived in Patna with strong ideas about the need for austerity to reinforce the spirituality of her future life and very concerned with the hours of prayers, penance and fasting; the Medical Mission sisters taught her much of practical use. Most important was diet; Sister Teresa originally wanted to exist on no more than rice and salt, like the poor, but the Medical Sisters explained that without regular, if simple, balanced meals with sufficient protein, they could not perform their work. They also needed adequate rest and a strong emphasis on personal hygiene. From their own experience of hard work in poor conditions they too accepted strict rules of prayer but with nothing later than 9 p.m. They wore white cotton habits and veils which were changed daily, even twice daily, and head covering was kept to a minimum with no starch. They also imparted to her such basic procedures as giving an injection, helping to deliver a baby and making a bed with hospital corners.

Sister Teresa could not spend more than a few weeks in Patna as she had been given only a year to prove herself. In December she returned to Calcutta alone, to start her new life.

CHAPTER FOUR

EARLY HELPERS

In December 1948, Sister Teresa moved in with the Little Sisters of the Poor, a group of nuns who ran St Joseph's Home. After a few days helping to look after the 200 or so aged, impoverished inmates, Sister Teresa began her new life. The slums she knew best, which cried out for help at every level, were near her old school, at Moti Jhil. So she set off, with some meagre rations in her bag, and walked for an hour to the other side of the city.

She immediately gathered a group of children around her, all eager to learn, and did what she was trained to do: teach. But as she had no desks, blackboards or books she just took a big stick and wrote the alphabet in the mud. Next, she taught the young children something about cleanliness and then, of course, Godliness. She slept little because at night she often wandered the streets and went into some of the slums to help with the cleaning or washing or to look after a sick child.

During this time, at Archbishop Perier's request, she kept a diary. Fragments of it have often been quoted because the radical nature of her vision is starkly and humbly expressed. Her utter conviction and trust in God never faltered and were strengthened by the urgency and need she was now encountering. 'Oh God! If I cannot help these people in their poverty and their suffering, let me at least die with them, close to them so that in that way I can show them your love,' she wrote. The diary, however, has apparently not been preserved. According to Eileen Egan, it was in Father Van Exem's hands for many years until she persuaded him to return it as she wanted to destroy it. 'There may have been revelations of her own reactions and emotions that she preferred not to share,' explained Egan. It is not a surprising decision for anyone concerned with how posterity might view them and is very human. Yet why should Mother Teresa be any the less saintly for being seen as a fully rounded human being, like the rest of us, complete with doubts and worries, ambition and determination? Her action could merely reflect an understandable desire for privacy once she realised that millions of people would be interested in reading such a diary but seems also to indicate a concern for shaping the image perhaps not anticipated in traditional concepts of sainthood, where the ego is expected not to intrude.

Soon, Sister Teresa began looking for new living premises. It had not been easy leaving Loreto but she had done so to create a new entity, not merely to be absorbed into another existing order. Initially, she had an idea that she should be living among the people she was trying to help, in the slums. But Father Van Exem persuaded her she would tire herself out unnecessarily, made enquiries among the local community and discovered that Michael Gomes, a Roman Catholic Indian, had a large three-storeyed colonial house at 14 Creek Lane, grand but somewhat faded and now half empty as two of his brothers had moved to East Bengal in 1947 to help support the Christian population there. There was a large room available on the second floor for which he wanted neither rent nor money for food. In February 1949 Sister Teresa moved in. Her first full-time helper was a widow called Charur Ma, who had been the cook at St Mary's, and was to stay with Mother Teresa until she died.

Next, Sister Teresa found a hut in Moti Jhil – for which she paid five rupees a month rent – in which to teach the children. Many of the older priests said privately they thought she was mad. But she must have been popular as many poor and dirty children also came to seek her out at the house in Creek Lane. Some people, hearing of this nun's pioneering work, also started delivering small gifts, but, as the need was endless, Sister Teresa worked to attract others.

There is a story of how she visited a pharmacy at this time with a long list of medicines and the pharmacist told her he could not possibly help. However, she simply sat down to wait and recited her rosary. At the end of the day the pharmacist took a fresh look at the list: 'Here are the medicines you need. Have them with the firm's compliments.'

Within weeks of moving to the Gomeses' house, she was joined by her first would-be novices, mostly girls from the school where she had been headmistress and who all continued to look upon her with enormous respect, verging on adulation. The first was Subhasini Das, a quiet girl from a wealthy Bengali family who had been a boarder at St Mary's from the age of nine. She admitted she had always been deeply influenced by her headmistress and later took the name Sister Agnes, Mother Teresa's baptismal name, out of respect for her. The first to become a Missionary of Charity sister, she remained for years one of Mother Teresa's most treasured helpers. In fact there were many vocations from Sister Teresa's classes, although some joined older-established orders such as Loreto or the Carmelites. Sister Teresa had clearly been an unusually persuasive and charismatic teacher, and not simply during formal class periods. By May 1949 she had three followers; by November, five, and at the beginning of 1950 seven. News of her work was spreading so fast that she soon had her first recruit from Dacca, East Pakistan (now Bangladesh), Sister Margaret Mary.

Four of the early recruits to Sister Teresa left school in their last year before they had taken their final examinations, causing considerable anguish for their parents, who were distraught to see a daughter leaving school without a secondary-school diploma. Sister Florence recalled: 'After she had been to Patna, soon she came fishing to our homes talking to our parents and to us. We were sitting for our School Final exams then, so our parents thought study was more important than anything else. But Mother said, "No, no. The sooner you come the better." She was young looking and very dynamic; she inspired us. So we joined her.'[1] At least one set of parents severed contact completely with their daughters for a while, so upset were they at seeing their girls being asked to undertake such revolutionary work – going into the slums to help the poor – on behalf of someone virtually unknown, and giving up their families and school work in order to do so. Sister Teresa did try to find time to coach some of these young girls for their school finals. In addition, she encouraged Sister Gertrude, who became the first Missionary of Charity doctor, to complete her medical studies. Although two early candidates decided to leave after experimenting with the new life, the majority stayed and are still working as Missionaries of Charity today.

According to Desmond Doig, a journalist who knew both Mother Teresa and many of the first sisters, 'Hers must have been inspiring words, words not so much calculated to impress profoundly a sensitive young girl, but words coming straight from the heart of a woman deeply moved and already aware of God's need for her.' Doig, an Indian Christian of Anglo-Irish origin, was born and brought up in India, served with the Gurkhas in the Second World War, then joined the *Calcutta Statesman* initially as an artist and later as the paper's roving reporter. It was in this capacity that he met and wrote about Mother Teresa just as she was starting out. 'I was tipped off by a Catholic functionary and fellow newspaperman,' Doig recalled later, 'to "watch this woman; she's quite extraordinary. She's going to be a saint." '[2] Doig is generally considered to have been the first Indian journalist to give media prominence to Mother Teresa. She always remained a very special person to him.

As more recruits arrived, the Gomes family extended the accommodation available and the little group now ventured out on buses and trams to their work. At the end of 1949 Mother Teresa applied for, and was granted, Indian citizenship and, once her year of exclaustration under obedience to the Archbishop was over, she set in motion her application to Rome to form a new congregation.

As she explained in her new constitution: 'Our object is to quench the thirst of Jesus Christ on the cross by dedicating ourselves freely to serve the poorest of the poor, according to the work and teaching of our Lord, thus announcing the Kingdom of God in a special way ... Our special task will be to proclaim Jesus Christ to all peoples *above all to those who are in our care*. We call ourselves Missionaries of Charity' (italics added). Mother Teresa never shrank from emphasising that she was working for Christ first and above all. The name, incorporating the word 'missionary' with all its resonance in Indian history, had been chosen with care and intent. Of course she hoped that by her actions she would win more converts for Christ. The constitution could not express it more clearly, even if conversion alone was never a goal.

The sisters were to be ready always to serve the suffering Christ, whom they saw in the poorest of the poor. From the first, their day was to be strictly regimented, rising at 4.40 a.m. with prayers at 5, mass and sermon at 5.45, then breakfast and cleaning. From 8.00 to 12.30 they worked among the poor and needy with lunch at 12.30 followed by a short rest. From 2.30 to 3.00 they were allowed time for reading and meditation, then tea, and from 3.15 to 4.30 Adoration of the Blessed Sacrament. Afternoon service to the poor lasted until 7.30, followed by supper, evening prayers at 9 p.m. and bed at 9.45.

But perhaps the most important single aspect of the constitution was a fourth vow: 'to give wholehearted and free service to the poorest of the poor'. It was this extra demand which was to set them apart from other groups of nuns who had tried to 'do good' before. It is probably this radical requirement that has attracted so many idealist spirits to come and work with Mother Teresa and try to change the world.

Archbishop Perier sent the constitution to Rome for approval and on 7 October 1950, little more than a year after she had left Loreto, Pope Pius XII approved the foundation of the Order of the Missionaries of Charity. From this date on Mother Teresa, head of the new Order, becomes a player on the world stage.

The day I met Mother Teresa for the first time − 7 October 1995, was the usual sort of hot and steamy Calcutta morning. Not quite knowing how to greet such a holy person I stopped en route at the Calcutta flower market and chose a handful of simple red roses in a bucket which the young boy then took from me and, dexterously and swiftly, arranged into a most artistic posy. I made my way, clutching the already wilting bunch, to the Mother House, now at 54a Lower Circular Road, and, obvious tourist that I was, found myself set upon by the wretched who wait in this most obvious of all alleyways. Once inside the large, airy courtyard, having observed in the corner the statue of the Virgin Mary that marks each of Mother Teresa's convents, I followed everyone else upstairs as mass was about to begin. Suddenly, Mother Teresa rushed past me at the top of the stairs and I thrust the roses into her hands along with a copy of the children's book I had written fifteen years ago. She thanked me, she blessed me, she urged me into the chapel and told me there was adoration all day for the volunteers to celebrate the Pope's blessing on the Order. She would speak to me later, she promised. God bless you, she added. So I joined the dozens of shoeless European volunteers who string themselves out behind the tidy rows of Missionaries of Charity in the brown-shuttered chapel and the chanting began. In choosing this day I had no idea of its special significance until I read the small blackboard outside the chapel which announced the forty-fifth anniversary of Papal approval of the Order.

During the 1950s, the Missionaries of Charity flourished at a dramatic rate; as more sisters joined, Mother Teresa opened more free schools. Wherever she could gather one hundred children the Calcutta Corporation was by law obliged to erect a school building. Almost immediately after the constitution was approved, and with the free schools mushrooming, the sisters realised they would need to move on from Creek Lane and find bigger premises for their Mother House. 'Mother Teresa knew enough about God's providence by now not to be discouraged. She and her sisters simply added this latest need to their prayers and carried on as before. She also made a novena to St Cecilia and offered special prayers for this need,' was one author's account of what happened next.[3]

The story of how they acquired 54a Lower Circular Road, usually explained as if it was simply the answer to these prayers, is often told in biblical language. And so it was that ... that a Muslim was emigrating to Pakistan and selling his large house. Father Henry made an offer for it on Mother Teresa's behalf, the money having been authorised by Archbishop Perier. 'The largest figure that he could propose was less than the worth of the land on which the house was built; but miraculously, the offer was accepted.'[4] Truly a miracle? Or was the unnamed Muslim actually quite satisfied with the price he was paid for a building in need of repair in a no longer fashionable area?

Not long after this the small band of Missionaries of Charity decided to start a home for dying destitutes. The catalyst had been an unsuccessful attempt by Mother Teresa to take to hospital a desperately ill woman, lying on the pavement while rats and cockroaches ate her feet. She was turned away at every hospital she tried. Mother Teresa, displaying the awesome determination she was now learning she could use to such devastating effect, would threaten not to move with her patient until a bed was found. The woman was both too ill and too poor and the overcrowded hospitals, with sickness spilling into their corridors, either could not or would not take her and so she died, after all, on the streets. Death, for Orthodox Hindus, is associated with elements of impurity and pollution and so touching a corpse is a task reserved for the scheduled castes (or untouchables). Poor people thought to be at the point of death might be thrown out of their lodgings to die on the street so that the room in which they were living was not tainted. Not surprisingly, therefore, there were many wizened and emaciated figures to be found on Indian streets lying alone as they waited to die. Soon Mother Teresa addressed herself to the Calcutta Corporation and begged them to find a place where such people could 'die with dignity and love'.

She was already known to the health officer of the Calcutta Corporation as someone both serious and obstinate after she had tried to persuade the Corporation on more than one occasion to improve the water supply to the bustees. Significantly, she had also made herself known to Dr Bidhran Chandra (B. C.) Roy, Chief Minister of West Bengal from 1948 to 1962. Dr Roy had studied medicine in London at the turn of the century, was physician to both Gandhi and Nehru and continued to see patients free of charge most mornings. But he had a long-standing interest in politics, having joined the Swaraj (nationalist party) in the 1920s and, after a period of imprisonment during British rule, had twice been Mayor of Calcutta in the 1930s. His real career had started after Independence, interestingly coinciding with Mother Teresa's beginnings, and her canny political instinct recognised in Roy a man of stature, intelligence and great influence. From the start, dealing with politicians and business leaders never fazed Mother Teresa: she always recognised the importance of developing relationships with powerful men, which may seem extraordinary given that she had spent twenty years in a convent. But as convent headmistress she would have been in contact with important Catholic priests and have had discussions with influential men and women who were parents at the school. In addition, the first eight years of her life were passed in a vibrant household where politics and business were pursued with equal élan. Perhaps some of her father's political spirit had rubbed off on her.

At all events, the Corporation offered Mother Teresa the use of a former pilgrims' hostel, near the temple of Kali, in the heart of a bustling Hindu thoroughfare. Mother Teresa accepted as soon as she saw it, although it was at the time occupied by goondas – loafers and thugs who were using it as a place to drink and gamble – and it was filthy, because she knew that many of the city's destitutes went to Kalighat to die. For devout Hindus, this was one of the most sacred spots in the city to be cremated. Also the layout was ideal, with two separate sleeping areas, electricity and gas connections for cooking and a large enclosed courtyard where clothes and bedding could be hung up to dry. A key helper here was a niece of Dr Roy who had heard about Mother Teresa's work in the slums and remained a devoted worker until her death. When Mother Teresa went on retreat, it was she who took over the running of Kalighat.

Mother Teresa called the pilgrims' caravanserai Nirmal Hriday, a Bengali phrase meaning Pure Heart. It was opened on 22 August 1952, a feast day dedicated to the Immaculate Heart of Mary. Such 'coincidences' matter to Mother Teresa. As with most things she has started, there was never a clear plan as to how it would work when it opened, although in fact it has changed little since that time. Nirmal Hriday has became a symbol in the West of all that Mother Teresa stands for. It is an abode of last resort, a place to die with a roof and some food, never a hospice. Initially, there was considerable opposition to Mother Teresa being there, as she was on sacred temple precincts. There were demonstrations and the Brahmin priests were aghast that Catholic sisters had been given permission to work so near their shrine; they regularly petitioned the Calcutta Corporation to evict them as the agreement was only provisional. But nothing happened. Only after the Missionaries of Charity cared with devotion for a young Brahmin priest with tuberculosis, who had virulently opposed Nirmal Hriday, did a slow change of attitude begin.

At the beginning Mother Teresa tried to have a doctor oversee Nirmal Hriday. After making enquiries among the Catholic community twenty-two-year-old Marcus Fernandes was 'volunteered'. Dr Fernandes, whose sister had been a pupil at Loreto, was attached to one of the big Calcutta hospitals while completing his studies, but agreed to help Mother Teresa whenever he could.

Fernandes, young and inexperienced though he was, found the haphazard nature of the treatment contrary to good clinical practice and made several suggestions to Mother Teresa which he felt would improve the patients' chances. He pointed out that many inmates were suffering from malnutrition, not cancer, TB or even heart ailments, and that if fed dhal (pulses) and rice with vitamin supplements they could recover. He wanted a better diagnostic approach and a separate area for these people so that he could properly assess those who were starving and could be cured. 'He could not persuade her to treat them with vitamins,' explains his widow today. 'She did not want them treated; she expected people to die and would simply say, "Well, she's gone to God." She was not particularly interested in medicine.' Mother Teresa has made similar comments on other occasions. Once a visitor to the Home for the Dying described how, when asked by her sisters to try and save a sixteen-year-old on the verge of death, she blessed him and said, "Never mind, it's a lovely day to go to Heaven." '[5] Frances Meigh, while working for Mother Teresa with a view to joining her Order, was told after she had managed to get a young girl with a heart defect admitted to hospital, 'You have done the work, she has a place. Now it is up to God whether she lives or dies, that is all. It is nothing to worry about.'[6]

Dr Fernandes remained a helper on an ad hoc basis for about two years before going to London to complete his postgraduate training at the London School of Hygiene and Tropical Medicine. When he returned with his new English wife, he offered his services again to Mother Teresa but was appalled to see 'that a lot of money was being wasted and the facilities were not improving'. In particular he was upset by an expensive X-ray machine which had been donated new eighteen months previously but was now lying rusting. When he asked Mother Teresa about this she simply said that there was no one to use it. She may never have asked for this or other such equipment, but surely someone could have been trained to operate it.

Patricia Fernandes, who had been working as a medical statistician at the same London hospital, volunteered too and was asked to sort out medicines, which had been airfreighted as donations from America, now lying in a godown (warehouse). She recalls: 'It was all pretty chaotic. I was given the job of unpacking huge crates of medicines from the USA. Somebody in America had the bright idea of people emptying their medicine cabinets and sending the contents to Mother Teresa's charity. This must have been done at some cost. When I opened them they were full of slimming pills and blood pressure pills, tranquillisers and anti-depressants, many of them out of date. What we wanted was antibiotics, vitamins etc. When my husband pointed this out to her she just wasn't interested.'[7]

Mrs Fernandes then worked for a time with some of Mother Teresa's other projects. 'I met Mother Teresa on many occasions and, quite unusually apparently, she came to our flat.' The reason for the visits was that Dr Fernandes was treating a minor skin ailment for Mother Teresa. However, when the treatment finished and he sent her a bill, she declined to pay. At this point the young doctor severed all connections. 'My assessment ... was that she was an extremely ruthless and hard woman ... my husband had quite severe differences of opinion with her and she would never listen to or take any advice on anything ... she could only cope with uneducated people, the sort she could shout orders at.'[8] Dr Fernandes spent much of the rest of his life helping various groups of medical and teaching missionaries throughout India but he never revised his opinion of Mother Teresa. There were others, too, at this time who saw her as 'very determined and quite ruthless in getting her own way'.[9]

Major E. John Somerset worked as Professor of Ophthalmology at the Calcutta Medical College Hospital from 1939 to 1961. Having decided to stay on after 1947 he accepted mostly private patients but was renowned for the way he encouraged people to bring their animals to him, for which he never charged. He retired to England in 1961 and in 1979 wrote his memoirs (unpublished), which he deposited in the India Office Library in London. In the early 1950s, Somerset recalled, there were about five or six charitable homes for the aged and infirm in Calcutta – mostly for Anglo-Indians. 'I used to see anyone from them when I was asked to, free, of course.' Thus he was not surprised when a Catholic nun by the name of Mother Teresa started to bring him a few cases:

There were a lot of destitutes and Mother Teresa and her band of helpers would go into the streets and pick them up to die with dignity. She did a lot of good work for people but more important and significantly she set an example to the local Hindu population, who were normally only interested in their own family members. She also showed up the Calcutta Corporation, who were neglecting the running 'Duty' of taking collapsed and dying people off the streets. She used sometimes to come to me in an ambulance with several children suffering from gross Vitamin A deficiency whose eyes had been so severely affected that the corneas were melting away (Kerat Omalacia). The deficiency was mainly due to lack of milk in tiny children up to the age of three or four years. Several times I told Mother Teresa I would see as many cases as she liked and give her as much time as was necessary if only she would let me know beforehand and not come in the middle of the morning when I had a full quota of patients booked at half-hourly intervals, including people whose time was valuable and who wanted to be seen at their appointed time. Nevertheless she persisted in turning up without an appointment at the most awkward times. I thus regarded her as an unmitigated nuisance.[10]

Overall, however, there was a tremendous amount of goodwill towards Mother Teresa in 1950s Calcutta especially, but by no means exclusively, from the Anglo-Catholic community. Much of this was orchestrated by a young Englishwoman, Ann Blaikie. Blaikie was the daughter of an Anglican clergyman who had trained as a teacher and converted to Catholicism before marriage. But at the beginning of the 1950s she and her husband, John Blaikie, a lawyer working for British American Tobacco, were posted to Calcutta. Ann Blaikie had been working in a mission charity shop until, having become too heavily pregnant to reach the bottom drawers, she looked for some other form of voluntary work. In 1954 she read an article about how Mother Teresa had rescued an abandoned baby from a dustbin and this persuaded her to offer any assistance she could give. As soon as she met Mother Teresa she was convinced that this was someone who would give direction to the rest of her life.

At first Blaikie's activities largely involved fund-raising and providing toys, food and clothes for the children. There was a pool of potential helpers among the expatriate European women in the capital upon whom Blaikie could easily call since most had time on their hands but little sense of fulfilment. Not all wished to become involved, however. One Calcutta wife told me she found it too exclusive for her taste. 'I remember being asked by Ann Blaikie to join the Marian Committee and make stuffed toys – mostly giraffes I think – but when I tried to introduce some of my friends who were not Catholic, eyebrows were raised and it was suggested, "Well not really." I carried on for a bit but as soon as I was pregnant with my first child I was pleased to have an excuse and give it up.'[11]

Ann Blaikie was a most loyal, convinced and influential supporter until she and her family returned to Britain in the 1960s. After that, she continued to work indefatigably for the cause, helping to set up the International Association of Co-Workers. Mother Teresa famously called Blaikie, who became her spokeswoman for a while, her 'Other Self'. They particularly complemented each other when it was necessary to give a speech: articulacy was never one of Mother Teresa's gifts, but Ann Blaikie found public speaking came easily to her. Blaikie organised the first, highly successful campaign to 'touch a leper with compassion' before she left Calcutta and spoke at the opening of the leprosy dispensary at Titagarh in northern Calcutta.

The attitude of the European, mostly English, wives is important. Many of them lived in the smart suburb of Alipore, frequented certain clubs and socialised only with each other. If they met Indians at all it was either through work or at an official level. 'Well, there doesn't seem to be any resentment – quite the opposite if anything,' says Basil Cox, the British boss invited to dinner at the Bengali home of a promising Indian on his staff in Vikram Seth's novel, *A Suitable Boy*. 'But I wonder what people like the Chatterjis really think of us ... After all, we're still quite a presence in Calcutta. We still run things here – commercially speaking, of course.' Seth expressed succinctly the continuing sense of superiority among the British, and there are those who believe Mother Teresa went a long way to providing a justification for the privileged lifestyle about which a number of them felt guilty in post-Independence India. As they stepped out of their cultivated surroundings and encountered the poverty and deprivation of the slum dwellers and beggars, they could say to themselves, 'We help Mother Teresa,' and then carry on with their tennis or bridge. Is this attitude any different from many of those who make donations to charity today?

Leonard Cheshire, the wartime bomber pilot and Catholic convert who devoted the rest of his life to helping the disadvantaged, thought about this colonial guilt factor rather more profoundly. Explaining why he felt the need to open homes in India, when he was still building up his charity in this country, he said:

> The call from India ... was so compelling that I should have been doing wrong to ignore it. Even though the odds seemed heavily against living up to the promise I felt an inner conviction that it was right to make it. But there was another factor too.

On my previous visit to India during the war, I didn't come into contact with the ordinary people, though I know I should have done. But I came away with the impression that England had gone to India more with a view to what it could take out than what it could put in. I don't mean to belittle what we did and gave in the field of administration and engineering and that sort of thing, but I don't really believe we did what we might have done for the poor and helpless.

This idea, that the British in particular wished to help Mother Teresa as a way of expiating imperialist guilt – whether justified or not – has never been entirely demolished. It was for some a potent motivating factor, but many Indians are aggrieved at the way the notion is promoted to imply that the Indian state and people are indifferent to suffering and it is only Westerners, symbolised by Mother Teresa and the Missionaries of Charity, who help the poor.[12]

And there were other Europeans who helped Mother Teresa not out of a sense of contrition or because they had time on their hands but simply because they saw the need and knew how to get things done. One of Cheshire's most hardworking and valuable supporters was Larry Donnelly, an engineer and a Catholic who had been in India since 1948, described in an account of the Cheshire Homes as 'the chap who is running the show in Calcutta'. Donnelly, living in India with his young family and working for Babcock and Wilcox, had been managing trustee of the Cheshire Indian Foundation for two critical years and had built up remarkable support in Calcutta for the home at Serampore. When around 1955 he was introduced to Mother Teresa by the White Fathers he was so impressed by her energy and directness that he immediately set about raising the money to build one of her first outpatients' clinics in Calcutta.

Not only is this clinic very real to me, so is the euphoria at the time of its opening. It was a simple one-storey building called the Loyola Dispensary built on to the back of St Teresa's Church in the parish of Entally, run by the White Fathers, open initially only on Tuesdays and Fridays. I know this because I have seen a home movie taken by the Donnelly family which captures its construction almost brick by brick, as well as the celebration when it opened. Mother Teresa herself was there, of course, looking younger and smiling, but hardly altered from today's familiar face. Other guests were Father Julien Henry, resplendent in his long white cassock, and the young Indian Archbishop, Cardinal Valerian Gracias. I saw this film, now transposed on to video, as a guest of the Donnellys, whom, it turned out, I had known for some years and who were near neighbours of mine. It was an emotional evening. David Donnelly, in the flickering cine film a child of eight or so playing with his father among the rubble that was to become the dispensary, has known Mother Teresa since he was a child in Calcutta and often saw her technique in action in those early days, as he told me over dinner. 'She would fix her eyes on you imploringly and say, "We really need such and such, I don't know where we're going to get it from," and you would find yourself rooted to the spot, writing out a cheque for whatever it was she wanted.'

By the late 1950s Mother Teresa was not the only European trying to alleviate the situation. A committed Catholic, Sue Ryder, now Lady Ryder of Warsaw, was another who got to know Mother Teresa at this time. Ryder had worked as a nurse in 1945 and had also helped rescue concentration-camp victims. Her subsequent mission and the Sue Ryder Foundation developed from this. But when Ryder visited India in 1957, two years before her marriage to Leonard Cheshire, and suggested some sort of co-operation between their ventures, Mother Teresa was already confident enough of the future to respond negatively. The two women visited slums together and there was even a possibility of using some Missionary of Charity sisters in Ryder-Cheshire homes. But it soon became clear that Mother Teresa, recognising the strength of her own numbers, was not interested in anything which might lead to a merger. The two women had a basic difference in their approach to the same problem. Sue Ryder, knowing from her war experience that nights are often when help is most needed, believed it was no good trying to live in two worlds and always felt strongly that, even if you get away briefly to pray, you must not leave those you are trying to help. Mother Teresa, however, has always insisted that the sisters must return to the convent to say the Divine Office and the Mass.

There was Dudley Gardiner too, a retired British major who for more than twenty years ensured that as many jobless pavement-dwellers and destitutes as he could reach should have at least one proper meal a day. Gardiner, a self-effacing man, set about his task with a mixture of army discipline and all the sincerity and solemnity of a monk taking holy orders. He was deeply religious, yet often said he was still searching for God throughout his life. Partly because of this uncertainty, he never considered himself suitable to join a religious community, yet he sought the same commitment as Mother Teresa and her Missionaries of Charity.

He envied Mother Teresa, whom he once described as 'my dear friend and source of inspiration', because she has 'at the centre of her dynamic work a complete and utter belief in God. Her burning faith is simple, uncluttered by theological nuances. She loves and trusts God and He has used her to accomplish miracles in Calcutta where one might be tempted to think that with so much poverty God had closed his eyes to human suffering and human dereliction.' Dudley Gardiner, in spite of his six-foot-two-inch, twenty-stone frame, admitted that he looked on Mother Teresa as 'a plain little nun who bullies me ... yes, she bullies me. Not unkindly, I hasten to add, but when she wants something badly she insists and one feels that one is arguing with God himself. It's an unequal struggle. I always capitulate.'[13]

After a lonely childhood, some of it spent in India, Dudley Gardiner joined the army and endured three years as a prisoner-of-war in Malaya and then Burma. But in 1957 he retired from the army and, as both his parents had died during the war, decided to return to India, which had gripped his emotions. 'Even Calcutta, ugly, sprawling, depressing Calcutta which assaults the senses with its noise, its smells, its chaotic disorder, its grinding poverty – has claimed my heart.' In 1958 he started a feeding project in the Lower Circular Road, initially for just fifty-five people. Fifteen years later the project, under the auspices of the Salvation Army, was feeding 5,800 men, women and children. Gardiner, who lived as frugally as Mother Teresa in his single room provided by the Salvation Army, denies his personal magnetism. But his energy and drive were never in doubt. Every morning he personally checked the food, ensuring that the correct vitamins were added, powders mixed, and then, every afternoon in an old jeep with the back doors open, he set off on a five-hour food run to deliver the steaming mixture at various designated food stops throughout the capital. He returned home, late at night, exhausted but exhilarated.

He was proud that, in spite of increasing pain in his swollen legs and other ailments, he had never for one day deviated from his promise to dole out this food. Like Mother Teresa, he was not ashamed to beg, and persuaded some large corporations to let him collect their leftover rice and curry on a daily basis for the poor. He set himself what he considered a simple goal: 'to feed as many of them as possible daily'. And yet it was neither simple nor easy for him. 'You see,' he explained in his memoirs, 'Mother Teresa has God to help her with her planning, God to discuss her triumphs and share her disappointments. God to me is very real, don't mistake me, but I've never honestly felt a close personal relationship, which Mother Teresa enjoys. As a result I've led a lonely life. As I grow older and less active I feel as if caught in a never ending merry-go-round, trapped by my feeling of responsibility to the hungry thousands I feed daily.' The problem for Gardiner was his failure to understand why a merciful God would want so much poverty. For him there was no simple explanation for why it could exist. Gardiner, a believing Christian, would never say, as Mother Teresa has, 'The poorest of the poor are the means of expressing our love for God.' He wanted to reach exactly the same people, the poorest of the poor, but his motive was purely to alleviate their hunger, not to help Christ.

Gardiner was never patronising. He understood only too well from his own, fairly loveless childhood the human need to feel wanted and loved. He even admitted he sometimes longed for the company of a woman. He loathed religious bigotry, having suffered isolation from grandparents who disapproved of the mixed marriage of his parents. 'No matter what their form of religion, most people are groping for the truth, searching for the purpose and meaning in life.' Although David Frost made a documentary about Gardiner in 1974, *Angel with a Bushy Beard*, commissioned by the Salvation Army for British television, few today know anything about him. He died in obscurity with only a handful of people attending his funeral. Why? Gardiner, who constantly underestimated himself, offered one answer: 'I can't compete in a popularity poll against Mother Teresa; I'd be a non-starter. The work I do in Calcutta is non-imaginative compared with the outreach of Mother Teresa into various areas of need.' But in fact his dogged determination to feed the poor did make a real difference to many, as Mother Teresa herself recognised. Perhaps he lacked some of Mother Teresa's charisma in addition to her certainty. Or was it more that he did not have the same band of helpers and volunteers, let alone anyone committed to carrying on the work after he died? At all events, it stopped abruptly with his death.

Meanwhile the buzz surrounding Mother Teresa was constantly growing. After the Home for the Dying, the next cornerstone of her work, the children's home, or Shishu Bhavan, opened in 1955. This house too, with a spacious courtyard and steps up to the wide front door, just a block away from the Mother House, had been the home of a Muslim who had gone away. Mother Teresa was able at first to rent it and soon started filling it with homeless, abandoned, sick or deprived children. By 1958 they had facilities for about ninety children. Initially, Mother Teresa accepted a government grant worth 33 rupees per child. But after a few months she decided to refuse this; she preferred to spend only 17 rupees per child on more children, but the government insisted on exactly 33 rupees per child. She found such rigidity unworkable. The issue was, in different forms, to become a familiar argument among her detractors: why did she spread herself so thinly if she then made so little difference? 'But there are so many of them needing help,' she would say.

Early in 1956, Mother Teresa organised her first mobile clinic to help those who could not get to the dispensary. Catholic Relief Services in New York paid the US$5,000 needed to convert an ordinary van into a mobile medical dispensary, which travelled to some of the poorest quarters around the city where free medical services were pathetically inadequate. One or two local doctors volunteered to help the sisters and a small laboratory was set up in Shishu Bhavan.

With a home for the dying, a home for children, a house of prayer, mobile clinics and schools, the pattern for the Missionaries of Charity had almost been set. But there was one other area of desperate need in India from which Calcutta was not spared: leprosy. There had been a leper hospital in Calcutta but, when that closed, there was nowhere for the city's 30,000 lepers to get treatment and they were still, in the 1950s, viewed with a mixture of fear and loathing scarcely different from biblical times. To help them Mother Teresa set up another mobile clinic, a blue van that could fit six people as well as medicines, disinfectants, records and food.

Mother Teresa was fast becoming newsworthy, at any rate for the local press, which included several English-language newspapers. The *Calcutta Statesman* featured a photograph of the second van along with Archbishop Perier and Mother Teresa on 27 September 1957. The reporter wrote: 'Mother Teresa's mobile leprosy clinic was opened by the Archbishop of Calcutta, His Grace the most Rev. Dr Ferdinand Perier at Shishu Bhavan on Lower Circular Road on Wednesday. A mobile van with medicines and equipment will visit four centres weekly in the bustee areas of Howrah, Tiljala, Dhappa and Moti Jhil from where Mother Teresa and her Sisters of Charity have received requests for leprosy treatment.' Within a year there were eight leprosy stations where the mobile clinic called.

This article was not quite the beginning of what has become an exceptional relationship between Mother Teresa and the Indian press. A few years before, Father Van Exem had placed an advertisement in the *Statesman* describing the work of the small group of women. The first gift in response, 100 rupees, came from B. C. Roy; successive articles brought continual help in a variety of forms. Roy was so utterly won over by Mother Teresa that, when asked by a journalist in 1962 how he felt on the occasion of his eightieth birthday, he spoke not of himself nor of his political colleagues, but of her. 'As I climbed the steps of my building leading to my office, I was thinking of Mother Teresa, who has devoted her life to the service of the poor.' The *Statesman* considered this story important enough to make Mother Teresa front-page news for the first time.

As Mother Teresa became better known there were increasing numbers of Indian supporters. Aruna Paul, wife of the British-based international businessman Swaraj, now Lord, Paul, had been a Loreto schoolgirl in Calcutta and therefore felt a natural sympathy towards the nuns. As a teacher herself, it was not surprising that her first involvement was with the children's home, trying to teach the orphans and abandoned babies with very limited resources, and she also helped to organise Christmas parties. After her own children were born, she made a habit of giving a small party in Shishu Bhavan on the morning of their birthday parties and taking her children with her so they could learn how privileged they were. In addition, there was a family pharmaceutical company through which Aruna Paul was able to donate some medicines. Most usefully, she had access to a textile factory and, once a year, arranged to have new saris woven for the nuns. 'What I admired most in Mother Teresa was that she never gave the feeling of being harassed or stressed; that was a big motivation. In the days before she travelled, she always had time for everyone,' Lady Paul said.[14]

The 1950s had been an extraordinary decade for Mother Teresa. Why was she able to persuade Donnelly, Blaikie, B. C. Roy, Aruna Paul and many others that she was worth supporting? Was it her energy, her hard work, her simplicity, her austerity, her utter certainty, her determination or her charisma? It is hard to pinpoint any one aspect but, like many a natural leader, her clear-sighted determination to be doing something, which brooked no opposition, could also antagonise those who might have supported her. As the size and scale of her operation grew, so the need for centralisation and rigidity increased and the seeds of controversy took root. Perhaps there was no alternative.

CHAPTER FIVE

EXPANSION

Las Vegas must be the least likely city in the world for an association with Mother Teresa. But in 1960, when she left India for the first time in more than thirty years, this was her destination.

She had just turned fifty, she had 119 sisters following her rule, all but three of whom were Indian, and she wanted to spread her message further. According to canon law, new institutions have to wait ten years before they are allowed to open further houses. This seemed an interminable wait for Mother Teresa who, just before the ten years were up, sent a group of sisters to Ranchi in Bihar, an extremely poor state north of Calcutta, which had provided her with many girls from tribal groups to join the Missionaries of Charity. The next foundation was in the capital, Delhi, and then, during 1960, Mother Teresa started foundations in Jhansi and Agra in Uttar Pradesh.

But in the autumn of 1960 she looked beyond India for the first time and decided to accept an invitation to address the National Council for Catholic Women at their national convention in Las Vegas, leaving her first disciple, Sister Agnes, in charge. From there she arranged to travel around other parts of America and Europe raising at least consciousness if not, overtly, funds. Already, by 1960, she was not an unknown figure. Following Eileen Egan's initiative she had appeared on the front page of an American photo-magazine called *Jubilee, a Magazine for the Church and Her People*, in February 1958. This publication had introduced her, if not to the entire American public, at any rate to the country's Catholic community – almost one in four Americans

(23 per cent) is Catholic. Flying in to Los Angeles airport she was met by her friend Katherine Bracken, who had worked as a volunteer for Mother Teresa during her time as US consul in Calcutta.

Mother Teresa had never spoken in public before but it was quickly apparent that this could be an advantage rather than a disadvantage; while she was no smooth professional giving a written speech, she was something much more. She was a natural. There was no need to prepare anything as it was not difficult to tell her 3,000-strong audience about the work she and her sisters were doing and about the needs of the children in India. There were enough harrowing stories from the last ten years to stir the emotions of any group. She said what she was to say many times again in the next thirty years, that she was not going to beg for money as she did not need to; she was entirely dependent on the providence of God. But she did remind her audience that she was giving them, too, a chance to do something beautiful for God. This, rather than directly appealing for donations, was a far more powerful method of raising money, as she discovered after the speech. Sitting in a booth in the convention exhibition hall, most people could not walk past without putting cash into her bag. It was filled several times over.

Eileen Egan, who was with her on the trip, recalled that Mother Teresa refrained from passing any moral judgement on the gambling casinos and nightclubs that she passed on the road. Instead she made a point by taking home as a souvenir some long cactus spines from the Nevada desert which were twisted into a crown of thorns and placed on the head of the Crucified Christ hanging behind the altar in the noviciate chapel in Calcutta.

Mother Teresa went from Las Vegas to Peoria, Illinois, where the Catholic women were already quite familiar with the work of the Missionaries of Charity as they had been sponsoring Mother and Child Clinics of Mother Teresa for at least two years. She addressed another group in Chicago and then went on to Washington, where she collected more funds and had been due to meet the Kennedy family – Senator John F. Kennedy was a presidential candidate at the time – but this encounter did not take place.

In New York, staying at a Catholic hospice in the city, she spent some time with Mother Anna Dengel, the Austrian-born foundress of the Medical Mission Sisters, who had been so hospitable to Mother

Teresa when she had first left Loreto for Patna. She then paid visits to the offices of Catholic Relief Services, which had channelled such vital funds to India; to Bishop Fulton J. Sheen, an influential religious broadcaster who was also head of the American section of the foreign mission organisation called the Propagation of the Faith; and to other Catholic groups. But one of the most important contacts she made during this trip was with the World Health Organisation (WHO). She met the then director, Marcolino Candau, and told him of the urgent needs of the leprosy patients and their children in India. He advised her that if, on her return, she made the same appeal through the Indian government, medical supplies could then be obtained from WHO.

From New York she went to London, where it rained all week, but she was helped by having a car at her disposal provided by Catholic Relief Services. She was invited one evening to the home of the Indian High Commissioner, Vijaya Lakshmi Pandit, sister of Prime Minister Nehru, who apparently encouraged Mother Teresa to expand her work in the voluntary sector and said she hoped that 'such work in the Ghandi spirit would keep growing'. Mother Teresa met a representative of Oxfam, the voluntary aid agency, and she also had her first television interview during this stay, arranged by Lady Hamilton, with the journalist Derek Hart on the BBC.

Germany was the next stop, where Mother Teresa was better known than in the United States or England. Misereor, a Catholic overseas aid agency, had the previous year published a major feature on Mother Teresa in its magazine *Weltelend* (World Misery). In it there were scenes of starving people with wide-open eyes on the streets of Calcutta as well as dying people with all but closed eyes in Nirmal Hriday. Another photo-magazine, *Erdkreis*, had also published harrowing photographs of Kalighat. As she arrived at Frankfurt airport with only a rough woollen blanket wrapped around her cotton sari on a freezing-cold day, she found a horde of press photographers waiting to greet her. It was the classic photo-opportunity.

Misereor was keen to help Mother Teresa in any way it could. She had in mind a new home for the dying in Delhi – she already had land set aside for it – and to this it acquiesced even though, as a general principle, it preferred to fund self-help projects in the developing world. In addition its representatives asked Mother Teresa if someone in the

Missionaries of Charity would be able to send accounts regarding the project to Misereor. Mother Teresa, not for the first time, told them frankly that this would not be possible as the sisters did not have time to spend on complicated financial forms but assured them that every penny would go into the Home for the Dying. According to Eileen Egan, who was travelling with Mother Teresa at the time, she had decided early on that separate reports to numerous sponsors would be so time-consuming that the poor would suffer. 'Every donation was scrupulously recorded and acknowledged and put into the stream of resources to support centres already in operation or to start new ones.' Having a set of accounts, however, is not quite the same as separate reports to numerous sponsors.

Before the two women left Germany, Egan recounts in an oddly revealing paragraph or two how Mother Teresa then accepted her suggestion to visit Dachau, the former concentration camp. 'Mother Teresa was speechless before the details of mass persecution and murder conjured up by Dachau. After a long while, she said one word, "Colosseum. This stands for the Colosseum of our day. But then it was the pagans who threw innocent people to their death. It was not idolators of those pagan gods who threw these lives away – and how many millions of them. We are getting worse not better."'

After Germany, there was a brief visit to Switzerland and then on to Rome, where her reputation preceded her. Mother Teresa was making a formal and almost personal application to Pope John XXIII for the Missionaries of Charity to become a Society of Pontifical Right. The significance was that only once this had been granted could the sisters move out to begin working in other countries. She took her statement to the magnificent palace that is home to the Sacred Congregation for the Propagation of the Faith, Propaganda Fide, and sat on a red-plush settee to discuss the matter with Gregory Cardinal Agagianian and Archbishop Pietro Sigismondi.

Propaganda Fide, an institution founded by Gregory XV in 1622, stands on the right-hand corner of Rome's Piazza di Spagna. The square is thronged by tourists at all times of the year, most of whom sit, stroll or spend money around the eighteenth-century Spanish Steps. The façade is on one side the work of Gian Lorenzo Bernini and on the other of Francesco Borromini, and directly in front stands a statue of the Virgin Mary, erected atop an enormous column to commemorate the promulgation by Pope Pius IX of the dogma of the Immaculate Conception in 1854. Since then the Pope comes annually, on 8 December, to pray by the column. At right angles to the Collegio di Propaganda Fide is the Spanish Embassy to the Holy See, an exquisite building hidden behind a flag and a courtyard; it is the oldest embassy in the world still in use. Built in the fifteenth century, long before the days of Italian Unification, it is still full of dazzling state rooms with marble floors, portraits of Spanish monarchs and Bernini busts, including a self-portrait, executed when he was eighteen and justly known as *The Enraged Soul*.

By a series of fortuitous coincidences, I was invited here in 1996 and found myself discussing, with the present Ambassador, Pedro López Aguirrebengoa, the significance of Mother Teresa for the present Papacy. What could I expect from a diplomat other than diplomatic answers to my questions? However, not everyone I talked to in Rome saw Mother Teresa and the present Pope, John Paul II, necessarily as collaborators. Frequently I was told that his towering intellect and philosophical urges would leave her miles behind in the streets of history. The Ambassador, a charming and cultivated man who had served his country in many posts, including Jerusalem, where he was Spain's first Ambassador to Israel, told me: 'Especially for this Pope she is important because she gives a sense of looking at the world through a charitable character and not the traditional conversion which is associated with missionaries. I think history will link them because they are both innovators in a troubled world lacking statesmanship. They are both people who give moral leadership and offer specific ways to reply to the problems of the world.'

Señor Aguirrebengoa believes that the potential importance of Mother Teresa to the Catholic Church was immediately recognised during this visit to Europe. He is certain that she still receives counselling from the Vatican and has done so ever since her first trip to Propaganda Fide. 'Of course people help her to organise things, to manage whom she sees and prevent her falling into traps. She is a most powerful asset.'[1]

While Mother Teresa was in Rome in 1960, she arranged to see again, after more than thirty years, her brother Lazar, then fifty-three, who lived in Palermo, where he was the representative of a pharmaceutical firm. Lazar was married to an Italian, Maria, and had a

75

ten-year-old daughter. He had joined the Italian army after the Italian occupation of Albania in 1939 and after the Second World War was condemned to death *in absentia* by a military tribunal in Tirana. He could never return to Albania and he died in 1981, aged 74. Age, Mother Teresa's sister, had left Skopje in 1932, working first as a translator from Serbo-Croat to Albanian and then as a radio announcer. Two years later, her mother came to join her. Lazar and Agnes discussed the predicament of their mother and Age in Tirana but there seemed no way for either Lazar or Agnes, who had been continually refused a visa, perhaps because of her brother's connections, to help the two women languishing in the isolated, impoverished and totalitarian outpost of communism that Albania had become. As an atheist state with a vengeance, whose borders were virtually closed to traffic in or out (since 1948 it had alienated itself even from Yugoslavia) the last person the authorities wanted to let in was the representative of a religious order.

In February 1965, Pope Paul VI finally gave his permission, after more than four years and a few small problems, for Mother Teresa's Congregation to become a Society of Pontifical Right. Mother Teresa described this as the 'biggest miracle of all because, as a rule, Congregations are not raised to the Pontifical Order so fast; it takes most of them many years, thirty, forty years sometimes ... This shows the great love and appreciation the Holy Father has for our work and for the Congregation.'[2] Yet, even before the permission had come through, Mother Teresa knew exactly where her first batch of sisters would go and had already been on an exploratory visit. The Bishop of Barquisimeto, Venezuela, had been talking with the Papal Internuncio to New Delhi, Archbishop James Robert Knox, about his need for a group of nuns to live among some of the very poorest people in his community who lacked medical care, education and almost every other requirement for a civilised life. Archbishop Knox, an Australian, had spent ten years in India and had been a most vocal and practical supporter of Mother Teresa and her Missionaries of Charity. The Archbishop Knox High School in Calcutta is named after him and was opened by Mother Teresa for children deprived of secondary school who could catch up only by attending school in the evening.

It was Knox who had organised the visit of Pope Paul VI to Bombay for the Eucharist Congress in 1964 which resulted in the Papal gift to

Mother Teresa of his white Cadillac, used for the trip. She had decided that as it could not be converted for use as an ambulance the best thing to do was to raffle it. She raised 460,000 rupees (US$100,000) from this. Now, when Knox was asked who he would recommend to serve the poor in Venezuela, he told his colleague he knew the ideal candidates for the job.

And so, in July 1965, the first Missionaries of Charity home outside India opened in Cocorote, Venezuela, largely following a pattern already set by the several institutions now in operation in various parts of India and which deviated little from the Calcutta norm. There were by now further teams in the Punjab, in Bhagalpur in Bihar and Amravati in Maharashtra. In 1963 homes were opened in Patna and Madhya Pradesh, in 1964 Darjeeling, Jamshedpur, Goa and Trivandrum in Kerala, South India. One of the most significant developments came in 1961, when a new mobile-clinic leprosy service started in the Asansol district of West Bengal, which eventually led to the founding of a town for lepers, Shanti Nagar.

Mother Teresa chose the small town of Cocorote as a base for her sisters since it was near a church where a priest said mass regularly; the disused rectory would serve as a convent. Within a year arrangements had been completed, although there was a small hitch as the Indian government would not allow sufficient rupees to be taken out of India. Fortunately the Catholic Women of Brooklyn stepped in with pledged funds and agreed to sponsor the venture. Four sisters were chosen as pioneers and within months three more, all Indians, went out from Calcutta. The sisters encountered no shortage of need and were much in demand.

Over the next few years, other homes opened around the world; in December 1967 it was Colombo, capital of Ceylon (now Sri Lanka); August 1968, Rome, in the slums of the city; September 1968, Tabora in Tanzania – this was in a compound handed over by the diminishing White Sisters who had done so much for Africa but now, in a pattern that was becoming only too familiar to other orders, could not get enough vocations to continue; and, in September 1969, Bourke, Australia, where the Missionaries of Charity opened a centre for Aborigines. From this time on, and increasingly into the 1970s, a new centre opened somewhere in the world approximately every six months.

At the same time Mother Teresa's Congregation was expanding in yet another direction. In March 1963 the Archbishop of Calcutta gave his blessing to the establishment of a new branch, the Missionary Brothers of Charity. At first this group, twelve young boys and one priest, lived on the first floor of Shishu Bhavan, the children's home in Lower Circular Road. Their principal task was to work among the homeless and hungry boys who came to Calcutta by train seeking, if not gold, then scraps and often never got further than scavenging around the stations of Sealdah and Howrah. Early in 1966 a charismatic Australian, Father Ian Travers-Ball SJ, then aged thirty-eight, left the Jesuits to take charge of the Missionary Brothers as Brother Andrew. Mother Teresa could not be head of the brothers as the Church does not permit a woman to be head of a male congregation.

Brother Andrew, who has since left the Order, had from the outset a different, less formal style than Mother Teresa. This was reflected partly in the way that the brothers have no uniform (they wear jeans and tee-shirts) and partly in the way Brother Andrew was always keen to delegate. Also the brothers were always much less centralised; some are trained overseas, and they are not required to spend time in Calcutta at all but can make their final profession of vows wherever they are working. On the whole the two organisations, which have separate constitutions, have complemented each other, but one serious disagreement arose when Mother Teresa established a contemplative branch of the brothers without securing the prior agreement of Brother Andrew. Her precipitate action caused a serious if temporary rift and when Brother Andrew refused to go along with such a step the contemplative branch was severed from the brothers and put under the direct supervision of a Roman prelate.

As soon as Brother Andrew took over, the number of Missionary Brothers increased, as did the scope of their work; they took charge of the men's ward at the Home for the Dying, for example. They also moved out of Shishu Bhavan to a three-storey house in Kidderpore, Calcutta. The brothers became particularly involved in leprosy work, especially at the Titagarh refuge, a long stretch of land an hour or so outside Calcutta bordering a railway line on one side and with the municipal sewage-pumping station on the other. Mother Teresa had promised to keep lepers out of her Home for the Dying at Kalighat and started working at Titagarh in 1958 for an already existing community of people with leprosy. Two years later the Titagarh

Municipal Authorities gave her a parcel of land to establish a permanent home and treatment facilities. In 1975, as part of Mother Teresa's Silver Jubilee celebrations, the brothers took over the running of the Leprosy Centre, twelve years after their foundation. The centre was also renamed at this point the Gandhiji Prem Nivas, with the inaugural celebrations taking place on 2 October, Gandhi's birthday. This clever choice of date enabled Mother Teresa not only to honour Gandhi but also to ensure that the governor of Bengal, A. L. Dias, and his wife came to the ceremony and mingled with patients.

Titagarh is a bustling, lively market town. I walked from the level-crossing past the dwellings of several poor families where young children made themselves useful by kneading circles of cow dung and leaving them to dry for use as fuel. Today the brothers, some of whom are doctors and medical aides, serve close to 300 patients needing full care in the hospital on one side of the railway line. Across the tracks there are about 400 rehabilitated leprosy patients all trained to make sandals, weave saris and farm. They are today entirely self-supporting, and the vegetable garden, fish pond, piggery and poultry barns are a clean and orderly oasis in the fume-submerged town. Leprosy is still a major problem in several developing countries, but with the relatively cheap Multi Drug Therapy (MDT) it is possible to see leprosy as an illness on the retreat.

Why was Mother Teresa so determined from the outset to expand and send her sisters to other parts of the world when clearly the need in India was still enormous, possibly, even greater than when she had started through demographic reasons alone? It is not enough to say that her first trip to Europe whetted an appetite for travel, although it might have done, as clearly she already had a vision of the need to spread her work before she set off, implicit in her application for Pontifical Right. When she returned to Calcutta after that trip she must have been aware that she was awakening a massive if dormant response. Call it faith, call it confidence; doubts she may once have harboured were now banished. There was a tremendous momentum about Mother Teresa's operation at this time. She started to win international awards for her work, many of them with large cash prizes attached. In September 1962 it was the Padma Shri Award from the President of India as well as the Magsaysay Award for International Understanding given in honour of the late President of the Philippines. The latter came with a cheque amounting to approximately 50,000 rupees (£877). These were the first of many. It was, after all, the 1960s and there was a potent sense of idealism around, which she harnessed better than anyone else. There was a distinct feeling that here was someone who was actually doing something to right the ills of the world instead of merely demonstrating, or smoking dope, while talking of doing something.

Anyone who lived through the 1960s must remember the experimentation, the restlessness and the confusion, especially among the young. Sometimes this took the form of searching for a new wonder drug, hence the ghastly tragedy of thalidomide; sometimes for a spiritual leader or guru such as Marshall McLuhan, the Canadian professor who offered a new worldview, or the Indian mystic who called himself the Maharishi. All ages react against their parents, but the 1960s were particularly vocal in dismissing the false conclusions of the previous age and in continuing to seek for certainty or reassurance for themselves. Nowhere is this attempt to find elusive inner peace epitomised better than in the four singing Beatles; curiously, where did their search take them and many other hippies, but to India, the very epicentre of spirituality. Malcolm Muggeridge appeared to many publicly to personify this quest for true goodness, or saintliness or moral truths.

Muggeridge was, in the early 1960s, not merely an agnostic but a mocker of religion in general, while at the same time struggling to find religion. Born in South Croydon in 1903, he represented himself as an agonised seeker after the truth who in his youth had flirted with the notion of becoming a priest. His latest and highly sympathetic biographer, Richard Ingrams, portrays him as a man who had long wrestled with his conscience and had deep Christian leanings from a young age, not a poseur who turned to Christianity in later life when it suited him. He made his name as a journalist on the *Manchester Guardian* and in 1934 had gone, for the second time in his life, to live in India, this time working on the English-language *Calcutta Statesman*. On his return, he worked for the *Evening Standard* and became himself a feature of London literary life partly because he had by now found his form as a writer but also on account of the regularity with which he had affairs or made passes at women. According to his fellow journalist Bernard Levin, 'Muggeridge ... in some ways epitomised the riven nature of the decade, for as much as he was sinner when it started he was saint at its end, and although his formal canonisation was expected to be somewhat further delayed, many lived in the immediate expectation of his assumption into heaven as the Blessed Malcolm, while some claimed that the process had already started, and swore they could see light under his boots.'[3]

In 1968, in a rather inspired piece of casting, Oliver Hunkin, then head of Religious Broadcasting at the BBC, called up Muggeridge to ask him if he would do a short televised interview with a little-known nun from India. 'I remember he came up rather reluctantly from his home at Robertsbridge in Sussex,' Hunkin recalls. 'He was rather put out because it was such short notice and she could only spare us an hour next Tuesday afternoon. But having produced him before, I knew they would make an interesting pair to get together.'[4]

Prior to this, Muggeridge had not heard of Mother Teresa, but he read up the biographical notes provided by Hunkin and agreed to come to a small religious house, the Holy Child Convent in London's West End, to shoot the interview. There were no intellectual fireworks; Mother Teresa, already small and wrinkled, appeared slightly halting and nervous as Muggeridge put the expected kind of questions. When did she first fell this special vocation? Any doubts or regrets, etc etc? 'It would be easy to produce a little all-purpose set of questions to be used with anyone at any time,' Muggeridge explained later. 'Mother Teresa's answers were perfectly simple and perfectly truthful; so much so that I had some uneasiness about keeping the interview going for the required half hour. Controversy, the substance of such programmes, does not arise in the case of those who, like Mother Teresa, are blessed with certainties.'[5] So ordinary was the interview that there was even some question about whether it should be broadcast after all, according to Muggeridge. But it was transmitted in May 1968 in a BBC Sunday-night series called *Meeting Point*.

Afterwards, there were critics who recognised the extraordinary personal chemistry at play between the two protagonists, but there were many more members of the public who, so moved by Mother Teresa's account of her work for the sick and poor of Calcutta, sent, according to one account, £9,000 within ten days, although no appeal had been made for money during the programme. In another version of the story, some £25,000 resulted from this single interview. All the accompanying letters, many of them sent directly to Muggeridge, made similar remarks about how Mother Teresa's words had spoken to them in a way no one else's ever had. Bemused BBC executives decided to repeat the programme rather quickly – with an even greater response. It was a clear example of the 1960s' search for certainty, which gimmicks in religious broadcasting such as pop versions of the psalms or dialogues with atheists had clearly failed to satisfy.

Muggeridge himself said after it was over that he never imagined that anything particularly memorable had been recorded. 'I assumed that, as usual, the camera would have drained away whatever was real and alive in what it portrayed.' And yet he was smitten. He had known that from the moment she walked into the room. 'It was for me one of those special occasions when a face, hitherto unknown, seems to stand out from all other faces as uniquely separate and uniquely significant, to be thenceforth forever recognisable.'

Almost immediately, he worked to persuade the BBC to send him with a film crew to Calcutta to record Mother Teresa in action. In the spring of 1969 he went with Peter Chafer, the producer, and Ken Macmillan, the award-winning cameraman (who had recently received huge critical acclaim for his work on Kenneth Clark's Civilisation series), to make three religious films in India. Although initially reticent, Mother Teresa had apparently been persuaded to co-operate by Cardinal Heenan, Archbishop of Westminster. She agreed, she told Muggeridge, 'If this TV programme is going to help people love better.' She then gave the British team her full co-operation.

In his account of the filming Muggeridge recounts how, while Macmillan and the sound recordist were setting up their equipment, Mother Teresa suggested going up to the chapel together and praying. 'I readily agreed ... We knelt side by side.' Thus, from the start, Muggeridge himself became part of the myth of the film he was making. Who knows what prayers were said in those moments, but the pair came down from the chapel together and the filming began. If only Macmillan had been on hand to catch that extraordinary scene.

The next five days are shrouded in a fairy-tale cloak of divine protection. That a fifty-minute documentary could be made at all in five days, rather than the normal two to three months, was, Muggeridge asserts, extraordinary to a miraculous degree. Secondly the filming proceeded with quite exceptional smoothness and speed, with none of the usual breakdowns and crises. 'All this, as anyone with experience of filming expeditions will know, amounted to a kind of miracle,' wrote Muggeridge.

But the 'actual miracle', which has prompted considerable debate since, concerns shots taken inside the Home for the Dying, which Macmillan was initially uncomfortable about filming. 'This Home for the Dying is dimly lit by small windows high up in the walls,' wrote Muggeridge. 'Mr Muggeridge's way with a fact has always been cavalier,' commented Bernard Levin in his essay, 'Mugg's Game'. But all the same, 'small'? I recall them as arched, mostly with three sections to them, approximately three foot six high and three foot across. 'High up in the walls'? Nothing is very high since the ceilings are low, but one bank of windows for example is approximately three foot above the patients. Facts do seem to be often ignored in this discussion, which usually centres around the nature of 'kindly light' which Cardinal Newman refers to in his well-known hymn. Muggeridge, convinced he had witnessed the first authentic photographic miracle, wrote: 'This love is luminous like the haloes artists have seen and made visible round the heads of the saints. I find it not at all surprising that the luminosity should register on a photographic film. The supernatural is only an infinite projection of the natural as the furthest horizon is an image of eternity.'

At all events, Macmillan was at first adamant that filming was impossible in the Home for the Dying: the crew had only one small light with them and to get the place adequately lit in the time at their disposal was impossible. In his own account he explains how he had just taken delivery of some new film made by Kodak which they had not even had time to test. But because of this he agreed to have a go. 'So we shot it. And when we got back several weeks later, a month or two later, we are sitting in the rushes theatre at Ealing Studios and eventually up come the shots of the House of the Dying and it was surprising. You could see every detail. And I said: "That's amazing, that's extraordinary." And I was going to say, you know, three cheers for Kodak. I didn't get a chance to say that though because Malcolm, sitting in the front row, spun round and said: "It's divine light! It's Mother Teresa. You'll find that it's divine light, old boy." And three or four days later I found I was being phoned by journalists from London newspapers who were saying things like, "We hear you've just come back from India with Malcolm Muggeridge and you were the witness of a miracle." '

With the filming completed, Muggeridge returned to England only to find the 'miracles' continuing when he discovered the film was already in the right shape and hardly needed editing. Mother Teresa wrote to him shortly after: 'I can't tell you how big a sacrifice it was to accept the making of a film – but I am glad now that I did so because it has brought us all closer to God. In your own way try to make the world conscious that it is never too late to do something beautiful for God.'

This phrase became the title of the black-and-white film, first shown in December 1969, which opens with a long shot of Indian poverty that is sadly only too easy to find. There are close-ups of emaciated men washing at the roadside, the noisy traffic and belching lorries. Then the camera turns to the Mother House in Lower Circular Road; 'Vote for Abul Hasan' and a hammer and sickle are daubed on the side. Nuns are singing and the novices taking communion and collecting buckets. The first voice of the film is Muggeridge's, telling his audience: 'They live in one of Calcutta's poorest slums. It's a natural place for them to be.'

It is a potent juxtaposition but although the Lower Circular Road is hardly a luxurious abode, it is not one of the city's worst slums either. It is the city's 'social service area' where the Mennonites, Salvation Army and others are based. As Ingrams comments, Muggeridge 'was never too careful with details of that kind'. Ingrams believes Muggeridge was completely sincere in his emotional response to Mother Teresa and that, as there may be hundreds of Mother Teresas doing similarly valuable work the world over, the importance of the Muggeridge film can hardly be overestimated. 'She comes over very well on the screen because she does exude humility, there is nothing bogus about her. She was a symbol and so was Muggeridge, in his case a symbol of someone searching for goodness in the twentieth century. The impact of the film was enormous and Muggeridge's attitude had a considerable amount to do with that. For example, the BBC television journalist John Simpson wouldn't have been the same at all, good though he is at his job, because Muggeridge was so personally involved he was trying to answer his own questions, for himself, which is not the normal reporterish sort of attitude, but which made for very engaging television.'[6] Ironically, Muggeridge was soon announcing his loathing of television, 'that repository of our fraudulence', and publicly did away with his television set. 'It was', explains Ingrams, 'a repeat performance of his attitude towards sex when having, it seemed, taken his full fill of the pleasures of the flesh, he turned around and denounced it all as a fantasy and a fraud.'

Peter Chafer, the producer, who describes himself as not a religious person, nonetheless insists that his own life was permanently affected by making this film. 'She is one of the most extraordinary people I have ever met ... very practical and running a very tight ship. I think she's awfully good at being a nun. The lady has such an enormous personality that for me, all other preconceptions went out of the window.' Chafer is not prepared to stake an opinion on the miracle debate but accepts that Macmillan was technically a brilliant cameraman with a vast understanding of the effects of light, trying out a new film with a new emulsion which he then exposed, on the basis of information on the packet, for longer than required, giving it maximum exposure. But Chafer does not accept even this for the simple explanation it might be, since, when the same film was used on a later occasion to shoot in a Cairo nightclub, the results were not nearly as good. 'All I know is I was extremely grateful to have my film. But it was not my film that put Mother Teresa on the map. No, it was her. If she had not had her own charisma it would not have worked. She definitely has something going on right.'*

Chafer was not alone in this view. It is impossible to know precisely what impact the film had in persuading young women to enter the Missionaries of Charity because, within Catholic circles, Mother Teresa was already fairly well known. Yet by 1970 they were flocking to join and in that year alone 139 new candidates were received into the society. There were, in all, 585 sisters of whom 332 were fully professed nuns, 175 novices and 78 postulants still in their first year. The girls came from Pakistan, Ceylon, Nepal, Malaysia, Yugoslavia,

---

* Chafer was to meet Mother Teresa once again when she came to England a few months later to open a home in Southall. She invited various people to a small service to commemorate the opening, including Muggeridge, Chafer and Cardinal Heenan. But the latter replied that, as he was busy and could not come, he would send along a deputy. According to Chafer, Mother Teresa wrote back and said, 'It is such a pity you cannot come as Jesus Christ will be there.' Cardinal Heenan relented and recounted the story to Chafer during the drive to the opening.

Germany, Malta, France, Mauritania, Ireland, Venezuela and Italy, as well as the various regions of India.

How important is it for Mother Teresa to be a miracle-maker? A saint these days is still, strictly speaking, required to have performed or been responsible for two miracles for beatification and two more after beatification for canonisation. If the case is based on 'virtue', rather than 'martyrdom', more might be required. And yet that is not what all the fuss is about, as the Pope can decide to dispense with the requirements. Muggeridge was not making a premature case for Mother Teresa's canonisation. He was trying to refute the then common assumption that science had all the answers, to the discredit of religion. But the story of the miracle was important because it set the agenda for the next twenty years whereby the assumption slowly grew that God's hand was directing Mother Teresa, and to question anything she did was therefore unacceptable. Peter Chafer described to me the process of anyone whom she felt was damaging the cause as being 'fingered by God'. The sisters' conviction that God is directing them, because their prayers are answered so often by clothes, medicines or money and even on one occasion by a snowplough to help during a hard winter in New York, has persuaded many of a less credulous bent to believe there must be some higher purpose to all that they do. This is the fundamental basis upon which rests everything else the Missionaries of Charity do, and the real importance of Muggeridge's film is that it gave credence to this fundamental belief. To challenge, to question or to doubt is to confront a much higher authority. All but the most ardent atheist does so at his or her peril. It is this, emanating from Muggeridge's film, which has given Mother Teresa what Christopher Hitchens calls a 'Niagara of uncritical publicity' and has helped to make her 'the least criticised human being on earth'.[7]

Two years later Muggeridge wrote a book called, like the film, Something Beautiful for God, which consists partly of a transcript of the film, with many black-and-white photographs. But there is also a longish introduction and afterword in which he agonises over his own religious position. Muggeridge as author plays a larger role than he did as interviewer. Here he shares with his readers the 'hesitations and doubts' which made it impossible for him at that moment to be received into the Catholic Church and yet describes how much he longed to do this. 'There are few things I should rather do than please her. So much so, that it almost amounts to a temptation to accept her guidance in the matter of entering the Church.' He wrote of the infinitely benign purpose of religions: 'Of all the purposes which draw people together – excitement, cupidity, curiosity, lechery, hatred – this alone, worship, makes them seem like a loving family; abolishing the conflicts and divisions of class and race and wealth and talent as they fall on their knees before a father in heaven and his incarnate son.'

The book has been a phenomenal success, rarely out of print and, over nearly thirty years, has sold more than 300,000 copies. It has been reprinted twenty times and translated into thirteen languages. The royalties were donated by Muggeridge to Mother Teresa, a sum amounting at the time of his death in 1990 to £60,000.

Yet it was this public flagellation which, while it made compulsive viewing, worried some people such as Colin Morris, the broadcaster, who had been a missionary in Africa before joining the BBC. 'Muggeridge was a parody of the religious commentator,' Morris explained. 'He was constantly engaged in this agonising dialogue with himself so that it was rather hard to see whether it was genuine or a performance.' Morris, who later became head of Religious Broadcasting, wrote in the *Observer*:

> To carry personal responsibility for keeping God alive in the modern world would be a grievous burden for anyone, even Muggeridge, whose search for the kingdom has been fascinating to observe but who, since he found it, has been sadly in danger of becoming Christianity's most bizarre exhibitionist. Face contorted, hands clawing in the air to pantomime his inner anguish, world weary and longing for an apocalyptic end to a Naughty Age, Malcolm reviles the medium which feeds him and begs reassurance that he is still loved from the assorted personalities who gather about him like Plato's disciples. 'Why?' his strangulated cry goes up – tempting a heavenly retort 'Why indeed?'[8]

The chemistry between Malcolm Muggeridge and Agnes Bojaxhiu may have been dynamic. But there was a small episode in Muggeridge's past which presumably Mother Teresa herself knew nothing about, although other Catholic Albanians have not forgotten, and which, had she known, could have threatened the entire relationship. In 1949 there was a joint British–American-sponsored mission to subvert and sabotage Albania's communist government. However this expedition was a tragic failure. Several young Albanians had been recruited to join the mission and, after training in Malta, were parachuted into Albania to operate in areas where they had relatives and friends. The aim was to secure local support to overthrow the communist regime. However, all these Albanians were captured almost as soon as they landed and were tried as spies or traitors. Hundreds of Albanian families which had been contacted by the agents were also rounded up, tried and imprisoned. It was partly as a result of this failed expedition that the infamous concrete bunkers were constructed by Hoxha throughout the country. Later it was discovered that the men had been betrayed by Kim Philby before he was known to be a Soviet spy.

'In connection with this failed expedition,' wrote Safete S. Juka in the *Albanian Catholic Bulletin*, 'there was still another betrayal. Albeit of a different order, this betrayal concerns Malcolm Muggeridge.'[9] Just as this operation was getting under way, British government officials decided to give a party in London for members of an anti-communist, pro-democracy Albanian National Committee. The aim of the party was to present the committee to some of London's leading writers and intellectuals in the hope they would publicise it. Nicholas (now Lord) Bethell takes up the story: 'The whole atmosphere was spoilt, though, by Malcolm Muggeridge, who declared in a loud voice that Albania was a ridiculous country anyway that ought to be partitioned as soon as possible between Greece and Yugoslavia.'[10] According to the article in the *Albanian Catholic Bulletin*, Muggeridge's remark was 'particularly disturbing'. Muggeridge's betrayal seemed much worse than Philby's. Pat Whinney of British Intelligence based in Athens considered the personalities of Philby and Muggeridge to be very similar. He remarked that both men were 'caustic, sarcastic, full of intellectual arrogance'.

From such small vignettes is history made. But history would be a harsh judge to conclude that Muggeridge's brazen comment was somehow worse than the actions of a Soviet spy who fed information that resulted in the capture and death of several anti-communist Albanians.

CHAPTER SIX

RECOGNITION

In retrospect it is easy to see the decade following *Something Beautiful for God* as leading directly to the award of the Nobel Peace Prize in 1979. In the 1960s, Mother Teresa had burst forth upon a world only too ready to receive her message; in the 1970s, international recognition consolidated her position and encouraged her in yet further growth.

Malcolm Muggeridge, even though he was still opposed to the institution of the Catholic Church and was not actually received into it until 1982, took to championing Mother Teresa as a personal crusade. At a party to launch his book of the film he explained his reason for including in it nine pages of Mother Teresa's own sayings. 'Mother Teresa will never write about herself or her work ... when she is considered for the Nobel Prize there should be something in print in her own words.' However, winning the prize proved not quite so straightforward as it appeared; the Nobel Committee rejected at least three applications proposing her.

While others were preparing submissions on her behalf to this prize committee or that, the sixty-year-old nun got on with her development programme. Throughout the 1970s new centres were opened; in 1970 it was Melbourne, Australia and, for the first time in the Middle East, Amman, Jordan. In December 1970 a noviciate was opened in England to train novices from Europe and the Americas, and six months after that a house opened in London's Paddington district. This was followed, a little over two years later, by what the UK newsletter called 'Mother Teresa's new adventure in Gaza'. She sent four sisters to work there as 'the people of Gaza are Arabic speaking, yet the solid barrier of Israel separates them from all other Arab nations. The silent isolation lies heavy on these people and life is defined by negatives – no future, no courage ... they have lost their villages, their property, their lands. The work that awaits the sisters is endless.'[1] In January 1971 there began the steady trickle of international awards with, first, the Pope John XXIII Peace Prize given by Pope Paul VI. Towards the end of the year, three separate American institutions told her that they wished to make her awards. She had hoped to be going to the United States in any case to settle her sisters in a new home in the Bronx district of New York, but a crisis in India overtook her and there was some doubt whether she would be able to make a US trip in the near future.

Calcutta, whose resources were already stretched to the utmost, was in the middle of 1971 suffering one of its worst ever batterings. Millions of homeless, most of them near death from starvation or exhaustion, were pouring in from what was to become Bangladesh as the long-standing differences between East and West Pakistan finally exploded into a bitter and bloody civil war in which three million people lost their lives. The emergency in East Pakistan had begun in 1970 with a cyclone followed by a tidal wave that swept away more than 300,000 lives in the province. Shortly after, fighting broke out with many brutal and vicious killings reported. The refugees, in desperation, tried making their way into India, to one of the world's poorest provinces – Bengal – and considered themselves lucky if they found shelter in a sewer pipe. There happened to be several of these in an area outside the city called Salt Lake – once a swampy expanse of lake – which the Calcutta Corporation was planning to turn into a housing development to relieve the congestion of the city itself. Conditions were appalling with cholera, dysentery and smallpox all rife. Voluntary-aid agencies throughout the world sent teams to try to help with the emergency, as well as food, medicine, tarpaulins, building materials, trucks and workers. Mother Teresa and her Missionaries of Charity took on various menial and filthy tasks including clearing up the hospital tents and tending the sick and dying. It was at this time that Mother Teresa met Senator Edward Kennedy when he visited Calcutta as chairman of the Committee on Refugees of the US Senate. Kennedy was on a tightly scheduled government programme but specifically asked to see the big camp at Salt Lake. Desmond Doig was there: 'Officials and people milled around him wherever he went so it was difficult for him to see much. But suddenly he spied something: a sister was washing clothes from the cholera ward. It was Sister Agnes and Senator Kennedy asked if he might shake her hand. She said that her hands were dirty but he went ahead and shook her hand saying, "The dirtier they are the more honoured I am. It is wonderful work you are doing here." I cannot forget that scene,' Doig added.

By September, although the crisis was far from over, Mother Teresa's 'usual resilience' had asserted itself, Egan explained, and she decided she would visit America after all. Three American awards in as many months emphasised how deep an impression she had by this time made across a wide swathe of US society. She enjoyed the support not only of the Catholic Democrat Kennedy family, but also numbered the Republican President Richard Nixon, a Quaker, among her band of admirers and supporters. However, she decided she would not go in person to receive the Good Samaritan Award in Boston – Egan went in her place – but would accept an honorary Doctorate of Humane Letters at a degree ceremony in Washington, the first of many honorary degrees to be conferred on her in the coming years. She also attended a ceremony in Washington DC to receive one of the international awards of the Joseph P. Kennedy Junior Foundation, named after the late President's eldest brother, who was killed in the Second World War. The awards were made at a conference entitled, 'Choices on Our Consciences', which gave her the opportunity to talk about her view of the sanctity of life, however damaged or limited that life might be, as frequently witnessed by her in Calcutta. She also told her audience of the millions of refugees from East Pakistan now struggling for existence in West Bengal and commented that each of them must be recognised as having the divine spirit and must therefore be loved and helped.

Coinciding with these awards and the opening of a home in the Bronx was the US publication of Malcolm Muggeridge's book. This resulted in a whirl of media attention, often with Muggeridge and Mother Teresa in a 'double act' such as the television interview in a New York studio with David Frost – who was, as Egan pointed out, the son of a Methodist minister. 'It was clear Frost found it hard to digest Muggeridge's reference to suffering as part of the everlasting drama between Creator and creature, a drama that enriches life and makes it more fascinating.' She found the next interview, with Barbara Walters, on the Today show, viewed by millions across the country, also less than positive. Walters, the supremely polished performer, was, thought Egan, 'not at her best, describing Mother Teresa as "a humanitarian" and filling in six minutes with flat, workmanlike questions that elicited straight answers from her'. Egan's comments leave one to wonder what sort of questions would have made Walters seem 'at her best'. Since Mother Teresa was used to the piety and adoration of interviewers such as Muggeridge, it may have been disappointing for Egan to have Walters approach Mother Teresa with respect but less enthusiasm. If Mother Teresa had made it a condition that she would appear only on religious programmes she could perhaps have guaranteed conversations being conducted only in reverential tones. But because she wanted her message to reach the widest possible audience she took a gamble and gave regular interviews. Not until the 1990s did anyone seriously break the unwritten rules.

By January 1972 it became clear that the crucible from which Bangladesh emerged had resulted in much more than the birth of one more nation. According to figures released by the international Roman Catholic relief organisation, Caritas, Pakistani troops raped some 4,000 women in Bangladesh before their defeat by India. Some estimate the number of women raped as high as 200,000. On 14 January Mother Teresa put out an announcement that she was going to Bangladesh with ten other nuns, including Sister Margaret Mary, one of her earliest followers whose family came from Dacca.

According to the official statement, her aim was to carry out 'a project of assistance in favour of the very many women who underwent violation from the Pakistan army and are now in a state of advanced pregnancy'. They went to Khulna, Pabna and Rajshahi as well as to Dacca. Mother Teresa admitted that there were not many girls coming to ask for help. 'But one thing I told them was that we would take all the babies and find homes for them. Killing, I said, is killing even if the child is not yet born.' The Missionaries of Charity were given a 300-year-old convent in Dacca by the local bishop as a home for the women who were prepared to come forward, and tried to arrange as many adoptions as possible.[2] Not all the thousands of women raped conceived, some others set about trying to abort themselves and in one rare case the girl concerned had her baby and was accepted as a single mother by her family. But for a Muslim girl who had been raped – one of the most serious crimes there is in Islam – the future seemed bleak indeed. Eventually the old convent was converted into a Shishu Bhavan, a home for abandoned and orphaned children as well as other malnourished children.

It was this latest horrific episode in the inventory of man's inhumanity which prompted the Australian writer Germaine Greer to become one of the first and fiercest critics of Mother Teresa. The unlikely pair met in the autumn of 1972 in the first-class section of an aircraft taking them both to a function at which Mother Teresa was to be given 'yet another award for services to humanity'.[3] 'By dint of using contacts, Mother Teresa has accumulated considerable power,' wrote Greer some years later. 'When she went to Dacca two days after its liberation from the Pakistanis in 1972, 3,000 naked women had been found in the army bunkers. Their saris had been taken away so that they would not hang themselves. The pregnant ones needed abortions. Mother Teresa offered them no option but to bear the offspring of hate. There is no room in Mother Teresa's universe for the moral priorities of others. There is no question of offering suffering women a choice.'

Greer had more to say: 'Secular aid workers told me at the time that women with complications of late pregnancy, caused by physical abuse and malnutrition, as well as women miscarrying, were turning up at clinics claiming to have been accused of attempted abortion and turned away by Mother Teresa's nuns ... When the new government of Bangladesh banned the export of Bengali orphans, Mother Teresa by some means, heavenly or earthly, was the only person who succeeded in placing Bengali babies abroad and they all went, of course, to Catholic homes.' Greer wrote to me subsequently: 'I was told about [the incidents] by people from the Family Planning Association of India, none of whom would allow me to name her. To bad-mouth Mother Teresa is to get a bad press.'[4]

Clearly Mother Teresa could not literally 'take all the babies and find homes for them'. Some were quietly stifled at birth,[5] others left to grow up in an institution, perhaps handicapped after a botched abortion. But as the new country had at the time no established non-governmental organisations (NGO)s – the network of non-profit making bodies supporting a wide range of activities – someone had to act fast. The new Prime Minister did set up a Rehabilitation Board for

Affected Women, which organised abortion services for some victims. These services were made available to women five months pregnant or less and were run by several volunteer Scandinavian doctors. Those women who were beyond five months of pregnancy were encouraged to have their deliveries in facilities provided by the Board, following which arrangements were made, where possible, to send the children for adoption, mostly to Scandinavian countries.

At the beginning of the Bangladesh crisis, when Mrs Gandhi, the Indian Prime Minister, said she would not turn the refugees back but would do all in her power to meet the situation, Mother Teresa had warmly applauded her decision: 'India has been wonderful in accepting and taking care of the millions of Pakistan refugees. In opening the door to them, the Indian Prime Minister has done a wonderful Christlike thing.'[6] In November 1972 came confirmation of the Indian government's need for Mother Teresa and its recognition of her international significance when they presented her with the Pandit Nehru Award for International Understanding, which had actually been awarded to her three years previously.

In April 1973 Mother Teresa travelled to London to receive the first Templeton Award for Progress in Religion, presented by Prince Philip. John Templeton, the US businessman who initiated the award, was concerned that religion no longer appeared to provide guidance for man at a time when society had 'become so topsy-turvy and when changes in direction were being taken without much reflection by most of mankind'.[7] He hoped his prize, which was to be an award for progress in religion, not saintliness or mere good works, would inspire young people to see a religious career as exciting, dynamic and varied. Templeton himself wanted the prize to go to 'a creative pacesetter in religion ... It is for achieving, for pioneering a breakthrough in religious thought and understanding.' The award was judged by a panel of nine representatives from the major world faiths who commented that, although they had received many nominations for the £34,000 prize, they had been inspired by Muggeridge's book and film in making their choice.

The award ceremony took place in London's Guildhall, which was filled with leaders of many beliefs. The Lord Mayor of London, Lord Mais, in chairing the ceremony, said that the prize was unique in crossing all traditional religious doctrinaire barriers. The judges, he pointed out, 'are all noted for their interest in relations between the world religions'.[8] Those who thought the first award of such an unusual multi-faith prize might provide a suitable occasion for an acceptance speech with an ecumenical flavour were to be disappointed. Mother Teresa's instinct was always to talk about Jesus and her faith in Jesus and to talk in a religious context on any other subject would have been, for her, a travesty. Subsequent prize-winners, including Chuck Colson and Billy Graham, have followed her lead and been unapologetically Christian. The next day, London's mass-circulation *Daily Express* carried a feature article on 'the nun with hope for the world' and various television news programmes included reports on the prize and Mother Teresa.

There was, however, one fiasco around this time, never publicly explained by the Missionaries of Charity. In 1971 Mother Teresa sent some of her nuns to open a house in the highly charged atmosphere of religious strife between a Catholic minority and Protestant majority in Belfast. After eighteen months, their work unfinished, the nuns suddenly and dramatically left in a great hurry.

In the short time of her presence in Northern Ireland, she became a legend; one story recounted how she spent more than an hour on the telephone to the Rev. Ian Paisley, but was unable to bring peace to the troubled province any nearer. The Roman Catholic priest in charge at Ballymurphy, part of the Roman Catholic outskirts of Belfast, Father Desmond Wilson, said,

> There is absolutely no doubt that in Belfast, where life had become in so many ways viciously irreligious, Mother Teresa's sisters, in the heart of what many people referred to insultingly as a Catholic ghetto, were a focal point towards which were attracted many people who very much needed an excuse to work alongside each other. There need be no doubt that whoever was responsible for withdrawing them acted in a manner which was cruel and arrogant and unnecessarily so. Whether the person was Mother Teresa or someone else is not the real problem. The real problem is that such things still happen in the Church.

Exactly what took place in Belfast may never be known but there was always a pocket of resentment that missionary sisters should come from India to the Irish. No doubt someone in the local Church hierarchy persuaded Mother Teresa she was not welcome and she moved out speedily.[9] 'Only a few people knew the explanation and it appears that Mother Teresa had bound them to keep silent.'[10]

In June 1974, she went again to America for the presentation of the 'Master et Magistra' Award and in August 1975 the Food and Agriculture Organisation of the United Nations (FAO) issued its 'Ceres' medal, bearing on one side the image of Mother Teresa as engraved by British artist Michael Rizzelo, and on the obverse a picture of an undernourished child about to be embraced by two outstretched arms. This was given in recognition of Mother Teresa's 'exemplary love and concern for the hungry and the poorest of the poor' and the linking of Mother Teresa with Ceres, Mother Earth, could hardly have been a more potent way of reinforcing the message that Mother Teresa was the source of that which was good and helpful for the poor. The Missionaries of Charity did not benefit directly, but the income from the sale of the medal was utilised for financing FAO projects in the third world. Also in 1975, Mother Teresa was given an important present from the industrial conglomerate Imperial Chemical Industries (ICI) of Calcutta. The company made available to her its enormous but obsolete compound of buildings at Tiljula, just behind Calcutta's Bridge Number Four. The Missionaries of Charity rechristened the complex Prem Dan, 'Gift of Love', and have used it for a variety of purposes including housing for overseas volunteers.

The more awards won, the more the newspaper articles increased and vice versa. There was, of course, a vast and dramatic pool from which to pick a 'human interest' story and Desmond Doig was responsible for digging up and making known many of these. In 1967, Doig became the founder editor of the Calcutta-based news magazine *Junior Statesman*, soon known as JS. A colleague of Doig's, Jug Suraiya, who was senior editor of JS until its closure in 1976, described it to me: 'This magazine featured articles about everything from the Beatles phenomenon to Mother Teresa's crusade in its efforts to make its readership better informed about our multifaceted world. JS became a magazine for everyone who thought young and had a readership that cut across age barriers.'[11] According to Manneka Gandhi, daughter-in-law of Prime Minister Indira Gandhi and widow of her son Sanjay, 'the group at the *Junior Statesman* were very powerful people and influenced young people from about thirteen upwards. Many icons were created by them – singers and dancers too; they influenced a whole generation. The paper went all over India and there were many regular pieces about Mother Teresa. To an extent they invented her.' Manneka added: 'We Indians always need hero worship; we like to feel there are saints in our midst, that's why we have 332 gods – and they felt she was a very good person at a time when there were hardly any NGOs in India.'[12]

In 1975 Doig published a slim biography of Mother Teresa and persuaded Indira Gandhi to contribute the foreword, in which she wrote of Mother Teresa's gentleness, love and compassion and compared her with Tagore, saying: 'Tagore wrote "There rest thy feet where live the poorest and lowliest and lost." That is where Mother Teresa is to be found.' Only three months previously Mrs Gandhi's government had declared a period of Emergency during which she oversaw the forced and indiscriminate sterilisation of tens of thousands of people across the country, something Mother Teresa felt bitterly opposed to as she only ever sanctioned natural family planning. In spite of this most fundamental of all disagreements Mother Teresa managed to retain the most cordial of all friendships with the Prime Minister.

But apart from the endless possibilities of writing about babies rescued from dustbins – and it so happened that the first-floor balcony of Shishu Bhavan in Calcutta overlooked a major refuse area, as one of the Indian unpaid helpers pointed out to me, where several babies had been found, rescued and then sent to happy 'well-to-do' families abroad – Mother Teresa herself made an unusually strong story of human interest. A European nun who counted presidents and prime ministers as her friends, who denied herself every comfort, who got things done with a zeal that was the envy of businessmen and who claimed it was all mandated by God, had to be a formidable individual. By 1975 the Missionaries of Charity had thirty-two Homes for the Dying, sixty-seven leprosariums and twenty-eight children's homes around the world. Her story made good copy, as the editor of Time magazine recognised in December 1975, when he made her the cover story.

Producing this feature involved Mother Teresa posing for a photograph, from which the cover portrait was then painted. She agreed to this, she explained, only because on the morning of the sitting she had prayed for a special favour at mass if she did it. For every picture the photographer took she had asked God in exchange to 'free one

soul from purgatory'.[13] According to the unsigned article entitled
'Saints Among Us', 'Mother Teresa's own loving luminosity prompts
many to bestow on her a title that she would surely reject. She is, they
say, a living saint.' However, the article maintained, saints tend not to
be normal. Quoting University of Chicago church historian Martin
Marty, it went on: 'A saint has to be a misfit. A person who embodies
what his culture considers typical or normal cannot be exemplary.'
Father Carroll Stuhmeller of Chicago's Catholic Theological Union
agreed: 'Saints tend to be on the outer edge, where the maniacs, the
idiots and the geniuses are. They break the mould.'

It was a powerful article which took for granted Mother Teresa's
saintly qualities, her mix of shrewd organising sense combined with a
deep compassion for the poor, which made her unique in many ways.
Yet the author went on to make a strong point about the many other
men and women in the world who share her kind of faith and fervour,
and the second half of the article described the work and beliefs of
other equally saintly people who had not become household names in
the same way as Mother Teresa. They included Dorothy Day, founder
of the Catholic Worker Movement; Brother Roger Schutz, founder of
France's Protestant Monastery of Taize; the Norwegian medical missionary Annie Skau in Hong Kong; Schwester Selma Mayer, of Jerusalem;
Dr Cicely Saunders, the Anglican founder of the hospice movement;
and the Coptic monk Matta el Meskin, or Matthew the Poor.

In spite of the growing international praise there were those,
especially Muggeridge, who felt Mother Teresa still had not had her
due and were clamouring to propose her for the ultimate award, the
Nobel Peace Prize. As early as 1972, Lester B. Pearson, former Canadian
Prime Minister, who had won the Peace Prize himself in 1957,
submitted Mother Teresa's name, with Muggeridge supplying additional
documentation. She did not win it that year but Muggeridge was tireless
in his continuing communications with the Norwegian Committee. In
1975 she was nominated again, this time by an extremely powerful
team headed by the Rt. Hon. Shirley Williams, then a member of the
British government, a nomination supported by Maurice Strong,
another Canadian, head of the UN Environmental Programme, and
endorsed by Senator Edward Kennedy, Robert McNamara, a Presbyterian
and President of the World Bank from 1968 to 1981, and three other
US senators, Mark Hatfield, Hubert Humphrey and Pete Domenici,

who were all familiar with her work in Calcutta. Several other organisations such as the National Council of Catholic Women and the US National Council of the Churches of Christ also wrote strong letters. When Mother Teresa's nomination was widely reported in the international press, many people wrote letters urging the Committee to give the award to Mother Teresa. The Mayor of Addis Ababa and the head of the UN Disaster Relief Organisation, Faruk Berkol, a Turk, wrote as did several other heads of relief agencies. It was even put about that half the nuns in Spain had taken pen in hand in support of Mother Teresa for the Nobel Peace Prize.

However, again in 1975 Mother Teresa did not win the award. This time it went to the Russian scientist and human rights campaigner Andrei Sakharov. In 1977 Mother Teresa's nomination was resubmitted quietly by Lady Barbara Ward, the author, who had devoted her life to environmental issues, and supported by Robert McNamara. When for the third time she was passed over in favour of another candidate she joked: 'I had a good laugh over the Nobel Prize. It will come only when Jesus thinks it is time. We have all calculated to build two hundred homes for the lepers if it comes so our people will have to do the praying.'[14]

There are seven categories of people with the right to nominate candidates for the Nobel Peace Prize. These include members of the International Court of Arbitration in The Hague, active and former members of the Nobel Committee of the Norwegian Parliament and advisers appointed by the Norwegian Nobel Institute, university professors of political science and jurisprudence, history and philosophy and those who have themselves been awarded the Nobel Peace Prize. The name of the person responsible for promoting Mother Teresa for the fourth and final time has never been divulged, although Robert McNamara is thought to be the most likely. McNamara had known Mother Teresa since the 1960s and had used her organisation to channel the enormous supplies of food and dairy products exported by the United States in the Food for Peace Programme. Normally these supplies went from government to government, but McNamara felt the poor would be better served if some went direct to organisations like the Missionaries of Charity who were closest to the poor. For more than fifteen years McNamara had been deeply impressed by the work Mother Teresa was doing and wrote in support of his 1975 nomination: 'More important than the organisational structure of her work is the message it conveys that genuine peace is not the mere absence of hostilities, but rather the tranquility that arises out of a social order in which individuals treat one another with justice and compassion. The long history of human conflict suggests that without greater recognition of that fact – a fact which Mother Teresa's concern for the absolute poor so strikingly illustrates – the prospects for world peace will remain perilously fragile.'[15]

On 16 October 1979 the Nobel Committee pronounced Mother Teresa as that year's recipient of the Peace Prize. Very little else is known about why she won the award that year and not earlier, because even where divergent opinions are expressed during the adjudication these may not be recorded in the minutes or otherwise disclosed. The deliberations of the Committee are kept secret and only the decision is made public immediately it is reached. In Calcutta she was mobbed. Photographers and journalists immediately came to the Mother House to seek her reactions and take her picture. 'I accept the prize in the name of the poor,' she told them. 'The prize is the recognition of the poor world ... By serving the poor I am serving Him.'[16] Then the telegrams started arriving. More than 500 were received from most of the world's leaders. For days there were either letters or people coming in person to offer their congratulations. 'JOY SWEPT CALCUTTA' was the banner headline of the Statesman, proud that after six decades another Nobel prize had come to the province of West Bengal. Jyoti Basu, the communist Chief Minister of West Bengal, held a reception in her honour and told her, 'You have been the Mother of Bengal, now you are the Mother of the World.' The Calcutta Corporation held a gathering in her honour and the government of India not only hosted a reception for her at which she was compared to Gandhi and told, 'It will take either a Shakespeare or a Milton to record her services to India. Indeed her services to humanity as a whole are beyond compare,'[17] but also issued a commemorative postage stamp.

In December 1979 Mother Teresa travelled to Oslo to receive the medal and a cheque for £90,000, as well as a donation of £36,000 raised by the young people of Norway. In addition, there was a further £3,000 which would have been spent on the customary banquet, but Mother Teresa had asked for the money instead to go to those who really needed a meal – a gesture that dented the complacency of a materialistic world. It was freezing cold that day and many in her audience were well wrapped in fur coats and hats. She wore a grey cardigan and black coat over her sari as she entered the building but shed these as she climbed the podium of the Aula Magna of Oslo University to give her response to the award. The room was filled with dignitaries, including King Olav V, Crown Prince Harald and Crown Princess Sonya. A symphony orchestra played Grieg and multi-coloured bouquets of flowers decorated the stage. The chairman of the Norwegian Nobel Committee, Professor John Sannes, in giving the address, explained succinctly why he believed Mother Teresa had become an icon for a troubled world: 'The year 1979 has not been a year of peace. Disputes and conflicts between nations, peoples and ideologies have been conducted with all the accompanying extremes of inhumanity and cruelty. We have witnessed wars, the unrestrained use of violence; we have witnessed fanaticism hand in hand with cynicism; we have witnessed contempt for human life and dignity ... The Norwegian Nobel Committee has considered it right and appropriate, precisely in this year, in their choice of Mother Teresa to remind the world of the words spoken by Fridtjof Nansen: "Love of one's neighbour is realistic policy." '

Mother Teresa, after helping her audience to pray, then launched into the speech that made headlines. Abortion, she told them, 'is the greatest destroyer of peace today ... because it is a direct war, a direct killing, direct murder by the mother herself'. She explained how her sisters had saved thousands of lives by telling all the clinics, hospitals and police stations, 'Please don't destroy the child; we will take the child.' 'And also we are doing another thing which is very beautiful. We are teaching our beggars, our leprosy patients, our slum dwellers, our people of the street, natural family planning.' Mother Teresa told the assembled dignitaries that by this natural method of abstaining from sex at fertile times of the month there were in Calcutta during the last six months 61,273 babies fewer from families who would otherwise have had them. She went on: 'The poor people are very great people. They can teach us so many beautiful things. The other day one of them came to thank us and said: "You people who have evolved chastity, you are the best people to teach us family planning because it is nothing more than self-control out of love for each other." And I think they said a very beautiful sentence.'

During the press conference following the prize-giving, one reporter boldly questioned Mother Teresa on the subject of religious persecution in Albania. Many Catholic Albanians living in the United States felt deeply let down by Mother Teresa on this issue, as evidenced by their letters to the *Albanian Catholic Bulletin* asking why she had never raised her voice in defence of Albanian suffering. 'I don't know what to say since I don't know what is happening there. I can say only one thing. My Albanian people are always in my heart.' Her repeated attempts to remove her mother and sister might be sufficient evidence that she did in fact know what was happening in Albania. Also in 1979 she had a meeting in New York with Queen Geraldine of Albania, widow of King Zog. But her defendants point out that she always backed away from involvement in political activity as incompatible with her primary mission. Disingenuously, these people ignore the fact that a woman's disputed right to an abortion is one of the most heated political conflicts of our age.

The speech was controversial. But Mother Teresa was giving notice that here was an issue she was never going to go soft on, one on which she would never lose an opportunity to proclaim her views. In spite of her acceptance of natural family planning, she was never to understand those who felt with a moral conviction equal to hers that the world might be a better place if it were less populated. This was truly a new era for the Missionaries of Charity.

CHAPTER SEVEN

GLOBETROTTING

It was fitting that of the four women who supported Mother Teresa in Oslo, two were Missionaries of Charity, Sister Agnes and Sister Gertrude, her first two disciples, and two were from the loyal band of lay helpers known as Co-Workers, Ann Blaikie and Jacqueline De Decker. From the 1960s onwards, Mother Teresa received vital additional support from the growing number of Co-Workers around the world. In March 1969 the dramatic growth of this organisation, developed by Ann Blaikie and others in the Marian Society in Calcutta, was given Papal recognition. Ann and John Blaikie, who had by then returned to live in England, went with Mother Teresa to Rome to present a constitution to Pope Paul VI. He blessed the three of them and recognised the Co-Workers of Mother Teresa as an Association in All the World Affiliated with the Missionaries of Charity. Ann Blaikie was given the title, International Link. Thus, ten years before the award of the Nobel Prize there was already an understanding of the importance of globalising the message. Some months later, Mrs Patty Kump, a former airline stewardess married to a doctor and living in Minnesota with four adopted children, was made chairman of the American branch. Patty Kump had first become aware of Mother Teresa after reading about her in the 1958 article in Jubilee.

This was not the first lay organisation to be associated with a religious community – the third order of St Francis was linked to the Franciscans and the third order of St Benedict to the Benedictines. But the Co-Workers of Mother Teresa were different. In the first place they were to be of all denominations and religions, not just Catholics, as was the case with the earlier organisations. Secondly, and partly as a result of the first, they exceeded other associations in sheer size. Above all, Mother Teresa hoped to create something new, unique even. She did not want a body of well-meaning women dedicated to collecting funds and supplies. She had sufficient foresight to realise how easily this could degenerate into a ladies' lunching club, losing sight of the real goals and totally inappropriate for the problems it was trying to solve. In fact, no food or drink of any kind was to be offered at meetings. Only water could be consumed. In any case, she was utterly confident, as always, of God providing money and materials. She envisaged a spiritual family which would be united in its understanding of the poor, the suffering and the sick as a 'repository of the divine'. The core of the association was to be prayer, and the constitution carried the text of two prayers which the Co-Workers were asked to offer daily in union with the Missionaries of Charity, one of which begged for the grace to merit serving the poor, who were seen as 'the Ambassadors of God'. The actual name, Co-Workers, was a direct reference to Gandhi, whom she had never met, but admired greatly. He too called his helpers Co-Workers. There were other echoes of his desire to identify with the poor, principally the wearing of simple, home-spun clothes.

Mother Teresa herself may have called the Co-Workers 'a most disorganised organisation', but there was a regular *International Newsletter*, put together by Ann Blaikie, then typed, copied on a mimeograph machine and mailed around the world, describing the work of the sisters and brothers. In the 1970s this was still just a couple of roughly typed and stapled sheets − by the late 1980s it was a glossy, two-colour brochure. One innovative feature was the link with Sick and Suffering Co-Workers, a role which Jacqueline De Decker, the severely ill Belgian woman who had wanted to join Mother Teresa as early as 1948, assumed. The Sick and Suffering Co-Worker loves one sister or brother so much that they offer their suffering for her or him and so share in the work. 'It is both a call and privilege,' De Decker explained, describing Sick and Suffering Co-Workers as the spiritual powerhouse of the Missionaries of Charity. Mother Teresa herself has always put great emphasis on the link with suffering. 'There is a power in this offering of suffering, a force so great it could change the world. May many more be called to join this link,' she wrote in 1973.[1]

There is no doubt that, thanks to the efforts of Co-Workers world-wide, Mother Teresa was able to expand the activities of her sisters throughout the 1970s and 1980s. Several ambulances, the core of the mobile dispensaries, were paid for and sent to India by Co-Workers. They organised film showings, concerts and pantomimes, sold books and pamphlets and made available recorded talks with Mother Teresa. According to a 1982 report, British Co-Workers sent £10,000 a month to Calcutta for flour to make bread, and arranged for one million Dapsone tablets to be sent each month for the treatment of leprosy patients in India. They also sent £10,000 annually for many years to pay for Christmas meals for the poor in various countries. This was in addition to the hundreds of donations and gifts in kind that they took or sent to the then four Missionaries of Charity houses in London and Liverpool.

The Co-Workers galvanised schoolchildren, thousands of whom gave money, old clothes and toys or organised school cake or jumble sales to help the starving children of India. One particularly successful idea in the UK was the 'bread campaign'. Schoolchildren saved enough pennies to give 5,000 Indian slum schoolchildren a daily slice of bread. In fact, this was sent as money to buy flour to make the bread but it was obviously easier for the children to visualise it as a slice of English-style, readymade and processed bread. This was so successful that children in Germany 'have readily accepted to make their little sacrifices'[2] to provide a daily vitamin pill for the slum schoolchildren and many thousands of Danish children 'made beautiful sacrifices' to provide a daily glass of condensed milk. In addition, several churches had, and still have, permanent collecting boxes organised by the Co-Workers. According to Eileen Egan, 'The generosity of the American people increased each year until for several years the donations exceeded $1,000,000 annually. In Germany contributions built up over the years until they often reached a total of $1,500,000.' The amounts were less but not insignificant from Ireland, Holland, Belgium, France, Denmark, Sweden, Italy, Australia and other countries where Co-Worker branches were eventually set up.

One of the reasons the Missionaries of Charity attracted funds so easily was the visible austerity of the nuns. Overheads at all the institutions do not exceed 2 per cent of total expenditure. Each sister has two sets of clothes and the food per head works out at roughly £4 a month. People have trusted them, believing that, unlike some other charities, the maximum amount of the money given was going directly to 'the work'. But the question is, what areas of 'the work'? Clearly the sisters themselves require very little to live on and much of the food they eat is donated. Some money is obviously spent on maintenance of buildings and other normal living expenses, however pared down, and educating the nuns is another cost which increased naturally as the numbers grew. In June 1970 the newsletter carried an appeal for novice sponsorships. Donations were urgently required to 'help the further education of the nuns and sisters, to enable them to carry out their work for the poor and the destitute'. Thirty-five pounds was estimated as the amount needed per girl for one year. Volunteers were regularly called upon to help teach English, the common tongue of the Missionaries of Charity.

In England, there were at least 20,000 Co-Workers by the early 1980s, although it was always difficult to gauge the exact number; 18,000 copies of the newsletter were distributed but many of the Co-Workers who received one actually represented a whole group such as a Girl Guide or Brownie pack, a knitters' or a school group. Compare this, say, to 4,000 volunteers for Sue Ryder Homes, similarly a Catholic-inspired charity with a dynamic foundress and international dimensions, and one begins to recognise the scale of Mother Teresa's success. And yet from 1975 Mother Teresa insisted, with increasing vehemence, that the Co-Workers were neither to solicit nor to collect money. She banned the sale of charity Christmas cards too. Donations, however, fell into a different category and the bread posters, encouraging schoolchildren to make donations, were still in use in the early 1980s. Eventually, in 1993, when Ann Blaikie was already seriously ill, Mother Teresa suddenly and without warning closed down the entire Co-Worker structure, which had registered charity status in the United Kingdom and therefore was required to produce accounts. She announced that in future donations were to go directly to the sisters.

The Catholic Media Office in London, besieged by questions from puzzled journalists, had not been told in advance of this and was as confused as the thousands of Co-Workers. In addition to closing down

Co-Worker bank accounts, there were to be no more administrative workers, gatherings or newsletters. According to some, Mother Teresa felt they had become too big and administratively unwieldy; according to others she did not think it necessary to be accountable at a human level despite the fact that the amounts of money being channelled through them were getting larger each year. She believed it should be possible to be a Co-Worker without being a member of an organisation and that those who wished to keep in touch through prayer meetings could still do so without the need of letters or too much travelling.

'Co-Workers can continue to be friends with each other within a country or around the world. Friendship is a gift of God,' she wrote to them on 22 July 1994, 'but these long-distance friendships can be kept on a private level as you do with other friends so there is no need to have national and international gatherings of Co-Workers to foster such friendships.' Two years later she was still having to write letters to her Co-Workers asking them 'to pray for the few who still find it difficult to accept my decision because they do not as yet see it as the will of God for the Co-Workers'.

Perhaps she always had had misgivings about letting a secondary organisation grow alongside her own which could never be subject to the same disciplines. The refusal to build institutions, other than her own Missionaries of Charity, is in any case entirely consistent with her attitude to building schools and hospitals. She wants nothing to come between her and her accessibility to the very poor. Also, by 1993, she no longer needed the Co-Workers. There was certainly no further requirement to publicise Mother Teresa's work. Schools wanting a lecturer could contact the local sisters directly. Ambulances could be donated by individual benefactors. The Missionaries of Charity had generated their own momentum and, as Mother Teresa maintained that divine Providence would bring them all they needed, there appeared to be a contradiction in having an enormous group of well-meaning people dedicated to bringing in gifts and cash.

The Co-Workers had flourished for nearly twenty-five years, but the necessary level of deprivation was one which many found increasingly hard to balance with the desire to be efficient. 'You have no idea how hard it is to persuade them to buy new PCs even when it's vital, because they're totally focused on spending the money on rice and medicine,' one charity executive in the UK said in 1995. 'But you can't deliver the rice or medicine without proper organisation, can you? We bite our tongues a lot.'[3]

Exactly how much financial help was generated by the activities of the Co-Workers worldwide over a twenty-five-year period is impossible to estimate. Mother Teresa always insisted that the practical help was secondary to the spiritual inspiration they could offer. She asked the Co-Workers to do the little things that no one else has time for, such as forming relationships with those in hospitals, geriatric homes, prisons and homes for the physically and mentally handicapped, or talking to the bereaved and elderly who wait often for days for the visit of a friend. She always wanted a predominantly prayerful gathering, that would seek out those within the neighbourhood who needed help, more of a family than an organisation, and, perhaps inevitably, when it developed in other directions, the only response was to dismantle it. If nothing else, the Co-Workers galvanised consciences in an extraordinarily effective way.

Following the award of the Nobel Prize, and, a year later, India's highest civilian award, the Bharat Ratna, Jewel of India, industrialists and politicians were falling over themselves in their often unseemly haste to beat a path to 54a Lower Circular Road, without any prodding from Co-Workers. Apart from the generosity of individuals, both Indian and European, several companies, such as the Bata Shoe Company, which donated leather for leprosy patients to make shoes, charities such as Help the Aged in England, which donated money for meals or specific projects and Rotary Clubs the world over all offered to help in some way. Recruits too, many of them with large reputations in tow, started flooding Mother Teresa with offers to help. These high-profile volunteers included Daphne Rae, mother of six, wife of the headmaster of Westminster, one of Britain's most famous public schools, who was bound to generate news stories when she left her children to go and work in the slums of Calcutta.

Mrs Rae became a Catholic convert in 1977, after she miscarried a twin and doctors advised her to abort the remaining twin as the risks of continuing the pregnancy were too great. However, she found a Catholic gynaecologist and was safely delivered of twin sons; it transpired that she had been carrying triplets. She said: 'They are the most fantastic children. When I think I might have been persuaded not to have them ... I would as soon have taken poison. You can't kill automatically – you must keep the life that is given to you.' In September 1979 Mrs Rae, who was born in Sri Lanka, was drawn back to her Asian roots. She tried to explain: 'I feel very moved towards the dying. I can't really say why people do things. I can't imagine ever wanting to go sailing. I'm sick if I look at a boat. Death is a very spiritual time; once you are born the only certain thing in life is that you are going to die.' Asked why she went to India to help those in need when there were plenty of those in England who needed help, Mrs Rae explained: 'It is much easier for me to help people in India than it is to help someone here who is spoilt and wealthy and overfed; easier for me to see Christ in the starving than in the gluttonous.'[4]

Daphne Rae, whose fragile English beauty must have been an extraordinary sight on the ward of Mother Teresa's Home for the Dying, went three times in all to help the Missionaries of Charity, taking with her large supplies of donated medicines and drips, melolin dressings and hypodermic needles. She wrote a book about her experiences called Love Until It Hurts, but then she suddenly stopped working with Mother Teresa and started to help much smaller Indian communities, with whom she is still involved. Reluctant publicly to explain her reasons for the break, she clearly feels her efforts are more valuable to these lesser-known charities, which have not benefited from the massive international publicity granted Mother Teresa once she won the Nobel Prize.

There are clues, however, to the change of heart both in her earlier life and in her book. Daphne Rae had wanted to be a doctor, but took a postgraduate diploma in Pastoral Theology instead. After the birth of her sixth child she worked part-time for two years at a home for the terminally ill and dying. Thus she was not short of practical experience of helping people to die in the best way possible. What she saw in India – for example, the same needle being used forty or fifty times, often a disposable one at that, distressed her. Daphne Rae was passionately anti-abortion and believed deeply in helping to save the lives of unwanted babies. For a while Mother Teresa gave her the job of visiting as many abortion clinics as possible and trying to save a tiny foetus, often weighing little more than a pound, that had somehow survived a botched abortion. This was work she believed in. But at Shishu Bhavan she noticed a different approach to unwanted pregnancies. As she explained in her book, for an Indian girl to be unmarried and pregnant was a huge scandal; it turned her into something worse than an untouchable and an abortion was often deemed imperative in these circumstances. Sometimes, these girls would therefore go to the Missionaries of Charity for help; the nuns would agree to keep them on an upstairs floor until their due date and then deliver the baby free of charge and keep it for possible adoption. In return, the girls had to help with domestic chores. A reasonable exchange, it might seem. But some of those who witnessed the arrangement have commented that the moral superiority of the nuns ensured that the girls were treated as the lowest type of servants and kept on sufferance in servants' quarters.

Jerry Brown, former Governor of California, was another who spent three weeks devoting himself to Mother Teresa and whose presence in Calcutta guaranteed plenty of newspaper coverage. Then, in 1980 at a rally in West Berlin, Mother Teresa was presented with a gift of $280,000 by the beautiful actress Maria Schell, her earnings from television appearances, providing a spectacular photo-opportunity. Throughout the 1980s and 1990s politicians of all persuasions and industrialists from all over the world came to give money to Mother Teresa. Barely a month passed without yet another notification from a world leader or would-be head of state suggesting a visit. The Vatican, too, now made an increasing number of requests for her to travel to conferences and give speeches, welcoming her traditional interpretation of theological matters. John Paul II, Pope since 1978, who soon developed a warm personal relationship with her, urged her to make her views known wherever and whenever an opportunity arose. The world's journalists flocked to listen to what she, as a Nobel Prize-winner, had to say. News stories about her visiting foreign capitals as well as outlying areas or refugee camps soon became regular occurrences. This gave her an unprecedented platform on which to air her views, available to few other religious leaders, Catholic or non-Catholic, and certainly to no other Mother Superior.

One of her first visits as a Nobel Laureate was in 1980 to Skopje for two days as a guest of the city authorities. She had meetings with Macedonian government officials before being declared a distinguished citizen of Skopje. A few months previously Mother Teresa had opened a house for elderly homeless people in the new city of Zagreb, the first time her Order had been able to operate in a communist country.

She had returned to the city of her birth in 1970 when she had met the Bishop, attended the Red Cross Centre for Macedonia and gone on to worship at the shrine at Letnice, which had been so important in her childhood. But she was disappointed to find that nothing remained of her home or her street following the earthquake.

However hard she insisted that her own lifestyle would not change after winning the Nobel Prize, the pressures on her to travel became increasingly insistent and she appeared to do so with relish. Sometimes she was away for ten months each year. At the request of the Pope, she attended a conference on family life in Guatemala and combined this with a visit to the desperately impoverished Caribbean island of Haiti, then ruled by Jean-Claude Duvalier and his new wife, the First Lady, Michèle Bennett Duvalier. The first Missionaries of Charity home opened in Haiti in 1977, the second in 1979; Mother Teresa desperately wanted more. A few months after Haiti she was in Egypt, where she urged Cairo housewives to 'have lots and lots of children'. This was not a popular message with the government, as Egyptian television had just finished filming a six-month series of cartoon films urging families to limit their number of children. Mrs Jihan Sadat, wife of the head of state, was Honorary President of Egypt's Family Planning Council, which was trying to stem the annual one million rise in the population.

How much did the constant travel and high-level meetings warp Mother Teresa's lifestyle in the last two decades of her active life? At the time of the Nobel award there were 158 Missionaries of Charity houses. The following year fourteen more were opened in Bangladesh, Belgium (two), Papua New Guinea, Nepal, Ethiopia, France, Yugoslavia, Spain, Argentina, Florida, Chile and Rome (two). In 1981 eighteen new homes were opened, in 1982 twelve, in 1983 fourteen. At the start of the 1980s the Missionaries of Charity boasted 140 slum schools, a daily feeding programme for nearly 50,000 people at 304 centres, seventy homes looking after 4,000 children and approximately 1,000 adoptions a year arranged; there were eighty-one homes for dying destitutes which, in 1982, admitted 13,000 people; 12,000 poor women were taught to earn their living and 6,000,000 sick people were treated by 670 mobile clinics. This was no small achievement, but it was largely India-centred. Young girls were flocking to join Mother Teresa as much for her own now legendary personality as for the work she did, which meant she was required to fly all over the world in order to see them all and oversee their work.

But although her workload increased dramatically, she never liked delegating. Hordes of visitors came to see her personally; if they were industrialists or politicians with cheques in their pockets, they would never be satisfied with seeing anyone else and often required a photograph with her. She managed on three or four hours' sleep a night, rising at 4 a.m. with mass at six; from 8.00 a.m. until 11.00 a.m. she visited her Calcutta homes in a station wagon, talking to the sisters or helping with the work, then back to her headquarters for lunch, followed by further prayers and some office work. After the 6 p.m. mass she went on another round of her homes, then had dinner. While the rest of the community slept she caught up with correspondence. It soon became apparent that her greatest skills included never being afraid to ask, and treating the world's political leaders in just the same way as she would a down-and-out; her drive and determination, which had lain almost dormant during her first forty years, were ferocious.

One of the most remarkable aspects of Mother Teresa's advancing age was that her capacity for work seemed to increase. In 1982 she plunged into the chaos of West Beirut, where many hospitals had been hit by Israeli artillery. In a dramatic rescue that captured world imagination, this seventy-two-year-old nun took thirty-seven half-starved children in a Red Cross convoy to East Beirut, where they could be cared for by her nuns. They had been left stranded in the squalor of a mental asylum in a refugee camp that had been blasted day and night by Israeli forces trying to drive Palestinian guerrillas from the city. An International Red Cross official said at the time: 'What stunned everyone was her energy and efficiency. She saw the problem, fell to her knees and prayed for a few seconds and then she was rattling off a list of supplies she needed – nappies, plastic pants, chamber pots. The problem is that in wartime most of the attention is focused on the casualties. But the blind, the deaf, the insane and the spastics tend to be forgotten just when they need help the most. Mother Teresa understood that right away,'[5] said the official.

At the end of 1984, one of the worst ever industrial disasters hit the Indian town of Bhopal in Madhya Pradesh state: 2,500 people were killed almost instantly by a poisonous-gas leak from a pesticide factory owned by a subsidiary of Union Carbide. Thousands more were choked by the toxic fumes and many had their health permanently damaged. State officials in Bhopal said there was no contingency plan to evacuate people from the city during the operation to neutralise stocks of the deadly methyl isocyanate gas remaining in the underground storage tank which had leaked. Mother Teresa took an early plane to Bhopal and, greeted at the airport by large crowds of angry relatives of the gassed victims, advised them, 'Forgive, forgive,' a comment that seemed to offer little tangible comfort to the victims. As she toured the hospital she explained, 'I am here to give love and care to those who need it most in this terrible tragedy.'[6] Five years later, the US owners of the plant agreed to pay the Indian government $470 million compensation; in return the government agreed to drop criminal charges against the company and its former chairman.

Mother Teresa plunged into the AIDS crisis with similar gusto. She opened a hospice in New York's Greenwich Village to be run by four of her nuns to care for American victims of the disease, which she labelled 'the new leprosy of the West'. The story became headline news in the US because, after some forceful campaigning with the city authorities, she obtained the release from the notorious Sing Sing Prison outside New York of three tough young men serving up to nine-year sentences for violent crimes. Antonio Rivera, Jimmy Matos and Daryl Monsett each had irreversible AIDS. Repeated attempts to have them transferred had failed and they faced certain and agonising death behind bars. But then Mother Teresa visited them in their cells and immediately telephoned New York Governor Mario Cuomo. 'In God's name, please let these men die in peace,' she pleaded. Cuomo, who had turned down similar appeals, felt obliged when pressed by her to sign the release order within twenty-four hours, which allowed the three to transfer to the Greenwich Village hospice. As she explained: 'We are hoping these poor unfortunate men will now be able to live and die in peace. We plan to give them tender loving care because each one is Jesus in a distressing disguise ... we are not here to sit in judgement on these people, to decide blame or guilt. Our mission is to help them to make their dying days more tolerable and we have sisters who are dedicated to do that.'[7]

Anthony Burgess, the novelist, wrote in a newspaper article of the comments of the doctor appointed to supervise the medical side of St

Clare's Hospital. Terry Miles, he reported, was appalled by the ignorance of the sisters there, who had no idea what AIDS was. 'The Crucifix on your chest isn't going to protect you,' he warned them. 'God will provide,' Mother Teresa kept saying. Burgess concluded: 'But God never provides knowledge or skill. God in fact is never enough.' He questioned the nature of sanctity, which 'seems to consist of an unwillingness to accept the existence of evil, despite the Church's insistence that it is alive and kicking in the world. It rampages in New York, but the Teresan community sees it as a sickness that can be assuaged with loving words and a little hot soup.'[8]

In 1985, the world was shocked by stories and pictures of starving Africans. Mother Teresa already had nuns working in Ethiopia in the shanty towns of the capital and others in the famine-stricken province of Wollo, where they ran a feeding programme and hospital and cared for the old, the blind, the disabled and the incurably ill. In 1985 she toured Ethiopia at the height of its famine, a visit which coincided with one from pop singer Bob Geldof.

The meeting of these two, widely dubbed the saint and the sinner, was a good story, and not just for the tabloids. Geldof, born into a Catholic family and educated by priests whom he came to loathe, unable to utter a sentence without several expletives, had shaken the world's charities by his success in raising millions for the poor in Africa. He rallied the forces of rock performers around the world to create Band Aid and then, in 1985, was persuaded to go to Ethiopia to help arrange for the millions to be spent. Sitting in the departure lounge at Addis Ababa airport in January 1985, he saw Mother Teresa. 'She was astonishingly tiny,' Geldof recalled. 'When I went to greet her I found that I towered more than two feet above her. She was a battered, wizened woman. The thing that struck me most forcefully was her feet. Her habit was clean and well cared for but her sandals were beaten-up pieces of leather from which her feet protruded, gnarled and misshapen as old tree roots.' Geldof then bent to kiss her, because it seemed the right thing to do. 'She bowed her head so swiftly that I was obliged to kiss the top of her wimple. It disturbed me. I found out later that she only let lepers kiss her.'

It was not long before the photographers crowded around the odd couple. Mother Teresa started to tell Geldof of the Missionaries of Charity work in Africa and Geldof told her that his band, the Boomtown

Rats, had played in India and he would be very happy, next time he was in India, to do a benefit concert for her mission. But she promptly declined his offer. 'She said that she did not need fund-raising activities – God would provide.' Geldof then witnessed a clear demonstration of the way in which God provided. While the television cameras in the departure lounge were rolling, she snatched the live opportunity to say that she had noticed on her way to the airport some palatial old buildings which appeared vacant and wanted to know if she could have them as orphanages. A government minister brought in to the discussion stalled, too embarrassed to say no, especially when it became clear that Mother Teresa had done her homework beforehand and in fact knew all about the buildings. He replied that he would try to find her suitable premises for an orphanage and she quickly interjected: 'Two orphanages.' 'Two orphanages,' he conceded.

Geldof commented that the moment he met Mother Teresa, 'she struck me as being the living embodiment of moral good', but added, 'There was nothing otherworldly or divine about her. The way she spoke to the journalists showed her to be as deft a manipulator of media as any high-powered American PR expert. She does a sort of "Oh dear, I'm just a frail old lady" schtick. She was outrageously brilliant. There was no false modesty about her and there was a certainty of purpose which left her little patience. But she was totally selfless; every moment her aim seemed to be, how can I use this or that situation to help others?'[9]

By the end of the decade, Mother Teresa recognised Eastern Europe as the new area of desperate need. In 1986 in the wake of the Chernobyl nuclear disaster, she was in the Soviet Union, and the following year, at the invitation of the Official Soviet Peace Committee, returned in the hope of establishing a mission there. On 22 December 1988, four of her nuns started work in a Moscow hospital helping victims of the Armenian earthquake. The Moscow venture was unprecedented because after the Revolution all voluntary organisations were disbanded and religious orders were forbidden. The Missionaries of Charity was the first religious mission to open a house since 1918.

Jill Braithwaite, wife of the British Ambassador, Roderic, in Moscow from 1988 to 1992, became aware of the nuns the following year. 'They kept a very low profile, determined not to draw attention to their presence, but when I read a small newspaper story about them I set out to discover where they were.' She found them, in the east of the city, living on the ground floor of an appallingly dilapidated old people's home and working with the old people, who were mostly about to die, on the top two floors. 'Unlike the other aid agencies, who soon started to flood the country with Western goods, they were not bringing in lots of money nor were they in any way proselytising. Russia is such a terribly difficult place to do anything but their approach, starting from the bottom and working up, was clearly the right one,' Braithwaite believes. So impressed was she with the quiet efficiency and cheerfulness of the Belgian sister-in-charge, Sister Chantal, that when Sir George Solti and the Chicago Symphony Orchestra came to Moscow for a concert and wanted to make a charitable contribution she suggested the Missionaries of Charity 'because with them you know it goes straight to the people you're trying to help'. She then organised a collection to buy the sisters a car. After a while the nuns moved out of the basement and into a redundant Portakabin once used by some Austrian builders. They took over a second one as a home for some handicapped children. But in spite of their attempts never to undermine local authorities there were difficulties over visas or opening up in other cities, and then Mother Teresa herself would appear and sort out the problems at a higher level. 'I've never had anything to do with nuns before,' said Braithwaite, 'but the Missionaries of Charity were incredibly impressive; they showed their own strength by example.'[10]

In 1988 Mother Teresa made a visit to London with not altogether happy consequences. The history of the Missionaries of Charity in the UK had never been entirely trouble-free. The first English hostel opened in 1971 to help down-and-out women, but burnt down in 1980 and nine women died in the fire. The hostel had no fire escapes – charity hostels for the homeless were exempt from the law which otherwise insisted on these – but there was controversy surrounding the deaths as the local council said it had given permission only for ten people to sleep there but there were in fact twenty-one residents. Then there was a problem in 1983 with a hostel for homeless women in Liverpool which Mother Teresa had to sort out personally. Liverpool City councillors had said that the women should be looked after by their own existing welfare homes. After talks with councillors and Roman Catholic Church representatives, the sisters agreed not to use the hostel for night-time accommodation but to concentrate on developing daytime services for those in need.

When Mother Teresa arrived in April 1988, she paid a much publicised visit to Prime Minister Margaret Thatcher, who, she insisted, was bound as a mother to see things from her point of view. After two nights talking to London's homeless community in Waterloo's 'Cardboard City', Mother Teresa told reporters: 'There is much more suffering I believe here, more loneliness, painful loneliness of people rejected by society who have no one to care for them. It hurt me so much to see our people in the terrible cold with just a bit of cardboard covering them. They were inside the cardboard box made like a little coffin. I did not know what to say. My eyes were full of tears.' She added: 'I find poverty in a rich country more difficult to remove than poverty in a poor country.' The nun then begged the Prime Minister to help her set up a new hostel for the capital's homeless, threatening, only half jokingly, that if she were not given a house she would bring all the drifters into the Great Hall of Westminster to sleep. Downing Street replied calmly that the Prime Minister had listened for forty minutes and told Mother Teresa about the work of voluntary organisations in London.

Mother Teresa's visit was controversial in other ways, timed as it was to coincide with a new hearing for the Liberal Catholic MP David Alton's Bill to reduce the upper limit for abortions from twenty-eight to eighteen weeks; she pleaded with Mrs Thatcher, in vain, to change her stance and back it. David Alton, who chauffeured Mother Teresa around for much of her visit, commented: 'We know her intervention at this very personal level at this crucial moment will be a decisive factor.'[11] Mother Teresa had one other aim while in England, which was to address the Global Survival Conference in Oxford. There she told her audience straightforwardly that couples who had practised contraception would not be accepted as potential adoptive parents for any of 'her' babies.

The day after she met Margaret Thatcher, Mother Teresa fell into the clutches of the *Daily Mirror* and its then owner, Robert Maxwell. Friends of Mother Teresa point out that the meeting was set up only the day before and she had never met him previously. Although her association with such a fraudulent self-publicist was subsequently to damage her own reputation, it is unreasonable to suggest that she ought to have known more about his business dealings than the bankers and lawyers who were working so closely with him at this time. Along with the Mirror women's editor, Christena Appleyard, Mother Teresa went to inspect a possible house as Maxwell launched an appeal for the Mirror's 'wonderful readers' to contribute to a new Missionary of Charity refuge. The idea suited them both: Maxwell because he loved the publicity and there were plenty of pictures of him with Mother Teresa launching the appeal, and Mother Teresa because she never liked being given houses with government strings attached. In all, £169,000 was sent in by readers of the Daily Mirror. Put into a high-interest account, it amounted to £263,000 by the time Maxwell died. In addition, a further £90,000 was contributed by readers of the Scottish Daily Record. The total was intended to be enough for two homes.

Over the next few years, Mother Teresa repeatedly complained that Britain's homeless had been let down by those in power and insisted that the rejection experienced by the poor in Britain was more painful for her than working with the destitute in third world countries. In 1990 she expressed her frustration to reporters about the lack of progress in finding a proper home for the homeless: 'I talked to the highest people but nothing has happened ... A number of people promised to do something but we have no home.'[12]

By the time of Maxwell's death, still nothing had been done. There was speculation that the money had been taken by Maxwell for his personal use. A spokesman for Mirror Group Newspapers, however, insisted that the delay was because Mother Teresa's nuns had not found the land or an appropriate property and denied that any of the money had gone missing. Mother Teresa had few doubts about anything she did in her lifetime, but using money garnered through Robert Maxwell's auspices and therefore becoming tainted with the accusations of fraud which fell upon him after his death was something she greatly regretted. Finally, five years after the appeal had been launched, a thirty-five-room hostel was eventually opened in London, and Mother Teresa, who came for the opening ceremony, thanked Mirror readers for their kindness.

From the start, the 1990s were not kind to Mother Teresa. It was not simply that the media coverage and world crises did not let up but in 1989 her own health began to deteriorate. In September she suffered a near fatal heart attack, almost fifteen years after the first sign of heart trouble, and underwent major heart surgery. She was fitted with a pacemaker in Calcutta that December. Two years later she was treated at the prestigious Scripps Clinic and Research Foundation at La Jolla, California, for heart disease and bacterial pneumonia. Next, she had been taken ill in Tijuana, Mexico, and doctors performed a balloon angioplasty to force open a blood vessel. But her increasing frailty never stopped her travelling and, in 1993, when she was in Rome, she fell and broke her ribs. In July she was in a Bombay hospital for two days with exhaustion and a month later, when she was in New Delhi to receive yet another award, she fell critically ill with long-standing malaria resurfacing, complicated by heart and lung problems. This time she was taken to the All India Institute of Medical Sciences intensive coronary care unit and soon recovered enough to go home. Only a month later she was back in hospital in Calcutta where doctors treating her for a blocked heart vessel said she had had a close call.

In 1990, she informed the Pope that she wished to resign because of ill health. However, no one else had been groomed to take over and the nun founds it impossible to elect a successor while their foundress was still alive. Why? It appears rather harsh to blame Mother Teresa for her own charismatic personality but cynics will claim that keeping Mother Teresa at the helm was crucial to ensure the continuance of international funds. At the same time, would not a more openly democratic system, not simply of voting but of daily living, have paved the way for a successor who did not feel intimidated by Mother Teresa still being around and who might even have been encouraged to start taking over long before this? Even some supporters have told me, while not wishing to be named, that they find this inability to accept the emergence of a successor a most serious failing. To allow a major institution to be built up worldwide with so much goodwill and money yet not to prepare for its smooth continuation is both short-sighted and egocentric. A member of the Conference of Major Religious Superiors, as it was then called, who also asked to remain anonymous, voiced the concerns of many Church people that a new, younger, more active leader was required as there was a danger that 'the good she has done will be negated by her health'.[13] Another sister, working in the Vatican, remarked that, had she resigned then, she would have been able to look at internal affairs such as governance and education, and might have avoided much of the criticism that has come her way since.

Ill health or no, she continued to respond to new crises, such as sending a team of nuns to Romania to help handicapped children abandoned during Nicolae Ceauşescu's regime, and she continued to be the recipient of largesse from the world's leaders. Yasser Arafat, Palestinian Liberation Organisation chairman, went personally to Calcutta in 1990 to present her with a cheque for $50,000. Today, he refuses to comment on the reasons for making such a generous donation.[14]

But her style seemed increasingly at odds with the politically correct 1990s. First there was Germaine Greer's attack, albeit referring to events nearly twenty years before in Bangladesh, in a new column at the back of the Independent Magazine called 'Heroes and Villains'. There was never any shortage of people wishing to write about their heroes, but those prepared to declare their villains became scarcer and scarcer. The frisson when Greer's article appeared was palpable. Then there was an announcement that Glenda Jackson, aged fifty-four and star of countless passionate sex films, was to play Mother Teresa in a filmed version of her life planned by City of Joy author Dominique Lapierre, who had spent more than a year masterminding the project with the Vatican. Lapierre insisted that Pope John Paul II was full of encouragement for such a film before Mother Teresa died in case it then became open territory to any undiscriminating film producer. Notwithstanding the Vatican's eagerness, Mother Teresa sensed this was not a plan with which she should be seen to be co-operating and declined.

Hardly discernible, perhaps, but there was a sense in which the Vatican wished to capture Mother Teresa as she was before old age took its toll and magnified the eccentricities of senescence. When I visited Rome, I received the unequivocal message that Mother Teresa had done stalwart service but the Pope was now looking for younger, more active women as role models for Catholic women into the twenty-first century. 'As a media figure, she's almost had her day as far as the Vatican is concerned,' one journalist from a Catholic newspaper told me. 'They're looking for dynamic young women who embrace all the tenets and are outward-looking, possibly professional women or nuns such as Mary Ann Glandon, with a North American order, who is part of the Vatican's team on Women's Issues.' A new book, Women in the Church Today, published in Rome in 1996, failed even to mention Mother Teresa.

The newspaper profiles which appeared with increasing regularity in England now included a new note of wariness – or worse – about her activities. The *Sunday Times*, around an unflattering cartoon by 'Gary' (Gary Smith) that was to win a second life four years on, concluded an unsigned profile in 1990 with a clear statement of what it tactfully called her fiery, secular spirit. 'Sitting alone, surrounded by bags, fuming on an airport luggage carousel two years ago, she was approached by a reporter who offered her a charitable hand. "Yes, I am very cross," she confirmed, scanning the almost deserted concourse. "My sisters were meant to be here to help me and they are not. Look at me: Mother Teresa with nobody here to help her." '

Perhaps she never uttered the words, but the point is the subtle change in the reporting of her. A few years ago no profile of the living saint would have concluded with such an overt display of the continuing robust health of her ego.

CHAPTER EIGHT

ATTACK

On the evening of 8 November 1994, the duty officer at Channel Four television was besieged until the early hours by nearly 200, mostly outraged viewers who bombarded his switchboard. They were desperate to voice their opinions on a half-hour film entitled *Hell's Angel*, produced by the author and broadcaster Tariq Ali. The Angel in question was Mother Teresa and the British media, which had already received previews of the controversial programme, had been trailing it well in advance.

During the programme, the presenter Christopher Hitchens, renowned for his trenchant columns in *Vanity Fair* and the *Nation*, accused Mother Teresa of 'simpering' to world leaders as she was more interested in her connections with them than in saving lives. 'For someone whose kingdom is not of this earth, Mother Teresa has an easy way with thrones, dominions, and powers,' he commented. He was critical, too, of the way she allegedly spent millions of pounds on convents rather than building new hospitals for the subcontinent. Accusing her of 'operating ... as the roving ambassador of a highly politicised papacy', Hitchens concluded: 'In a godless and cynical age it may be inevitable that people will seek to praise the self-effacing, the altruistic and the pure in heart. But only a complete collapse of our critical faculties can explain the illusion that such a person is manifested in the shape of a demagogue, an obscurantist and a servant of earthly powers.'[1]

Most, but not all, of those who phoned in were appalled. They slammed the programme as insulting, hurtful, offensive, obscene, untrue, pathetically sick, obnoxious, disgusting, disgraceful, biased, cowardly, unfair, evil-minded, shocking, satanic and ungodly. Some callers threatened never to watch Channel Four again or to boycott all products advertised in the breaks. Many commented that it was unfair to an old lady who had done nothing but good and who could not defend herself. But then there were some callers who praised Channel Four for being informative, refreshing, cogent and relevant. Channel Four vigorously defended its film, maintaining that it had never intended to make a current-affairs-style documentary and, not unduly perturbed by the response, pointed out that those in favour of a programme rarely ring in to say so.

The criticism rumbled on in the press for weeks, much of it as vitriolic and highly personalised as the film itself. 'There's a Jew mixed up in the programme,' said one caller, alluding to Channel Four boss Michael Grade. Hitchens was described as a Balliol Bolshevik and Ali as an Oxford-educated former Marxist revolutionary. Lord Rees-Mogg in The Times said it was lucky that the poor of Calcutta did not have to look to Michael Grade for their supper. The Roman Catholic establishment rallied to Mother Teresa's defence. Cardinal Basil Hume denounced the documentary as 'a grotesque caricature' of a woman renowned for her 'genuine holiness', and the contribution from Victoria Gillick, the veteran anti-abortion campaigner, was that it was a perverse and cowardly Muslim–Jewish conspiracy, a reference to Ali and Grade. According to the Catholic writer Paul Johnson it was a diabolical and mendacious attack 'by a group of left-wing propagandists ... By crude juxtaposition of film clips and slippery use of innuendo, it is implied that Mother Teresa supports dictators, crooks and mass murderers ... I have never seen a more unbalanced or one-sided programme on British TV ... Channel Four and Michael Grade have committed an outrage against justice by paying for and transmitting this programme and, if it is legally and humanly possible, they ought to be brought to book, if only to stop them turning their hatred on somebody else.'[2]

In The Times letters page, Rev. Andrew de Berry questioned those who defended her uncritically. De Berry had met her, fifteen years earlier, when she was visiting HM Prison Wormwood Scrubs and he was a trainee chaplain there. Addressing a group of inmates at the prison, he quoted her as saying: 'I say to the women of Calcutta: "Have as many children as you want!"' He went on: 'Those words are etched on my memory. Some of those dying on the streets of India are almost certainly the progeny of mothers who took her advice.'[3]

Several reviewers welcomed the discussion. The Guardian's television critic Hugh Hebert wrote: 'Hitchens is right to question the Teresa cult. Idolatry is bad for us, canonisation of the living worse. But despite the air of smug self-congratulation that is habitual to the professional iconoclast, he unwittingly reminds us that, as conscience salvers go, our credit card charity is cheap at the price. So Hitchens, the gadfly reporter of Vanity Fair, becomes another of Mother Teresa's accomplices.'[4] The comment in The Times from Rumer Godden – 'it is so easy to denigrate, so difficult to achieve' – seemed to find a broadly sympathetic response.

One hundred and thirty angry viewers from a total of 1.6 million who watched the programme went on to complain formally to the Independent Television Commission. But the ITC eventually rejected the complaint, saying that 'Mother Teresa has a worldwide reputation for her good works among the poor ... that does not mean what she does and has said should be beyond criticism.' Paul Johnson had touched on the same issue but drawn a different conclusion when he wrote: 'If a supremely good woman like Mother Teresa is not spared their slanders, who is safe?' Perhaps, in an open society, no one should be – especially where large sums of money are involved.

The idea for the programme had been developed following a letter to the production company, Bandung, from Aroup Chatterjee, a Bengali doctor living in London. Dr Chatterjee, born and brought up in Calcutta, was aggrieved that 'the discrepancy between her actual work and her mythological image in the West remains astronomical. We must not forget that her assets are more than those of many third world governments. In Calcutta itself, she is almost a nonentity, which I'm sure will be an incredible notion in the West.' Chatterjee added: 'The truth needs to be told: that Calcutta is not synonymous with Mother Teresa – culturally and politically it has a tremendous tradition; that Mother Teresa is essentially a fictional entity; and that there are a large number of people, mainly black and some white, both secular and religious, who are doing much more than she is, but have never been heard of.'[5]

Chatterjee's approach to Tariq Ali at Bandung was serendipitous. Taking its name from a small town in Indonesia which, in 1955, became the venue for the first meeting of the independent African and Asian states which were forming the non-aligned movement, Bandung had already, in its ten-year history, aired some grievances felt by native Calcuttans for the way their city was regularly portrayed in the West. Anyone watching its 1991 piece about the controversy surrounding Roland Joffé's film, The City of Joy, based on Dominique Lapierre's book and filmed on location in Calcutta, could be in no doubt about the strength of feeling of many Calcuttans about the way the poor are exploited to reinforce a view of the city as a dark pit of misery.

It is not hard to see why such views are offensive to native Bengalis, but this time Ali felt there were wider issues at stake and looked to a broader-based journalist to present its new programme on Mother Teresa. His eye fell on Hitchens because, two years previously, in an article headed 'Ghoul of Calcutta', he had written unsparingly on his views of Mother Teresa, 'the leathery old saint', whom he had met once in 1980: 'While touring one of the less fashionable quarters of the city, I scheduled a drop-by at the Missionaries of Charity in Bose Road. Instantly put off by the Mission's motto – "He that loveth correction loveth knowledge" [a motto apparently over the door which seems to have been removed by 1995] – I nonetheless went for a walkabout with Mother Teresa herself and had a chance to observe her butch style at first hand.' It was the orphanage which decided Hitchens once and for all. 'I was about to mutter some words of praise for the nurses and was even fumbling in my pocket when Mother Teresa announced: "You see, this is how we fight abortion and contraception in Calcutta." Mother Teresa's avowed motive somewhat cheapened the ostensible work of charity and made it appear rather more like what it actually was: an exercise in propaganda.'[6]

He went much further in the programme, which in any case reached a substantially greater audience, showing particularly unattractive footage of the ageing nun, very bent and looking down while saying her rosary, focusing on her connection with the subsequently deposed Haitian dictator 'Baby Doc' Duvalier, her meeting with the widow of Enver Hoxha, hardline communist dictator of Albania, and with other dubious international business figures. 'The Teresa cult is now a missionary multi-national, with annual turnover in the tens of millions.

If concentrated in Calcutta, that could certainly support a large hospital, perhaps even make a noticeable difference. But Mother Teresa has chosen instead to spread her franchise very thinly. To her the convent and the catechism matters more than the clinic,' he said. Against a background of the Gary caricature of her, used in the *Sunday Times* profile of 1990, now blown up for the occasion, he also referred to her as a 'presumable virgin', a phrase he subsequently regretted and did not repeat.

In Mother Teresa's adopted city, prominent Calcuttans rushed to their heroine's defence, although the film, to date, has not been shown publicly in India, apparently because the archive film extracts used by Hitchens make it too expensive to sell. Copies are available privately. Mother Teresa, who did not see the film, insisted she was unaffected by the negative comments, but nonetheless did agree to a rare interview with the popular daily *Ananda Bazar Patrika* in which she defended her work. 'It is for you to decide how you want to live. As far as I am concerned I know that I have to keep doing my work.' She said she had 'forgiven' both producer Tariq Ali and Christopher Hitchens, a comment that was to draw a wry response from Hitchens. Mother Teresa also cancelled a scheduled visit to Taiwan the day after the programme was shown. She gave no reason for cancelling but told Taiwan's Ambassador to the Vatican in Rome that she no longer required a visa as she could not come.

In a programme about the programme a few days later, *Right to Reply*, Hitchens was attacked for not having been to Calcutta recently and for not trying to get her side of the argument. He defended himself against accusations of lack of balance by explaining that he was simply trying to produce an essay. 'We set out to be the first media criticism of the woman ever to appear ... we put the case against – we didn't pretend to do other than that.' It is a defence which has echoes of Mother Teresa's response to critics who attack her for simply ministering to the poor and not doing anything to help them change their own lives. 'I do not pretend to do other than that,' she says. She is, one might say, also trying to produce an essay on the poor, not a whole book.

Kathryn Spink, the daughter of missionaries who has written about Mother Teresa in the past, said in the programme she thought there were valid points but they were not effectively made because the strength of polemic obscured them. David Alton MP said that Mother

Teresa was one of the unique people of the twentieth century and that the programme was ill judged and ill conceived. Cristina Odone, then editor of the *Catholic Herald*, said she would have expected any intelligent investigation of any icon, spiritual or cultural, to be tested against the opinions of others with facts and figures. 'But the only people you had were writers, journalists and cameramen.'[7]

And there the matter might have rested except that, in the intervening period between the film being made and shown, other, more moderate, voices of criticism were also heard. Dr Robin Fox, originally a thoracic specialist and now editor of the influential medical journal, the *Lancet*, wrote a stinging criticism of the poor medical facilities at her Home for the Dying in Calcutta and complained of powerful analgesics being denied to those in pain. In contrast, Mother Teresa herself has had access to the most modern medical treatment, sometimes in the United States, including heart surgery to fit a pacemaker. Clifford Longley, former leader writer and religious affairs correspondent of *The Times* and the most respected lay writer on religious matters in Britain, wrote a thought-provoking piece in which he warned of the dangers in Mother Teresa's reverence for the dying, which turned suffering into a goal. Many health workers questioned privately how anyone concerned with poverty could avoid being equally concerned with helping women control their own fertility and improving their reproductive health. There was renewed discussion generally about how valuable Mother Teresa's work was after fifty years, and positions seemed to be hardening on the extremes.

Some weeks after the programme, I was sent a batch of cuttings from Indian newspapers by a Hindu Resource Centre called Hindu Vivek Kendra,* which had learnt of my interest in the subject. As I read I was struck by the reasoned arguments in the Indian press (especially compared with the British) of those who believe that there is an important case to be made for debating the issues around Mother Teresa that have now become controversial. There were many Indian journalists who, like myself, think that much of the work of the Missionaries of Charity is praiseworthy to a high degree, but nonetheless

---

* Hindu Vivek Kendra outlines its goal as an attempt 'to increase the study of Hindutva in a socio-political context ... to build a reference library of both pro- and anti-Hindutva literature and to encourage scholars to undertake and pursue research ... Our centre is definitely not against anybody' (letter to author, 1 January 1996).

insist that that does not mean that issues such as medical standards, methods of contraception, abortion and adoption, the goals of missionary work both historically and currently, and the future direction of aid work should not be rigorously discussed. The Hitchens documentary made this examination more necessary than ever. Perhaps there are better ways of helping the poor, more suited to the demands of the twenty-first century. Or perhaps the need for old-fashioned Christian charity, as demanded in the Beatitudes and exemplified so perfectly by Mother Teresa, will never be eradicated.

Suddenly, Mother Teresa and her work seemed to be a touchstone for many people to question their own views of doing good in the world. She is a powerful figure and the world has to reckon with her. Yet why are so many people uneasy about her? What activities could make a difference? How should the developed world be working alongside the developing? What part could women play in breaking the cycle of poverty? What role can spirituality play in helping the dying? What is the future for nuns, many of whom today work as professional counsellors, nurses and social workers and much more besides, at a time when most of the older congregations are desperate for vocations and face serious problems of looking after ageing sisters? Beyond the obvious sincerity, devotion and determination, Mother Teresa's personality is hard to fathom, especially at this distance of time and space. Yet I concluded that by examining her work and her interaction with others during fifty years one could explore many of these issues and perhaps that way discover the basis for the myth that has attracted thousands of people to give her their love, their time and their money.

PART TWO

PART TWO

CHAPTER NINE

MEDICINE

I have one overwhelming memory of my visit to New Delhi. There have been few days since when I do not think of the baby with two heads.

This baby, nearly six months old, was lying on a cold, cement floor with a pillow underneath its rear head. I was unable to see how developed the second face was but I could see the front face clearly enough, and there was an open wound in the middle of its forehead. Both heads emanated from one tiny trunk and the body was curled in a foetal ball. I was rooted to the spot, unable to remove my gaze from this desperate accident of humanity.

'Is she in pain?' I asked the Missionary of Charity sister who was showing me round the Delhi orphanage. 'Of course,' the sister replied. 'She can never lift her heads at all, they are too heavy to move. But everything is in God's hands. There is nothing any hospital can do for the baby ... Nature has its way.' 'What about the mother?' I enquired. 'She must be in a state of shock. Does anyone know who she is or how she is?' If they did, I was not told. The mother seemed unimportant. It was not a case they wished to talk about and the conversation quickly turned to a discussion about poverty in the West – much more serious, the sister said, because it was emotional poverty.

This tragic, two-headed baby focuses for me the essence of the role of the Missionaries of Charity. Without doubt, had it not been for the Missionaries of Charity, this baby would have died at birth, or shortly after, wherever it was dumped, and that may have been a refuse bin or the street. Clearly she had been fed by the nuns – she was thin but not puny and would not have survived that long without nourishment. And she had been shown love. But what do we mean by love? Why, as I went around the orphanage, did I not see any toys in any of the cots, nor pictures on any of the walls, nor mobiles for any of the children, most of them too twisted and deformed to do anything other than look at an interesting object? As the sister told me, the baby with two heads would die soon, indeed is probably already dead as I write this. And how much will she have suffered by then, and what for? Why, if she was in pain, was she not given painkillers, and being looked after in a hospital bed by trained nursing staff?

I have discussed this subsequently with several doctors. Dicephalic babies are so rare in the United Kingdom – one may be born every five years perhaps – that the Office for National Statistics is not prepared to release the date, or any information, about the last such case lest, inadvertently, it revealed the identity of the parents. Today, all expectant women in Britain are routinely scanned at an early stage and, if such a condition were found, would be offered, but of course not compelled to accept, a termination. To give birth to a dicephalic baby, the mother would need a caesarean section and, even then, terrible damage may have been done to the womb, to say nothing of the psyche. In India there is a famous pair of Siamese twins, known as Ganga–Jamuna, who have separate heads and torsos but share two kidneys, two hearts, one liver, one uterus, a common vaginal passage and two legs. In a country where female infanticide is still practised, it may be surprising that they were allowed to survive. But they were, are now in their mid-twenties, and making a living being paraded at village fairs and festivals. Their uncle, who is also their manager, charges between two and five rupees for a gawping public to watch them perform such daily tasks as eating and washing. But the baby with two heads could not even hope for a life as ghastly as that.

There are no simple answers but the question remains: is it an adequate response to take in a sick person, child or adult, and offer care if you are not prepared to give the highest level of care society is capable of? Is it a form of arrogance to make an assumption that, although a body of knowledge exists, you do not need to make use of it? I have tried to resolve this problem on various occasions with people far better qualified than I. Take, for example, as I said to a

Catholic bishop, the parable of the Good Samaritan – at least he crossed the road and did something to help. Yes, replied the bishop, but if the Samaritan repeatedly crossed the road and helped more and more people, by design rather than accident, so that a form of institution was created to help accident victims, then the care owed should be the highest standard available in the world.

On the other hand, Professor David Baum, President of the College of Paediatrics and Child Health, Director of its Research Unit and a leading light in the development of children's hospice and respite care in the United Kingdom, sees it rather differently. 'Giving the best care has so many dimensions that you might never do anything ... Mother Teresa has had a vision that you don't just walk past a baby, you pick it up, and if the idea catches on ... it is an exceedingly difficult position to get into equilibrium but I can imagine, without being critical, that it's unstoppable. Her mission is not to think it through. It could be from where they are coming that this is the appropriate model.'[1]

Baum's view, and he has been to India and met Mother Teresa as well as devoting many years to a research project in rural Thailand, is that what India most needs, medically speaking, is not another big new hospital – 'the finest teaching hospital in the entire third world', as Hitchens suggests. The dilemma Baum encountered in India was: 'Can India afford high-tech state-of-the-art hospitals when nationwide nutrition and vaccination programmes in the villages are so desperately needed?' Yet those in authority frequently conclude that such hospitals are essential if India is to keep its best-calibre doctors, confident that they can sit at the high table of international medicine. For Baum, that makes sense. 'Yet coming from our background I wouldn't be doing transplant surgery in India because, for the same expenditure, one could have better-planned outreach community health services ... There are other high tables to be at, yet it is difficult to portray these programmes as tangible. To implement a successful immunisation programme does not grab headlines, but to have a big modern hospital strips and starves the villages and the places where what is really needed is someone to find which children lack vitamin D and which have partial hearing. It may have been a subliminal decision, but Mother Teresa's anti-edifice stance may be very well judged for India.'[2]

A small incident from the early 1970s graphically illustrates Mother

Teresa's secure belief that her role was not to oversee a medical establishment somehow incorporated into her Order. Ann King-Hall was initially a journalist interested in writing about a revolutionary method (for the nineteen forties) of treating handicapped children. So impressed was she with the work of Mrs Estrid Dane that over the years she became involved herself and eventually worked for her full time, mostly on the administration side. Mrs Dane had developed a system, based on the Neumann Neurode exercises for babies and young children, to correct congenital and acquired deformities. 'Many years' experience had demonstrated that even when these handicaps could not be entirely cured, regular treatment for just ten minutes three times a week could give such confidence that their disability became unimportant. Even those with quite severe mental defects could be rendered happier and better coordinated,' Ann King-Hall explained. 'Many of her ideas, such as relying on artificial supports only as a last resort, are today widely accepted.'

However, by 1970 Mrs Dane, a Catholic convert and not a trained physiotherapist, recognised that as she was losing her sight she would not be able to continue her work for much longer. She started to search for someone who might take it over. She felt there was a valuable archive of treatment history, much of it in photographic records, which could be useful to future generations. In 1970 Mother Teresa came to London, met Mrs Dane and Ann King-Hall and suggested that the pair might come out to Calcutta to set up a clinic where her sisters could work helping the many handicapped and deformed children in her care.

In January 1973 the two women arrived in the Indian city full of high hopes that, even though the London clinic had been wound down, their ideas would live on. 'It was all a bit of a muddle,' Ann King-Hall recalls sadly. At first, they were given a room in Shishu Bhavan to work from but were not allocated a specific clinic. Later they did have the use of a house, lent by the Bishop of Calcutta. 'The problem was that Mrs Dane wanted some sisters permanently allocated so that she could train them in her methods, which took time. But Mother Teresa does not work like that; she keeps it all flexible and fluid. We partially trained about thirty sisters and although some were less gifted than others the real trouble was we didn't keep the girls very long and then they were taken off to do something else.' The experiment continued until August 1974, when the two women came home to England. Ann King-Hall left Calcutta with a heavy heart, pessimistic about the chances of the clinic methods being continued. Ten years later she went back and with great sadness saw that it had not taken root. 'Yet I know that if the seed had been properly sown it could have.'[3]

Ann King-Hall, although not a Catholic, is a committed Co-Worker and a firm believer in the value of Mother Teresa's approach. She says, in retrospect, that Mother Teresa was evidently the wrong person for this work because she never wanted any structures other than her own and would not allow her sisters to be committed on a long-term basis to anything which might take them away from demonstrating the immediate love of God. She noticed that the refusal to give the majority of her sisters long-term projects, which in some circumstances might be a criticism, could also be seen as a strength. 'Many of these sisters are very young girls for whom it was probably important always to have an element of surprise and excitement in their lives. They never knew where they'd be sent; one day it's Bangalore, the next Bombay, and this immediacy, this feeling of never knowing what will happen next, is very important to them. It may be intuitive on Mother Teresa's part, but you only have to see the way their eyes light up.'

In 1994 Mother Teresa's attitude to the role medicine could play within her organisation became a matter of public debate when Dr Robin Fox, editor of the Lancet, who was travelling in India with his wife, paid a visit to Nirmal Hriday. This was at the suggestion of a doctor friend of his in Calcutta, who was himself a regular volunteer there. Dr and Mrs Fox spent a day at Kalighat working, doling out food mostly, in order to see for themselves. 'Because it's such a long-standing place, I was fully expecting something that would be setting an example of how to look after the dying,' explained Fox. His disappointment was intense. Although he had not initially intended to write anything he felt compelled. The resulting article was particularly shocking for its cool, measured tones, which reverberated rather more widely than he had expected. Fox had not known about Hell's Angel when he published the piece but in spite of the controversy aroused he commented later: 'I would write it again.'[4]

In the first place he found the standard of medical care haphazard, with sisters and volunteers left to take decisions on the basis of no diagnosis. 'How about simple algorithms that might help the sisters and volunteers distinguish the curable from the incurable?' asked Fox.

> Algorithms can help even those without a medical training to reach a reasonably accurate diagnosis and decide what drugs can be used. This is the way primary health care is going in India and it means that even those without a high degree of training can be taught how to diagnose common complaints and offer simple but effective treatment. However, such systematic approaches are alien to the ethos of the home. Mother Teresa prefers providence to planning; her rules are designed to prevent any drift towards materialism.

Fox believed that the way the place was organised encouraged errors, which might be fatal; he told me of a young man who was thought to have meningitis but in fact died of cerebral malaria. 'Could not someone have looked at a blood film?' he asked. 'What happens depends on chance; it could be a Dutch or Japanese nurse or even one of the volunteers who do much of the initial assessment and they might not immediately think of cerebral malaria.'

Fox had other criticisms. 'If you give money to Mother Teresa's home, don't expect it to be spent on some little luxury,' he wrote in the Lancet, referring to an electric blender he knew had been brought into the home as a gift to help those who had trouble swallowing their food. This was particularly apposite for a country where the most common cancer is that of the head and neck, directly related to tobacco abuse, both in its chewing and smoking. 'I was told it was not in accordance with their philosophy ... what shocked me most was ... the insistence on simplicity to the point of discomfort. Clearly there are many things which could make a patient more comfortable and yet keep the conditions consistent with those to which the poor were accustomed.'[5] 'Finally,' he wrote, 'how competent are the sisters at managing pain? On a short visit I could not judge the power of their spiritual approach but I was disturbed to learn that the formulary includes no strong analgesics. Along with the neglect of diagnosis, the lack of good analgesia marks Mother Teresa's approach as clearly separate from the hospice movement. I know which I prefer.'[6]

Among the letters in the next edition of the Lancet was one from a specialist cancer nurse who had spent the last five years working in conjunction with the World Health Organisation in India and then, in

1990, set up a registered charity called Cancer Relief India (CRI). The object of CRI was partly to educate doctors and nurses in palliative care and pain relief and partly to increase the provision of pain-relieving drugs, equipment and clinics for patients. Thanks to various fund-raising activities, Gilly Burn has managed to pay for training and translation into Hindi of relevant publications, as well as for certain equipment. Burn, who had not met Mother Teresa and who accepted that the British hospice movement was not evident in Mother Teresa's homes, nonetheless took Fox to task for failing to recognise the difficulties faced by Indian hospitals in acquiring adequate, strong analgesia. 'Even in 1994 most cancer patients whom I saw did not have access to any analgesia, because of lack of suitable drugs, of knowledge about the use of the drugs by the doctors as well as, in some instances, no understanding about pain management, and compounded by a lack of resources,' she wrote. 'Mother Teresa is to be commended for at least providing loving kindness.'[7]

Gilly Burn, like most people I have met who work in this field, has a deeply spiritual inner motivation; she exudes genuine compassion based on a high level of well-honed training and experience. This has included a spell as a Macmillan nurse as well as a peripatetic nurse tutor for Marie Curie Cancer Care. She is also extremely jolly. For the past few years she has spent several months of each year in India and has immersed herself in Indian culture and thinking; thus she has identified a variety of problems which she is doing her best slowly to tackle. The lack of education in pain control for both doctors and nurses is a particularly difficult problem where nurses are concerned because of the low esteem in which they are held. Most Indians assume Burn must be a doctor, because of her high level of knowledge.

Often considered little more than cleaners, or at best helpers, nurses in India are expected to show no initiative. This is compounded by the paucity of drugs available, and strict state government legislation often prohibits the use of strong analgesics, even to patients dying of cancer. Until 1989 there were no oral morphine tablets available in India, where at least 80 per cent of patients who do actually arrive for treatment come in the latter stages of their disease when cure is impossible. 'Most patients I have seen are diagnosed too late to be cured and are dying in agony in hospital. At the other end of the spectrum, some patients are inappropriately over-medicalised. I have seen terminally ill cancer patients dying on ventilators, without their family, without attention to total pain and not even receiving loving kindness.'

Shortly after writing her letter to the Lancet, Gilly Burn was travelling across India again, preaching the importance of palliative care and encouraging those centres to which her charity had already donated funds. Having stoutly defended Mother Teresa, she decided it was time to pay a visit to her Home for the Dying at Kalighat. 'This was enlightening,' she wrote in her CRI report afterwards. 'I managed to speak to one of the nuns who was working in the centre. She was unable to tell me exactly how many people were actually cared for at any one time, but it looked to me like there were probably about 100 men and women in the centre, all of whom had had their heads shaved, the reason being that their hair may contain head lice. Some of the patients were clearly ill mentally, and the nun in charge told me quite categorically that there were no cancer patients present. A doctor visits two to three times a week. If there are any patients with pain they are treated with paracetamol or ibuprofen. When I visited there were two volunteers who were delivering care to the patients, who sleep on small, stretcher-like beds.'

It gave her no pleasure to conclude: 'Having seen the centre I feel I am able to echo some of the sentiments written by Dr Fox in the Lancet.' Burn had, initially, been extremely angry over Fox's article; she felt differently now, even though she understood some of the difficulties. 'Many of those in Kalighat (approximately two-thirds these days) will be released and have to go home without any hair; to an Indian woman, this is one of her most important assets.'[8]

Of the thousands of backpacking volunteers who fetch up at Mother Teresa's at all times of year, few write home praising the high standard of medical care. Although most nationalities are represented, the vast majority are English and American twentysomethings travelling in the subcontinent either just before or just after going to university, searching for a meaningful experience. In the words of a cynical British newspaper columnist, many are treating Mother Teresa's as a finishing school where you can lose weight. 'The two failsafe methods for getting thin in one's early twenties are to go to India or to get engaged. The first is easier,' wrote Ysenda Maxtone Graham in a May 1995 article she called 'Indian Summer of the Saintly Sloanes' in the London Evening Standard. 'To become a fully-fledged India girl you must, at some stage in your travels, work for Mother Teresa ... the conscience of a girl who has lived a sheltered life on the private tennis courts of England is suddenly pricked. Doing menial tasks surrounded by the dying is a way of soothing it. The urge seems to be to stay for only a short time, but in that time to steep oneself in as much real life misery as possible.' Maxtone Graham mentioned Lady Georgina Murray and Antonia Potter, daughter of the novelist Joanna Trollope, as two among the many English volunteers who had gone to Mother Teresa's hoping to do good. She also said that those being prepared for conversion to Roman Catholicism by Father Alexander Sherbrooke, a priest who knows the Missionaries of Charity well, 'are sent to work for Mother Teresa and come back glowing with the joy of self-sacrifice.'[9]

There is certainly a camaraderie about the volunteers, many of whom, but by no means all, are young, pretty, blonde and what have become known in the last fifteen or so years as Sloane Rangers, those well-connected young girls from the upper echelons of English society. Many of them do have a family nostalgia for India, a grandfather perhaps in the Indian Civil Service or connected with the tea business. India has always been a source of romantic fascination for these girls, sometimes reflected in the silk and paisley clothes they wear, the curries they eat or the gymkhanas they attended as children. 'It is a deep and quite unconscious feeling,' according to the official *Sloane Ranger Handbook*. 'Kipling is the Sloane tribal poet.' But the volunteers come from an enormous range of backgrounds. At the Home for the Dying, I met an Indian boy from Essex who told me he had always wanted to come home and work for Mother Teresa, as well as many Americans, including older women leaving their families, and many students, both male and female, from Catholic Europe.

Most of the helpers, from wherever they originate, end up staying in cheap hotels with damp, peeling walls and cockroaches in Sudder Street – the YMCA or Modern Lodge are favourites – and make their way to the Mother House at about 5.30 a.m. ready for mass at 5.50. They get a card from the sister-in-charge of volunteers telling them where they can work, but they can usually choose; Shishu Bhavan, which is 200 yards up the road from the Mother House, is the most popular place to start. Others go to Prem Dan, a short tramride away, to help with the mentally handicapped, or Kalighat. Very few are interested in helping out at the dispensary at Sealdah; however important the work there, it does not offer the same possibilities for human contact. And only a handful want to work in other parts of India, where the need for volunteers is greater, because it does not have the same magic. There is less possibility of association with Mother Teresa herself, which matters to them. After mass, breakfast is provided in the parlour at the Mother House – a banana, some tea and a roll when I was there – and then they troop off to work from 8 a.m. to noon and 3 p.m. to 6. Many return to the Mother House for Adoration in the evening. Thursday is a day off when no volunteers work in any of the homes.

Little or no advice is provided in advance. But, even if it were, it is almost impossible to describe the stench of rotten flesh, urine, faeces and Jeyes disinfectant, and many helpers, young and middle-aged, are physically sick when they first start work at the Home for the Dying. One Co-Worker in Britain does send volunteers a sheet detailing some of the chores they might be expected to do, which include dressing wounds or sores in the early morning, cleaning ears, cutting finger- and toe-nails, helping with shaving or cutting hair short, feeding patients, brushing teeth, massaging stiff or painful joints or limbs with oil and helping patients to stand and walk again.

One of the difficulties experienced by many of Mother Teresa's unpaid workers is the inability to communicate either with the Indian paid workers (Macees) or with the patients. There are Macees working in all the homes who do the cooking, most of the cleaning and many other things too. The ones I saw looked far from cheerful, but perhaps they spotted how my jaw dropped as I watched the same, not very clean cloth being used to wipe the bottom of one child and, immediately after, the nose of another. There appeared to be no sister supervising, but an English-speaking volunteer explained that the babies, four or five to a cot, were nappieless as they were all awaiting baths. 'The Macees can seem a bit hostile, but you have to remember you are only one of hundreds of volunteers they see coming and going.'[10]

Because of the large influx of refugees to Calcutta, even a passing knowledge of Bengali is often no use – more than 40 per cent of Calcutta's residents speak languages other than Bengali, and about 60 per cent of the industrial workers in the city are migrants from other states. When Mary Loudon, an English volunteer, worked at Kalighat, the first thing she was asked to do was wash a woman dying of

The Bojaxhiu sisters, Agnes (on the left) and her sister Age in 1923 wearing magnificent Albanian national costume. The girls' father, Nikola Bojaxhiu, had been an ardent Albanian patriot.

Nikola (Kole) Bojaxhiu, Mother Teresa's father, an entrepreneur in Skopje with a wide range of interests. He was a keen amateur musician and the only Catholic member of the Skopje town council.

Agnes, seated, next to her brother Lazar and sister Age in Skopje, 1924.

Agnes (third from left) as a schoolgirl of 10 with some of her classmates.

Above Agnes Bojaxhiu as a young woman in Skopje shortly before she joined the Loreto sisters in Ireland and was never to see her mother and sister again.

Left Agnes (on the left) as a young novice just after the announcement that she was going to India. She sent this photograph home to her family from Darjeeling in 1929.

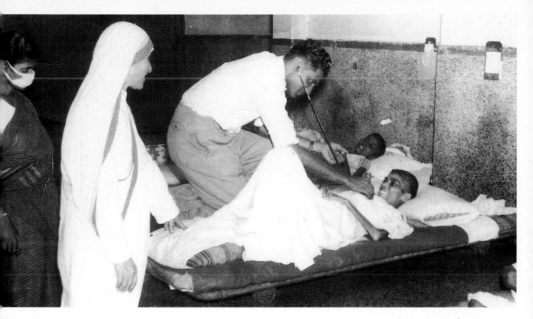

Marcus Fernandes, the young Catholic doctor who helped Mother Teresa in the 1950s, but left when he could not persuade her to use a better diagnostic approach.

Above A portrait of Mother Teresa in 1969. All the missionaries of Charity wear the simple crucifix on their left shoulder.

Left The entrance to the Mother House is down a small alleyway off Calcutta's busy thoroughfare, Lower Circular Road.

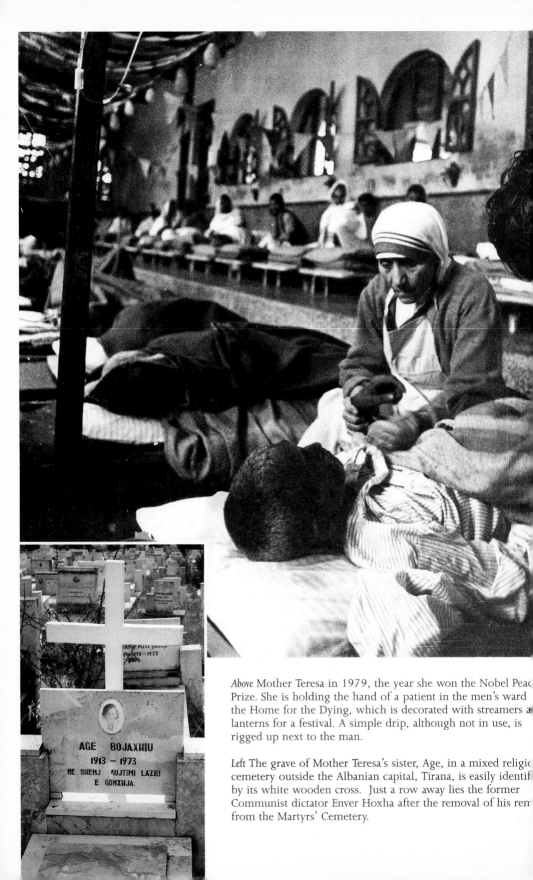

AGE BOJAXHIU
1913 – 1973
NE SHENJ KUJTIMI LAZRI
E GONXHJA.

Above Mother Teresa in 1979, the year she won the Nobel Peace Prize. She is holding the hand of a patient in the men's ward the Home for the Dying, which is decorated with streamers a lanterns for a festival. A simple drip, although not in use, is rigged up next to the man.

Left The grave of Mother Teresa's sister, Age, in a mixed religio cemetery outside the Albanian capital, Tirana, is easily identifi by its white wooden cross. Just a row away lies the former Communist dictator Enver Hoxha after the removal of his rem from the Martyrs' Cemetery.

Mother Teresa on her way to receive the Nobel Peace Prize in 1979.

The sisters doing their early morning washing in the yard of the Mother House in Calcutta. Aspirants, postulants and novitiates all work together, each using a tin bucket, one of their very few possessions.

Mother Teresa with Bob Geldof in Ethiopia in 1985, at the height of its famine. Geldof, there to arrange for the millions of pounds to be spent that he had raised through Band Aid, was impressed by Mother Teresa as a 'deft manipulator of the media . . . outrageously brilliant'.

A typical Calcutta street scene; three begg working together. The man at the back of this photograph is blind, the man squatti on the board holds the begging bowl wh the man with one leg (the other presum lost to leprosy) just rolls along.

Left A convocation of the Missionaries of Charity, 1980. Apparently, when Mother Teresa was asked who would succeed he when she died, she once pointed to this photograph as her answer.

Mother Teresa with Margaret Thatcher in London, April 1988. Mother Teresa came to investigate homelessness in the British capital and hoped to persuade the British Prime Minister to support a change in the abortion laws reducing the upper time limit from 28 to 18 weeks.

Diana, Princess of Wales, often described as Britain's answer to Mother Teresa.

Mother Teresa with the Pope during his visit to India in February 1986.

Right Mother Teresa, 85, flies to New Delhi to greet the new Indian Prime Minister Atal Biharai Vajpayee, within days of the spring 1996 elections. The meeting is considered front-page news by the *Asian Age*.

Above Mother Teresa listens to Hilary Clinton at a press conference to mark the opening of a new Missionary of Charity hostel for children in Washington, D. C., June 1995. Also on the podium is the once disgraced Mayor of Washington Marion Barry.

Left Mother Teresa, frail and wheelchair-bound, welcomed by nuns of her Order when she arrived in Rome in May 1997 for a meeting with the Pope. She brought with her to Rome four Indian babies being adopted by Italian families.

tuberculosis. 'She was in terrible pain, and so emaciated that the skin was hanging in folds from her arms. Nobody could tell me her name, so I told her mine instead. Nobody told me how to lift or hold her, so I improvised and said "Sorry" in English when she wept with pain. I still feel profound shame that a woman dying in agony spent the last hour of her life being washed by a frightened and incompetent stranger who couldn't even apologise in her language.'[11]

Washing may be central to Indian culture but another Englishwoman who went out to help will never forget the sight of a dying woman being carried unwillingly by two nuns, put on a tiled floor and literally hosed down with cold water. 'She was screaming out in agony ... that is a sound that doesn't ever leave you,' said Chris Oram Rayson, who was a social worker with one year's experience at the Michael Sobell Hospice in Oxford before she went to India in 1984. Many of the young volunteers she encountered had never seen anyone die before and suffered much more than culture shock with little or no counselling to help. Oram Rayson knew what death looked like but was shocked by other things. 'I saw a nun holding the hands of a dying woman in a praying position and I did not like this sort of forcibly Christian death. On another occasion an Indian woman was shouting and waving to get my attention and I was advised, "She makes a fuss that one, just ignore her," only to find she had soiled her bed which needed washing down with buckets of water.' One incident above all disillusioned her. 'I was making a bed and saw that a woman had put a crust of bread under her pillow, saved from breakfast presumably because she could not believe she would have any more. When the sister saw this she threw it away, which I thought showed an amazing lack of compassion.' Oram Rayson left after only two days, 'feeling that the patients were being given neither proper nursing nor loving compassion, so what on earth is the point ... all they were being given was a lot of rice.'[12] She now works as a counsellor in England.

Another volunteer with similar experiences left after a short time and went to work instead for the Missionary Brothers in Howrah. Flora McDonnell, an artist, was a university graduate of twenty-two when she went to Calcutta for a month. She felt that the influx of untrained volunteers, especially in the summer months, many of whom are there because 'It's the thing to do in your year off,' added to the very tense atmosphere created by the then sister-in-charge being over-stretched and under strain. 'I was holding the hand of a woman obviously dying, slipping in and out of consciousness, and Sister Luke said, "What are you doing? She's nearly dead." After that I left. All this talk about love ... I thought Mother Teresa's ethos was not being realised and the place was not full of love. They are giving no time to comforting people and are doing chores instead.'[13] McDonnell came away with an image of the patients in Nirmal Hriday as 'quite degraded really ... I see it almost as a milking parlour where they are kept clean and bathed but treated like cows rather than people.'

One of the most serious criticisms of Mother Teresa's medical care is the way disposable needles and syringes are reused literally hundreds of times, sometimes rinsed in cold water in between but not always. A former Missionary of Charity told me how she had been responsible for injecting five hundred children against polio with just a few needles. She might have protected them from polio, but what other dread diseases, including AIDS, might she inadvertently have passed on?[14]

In 1990, Wendy Bainbridge was a nursing sister in Plymouth, working at a purpose-built, twenty-bed hospice offering palliative and respite care to the dying and their families, when she and a friend decided to spend their annual leave as volunteers working in India. At the hospice, pain control was meticulously monitored with exhaustive attempts to suppress distressing symptoms. The individuality of patients was promoted and, where possible, they were encouraged to maintain control of their lives. On her first day at the Home for the Dying, she too encountered Sister Luke, the brisk Anglo-Indian nun who ran Kalighat for fifteen years, and she felt as if her senses were stunned:

By Western standards, dressings were limited and often inappropriate, instruments were washed after use and left in spirit, disposable needles and syringes were used many times ... The commonly used drugs were a limited selection of antibiotics, analgesics and vitamins ... There were no aids to mobility and aids to physical comfort were restricted to narrow, iron beds about fifteen inches apart, a blanket and a small pillow ... There were a few bedpans but toilet paper was not available. The toilet was an open gutter running behind the washroom and waste was washed away with a bucket of water.

And yet, in spite of the dramatic contrast, Wendy Bainbridge says, 'Smiles and laughter were a frequent means of communication and therapy. Much happiness was generated between the sisters, volunteers and patients in grim conditions. Emotional comfort was given with hugs, touching or stroking.' She and her friend were most struck with the 'gentle' deaths they witnessed. 'Perhaps [a] sense of spiritual direction facilitated the giving up of life ... as Western nurses we noticed how quietly and without anxiety the patients died ... The actual act of dying was quiet and without struggle or the benefit of analgesia or sedation. Spirituality seemed to have an extra dimension which overcame physiological deficits.'[15]

Another volunteer who experienced a heightened spirituality was Rose Billington, god-daughter of Malcolm Muggeridge and grand-daughter of Lord Longford. She spent a few weeks working for Mother Teresa between school and university in 1994 and was well aware of the criticisms levelled at privileged students in her position going 'to help in India'. In an article she wrote later about her experiences she described how a friend in India had felt a nagging sense of Western imperialism in her work, and recorded her own feeling that, had she been working for a development agency she would have been imposing Western standards on a less powerful country. But at Shishu Bhavan, she 'felt a great sense of release because I was absolutely confident that what I was doing was right. If I picked up a little boy with polio so that he could look out of the window – or just made him laugh – I knew I was being helpful. It was very strange to find how easy it was to be good.'[16]

Billington honestly recalled her reactions to a twenty-five-year-old, severely deformed woman who could only lie still all day in her cot. Her limbs were stiff and twisted, her head small and oddly shaped, her body hairy and her mouth overfilled with crooked and broken teeth. 'I had a horrible thought that maybe there was no point in keeping her alive. She couldn't speak or understand or move. And then suddenly her big brown eyes lit up and she made an excited squeaking noise and tilted her head backwards. I looked behind me and saw the physiotherapist approaching. The woman whose existence I had thought pointless had recognised her visitor and been made happy. I don't think I'll ever again be so arrogant as to decide whether a life is worthwhile or not.'[17]

For Billington, and hundreds like her, the sensation of putting their desire to do good into action without feelings of guilt or ambiguity in their motives has been a transforming experience in their lives. It is not only female volunteers who have benefited. Damian Furniss says he was an over-educated and inexperienced Englishman, like many others, when he went to Calcutta. 'Some do voluntary work there thinking that they are putting something back, although the prime motivation is more often ... a salving of conscience. So I suppose it was with me. My only claim to difference might be that I got more than I bargained for.' A year later, back in England, Furniss developed tuberculosis; although he recovered, he started writing poetry, including one poem for Mother Teresa 'that she might like' in response to the time he spent in India.[18]

Simon Weinstock, a one-time advertising executive in London more interested in the appropriate merits of teaspoon handles for yoghurt commercials than Indian spirituality, in the summer of 1988 discovered The Prophet, by the Lebanese poet and philosopher Kahlil Gibran. Inspired by his words on the nature of giving, he gave up his job and went to work with Mother Teresa, 'the only person who for [me] truly epitomises the meaning of Gibran's work'. The photographs he took during his time there were subsequently published as The Book of Giving – A Tribute to Mother Teresa. 'I am not a particularly religious person,' Weinstock wrote in the preface, 'and so I still struggle enormously with the significance of my experience yet I somehow feel blessed that this book has come to fruition.'[19]

Clearly such testimonies provide a key reason for Mother Teresa not simply encouraging the world's youth, many of whom stay for such short periods that they cannot possibly be of real help, but refusing to discriminate in favour of those who might be of some use and those who are clearly not at all suited to such work. 'I am so impressed with the young men and women who come to Calcutta from all over the world – Catholics, Christians and non-Christians,' Mother Teresa wrote in a recent newsletter to Co-Workers. 'Daily they come for Mass and Adoration. During the day they go to serve the poor. And not one of them goes back home the same.'[20] 'It is so beautiful to see how God floods them with "Grace",' said Sister Bethany of the volunteers. 'Some come as atheists but they don't leave that way.'[21] This helps to explain why no time or money is invested in their training and why so many of them report their utter shock at being told, almost upon arrival and with no preparation or advice about avoiding disease themselves, to bath a dying man or woman who may have leprosy, or bones sticking out of flesh, and with whom they are completely unable to communicate.

I discussed this with one of the occasional volunteer doctors, the British-born Nicholas Cohen. 'One of Mother's reasons is to touch people, that's what she feels. Obviously, the volunteers could be replaced by sisters doing the same job the world over.' Dr Cohen, who trained in London and spent eight years in Bangladesh before moving to Calcutta and has a high reputation as an epidemiologist, has tried to train and prepare the volunteers 'for being there' and performing such simple tasks as giving an injection. But even though he has watched some people stab themselves accidentally, which he admits is very dangerous, and recognises there are problems they have not solved – for example, some volunteers will get tuberculosis – he still insists the essential part is that Mother Teresa offers care, support and love which those who come off the streets would not have elsewhere. 'There is no alternative; they can't have hospice care, so what she has done has affected the whole world. It has meant other people have started things up too and that is what is important, not what medicines are given or not given. Millions of mistakes are made in modern medicine anyway.'

Cohen has watched tourist parties of up to thirty Japanese or Spanish being shown around the Home for the Dying as part of a sightseeing trip. But even if he does not like this voyeuristic aspect at the very high expense of both the privacy and dignity of the silent poor, he can see a purpose behind it. To give witness to faith. 'It's really a question of, "Are you going to accept it?" Because that's what I do. I do less and less medically. There is, okay, a tremendous amount I could do but each medical act requires the right follow-up treatment. For example, you only have two opportunities to give drugs in the Home for the Dying, but most drugs you need to give four times a day, every day. There's really no difference between me and the Japanese tourists, that's what I like.'

Of course Cohen does intervene if he considers his intervention could prevent imminent death, but he has been around and absorbed Mother Teresa's beliefs for long enough to echo her view that loneliness is one of the greatest diseases, and he feels his real value is here. 'I can sit with the patients, I speak the language, the Co-Workers and volunteers can't do that.' Cohen has a wide experience of the developing world and has seen several of Mother Teresa's homes in other countries. What always strikes him is 'the happiness and love amongst all the people who work there, which is extremely rare in the world anywhere and gives you a sense of peace and a feeling that you can do something without any personal reward for it. It's a very powerful feeling. Once you're there you're part of a brotherhood, you do your best but you are not judged. I like the idea of just caring for people but there's no judgement.'[22]

Many of the volunteers who are disillusioned with the lack of good medical practice in the Missionaries of Charity homes go on to work for another English doctor in Calcutta, Jack Preger, a Jew who converted to Catholicism and in old age is rediscovering his Jewish roots. Occasionally the traffic goes the other way; if a volunteer has come out to work with Preger but is looking for a more spiritual experience he or she might end up with Mother Teresa instead. 'I felt Dr Jack and Mother Teresa complement each other quite well,' explained volunteer Justine Long, an experienced nurse who spent six months in India working for Preger. 'Many Irish nurses start at Mother Teresa's and then leave because they had expected to work on a professional basis but are not allowed to, which is especially hard when there are curable cases. Those who stay do so because they feel they have a moral duty and there is a feeling that everyone who works for Mother Teresa is more virtuous because the emotional demands are so great.' Justine Long felt under moral pressure to do more, which is why she worked for Preger.[23]

Preger, born in 1930, came to medicine late having read philosophy, politics and economics at Oxford. He then took up farming in Wales and married for the first time, before deciding his vocation was to be a doctor and help the poor in the developing world. As a mature student he had difficulty finding a place at most British universities to study medicine but was accepted at the medical school of the Royal College of Surgeons in Dublin. He qualified at the age of forty-two and almost immediately, in the summer of 1972, arrived to work in Dacca, capital of the newly created and desperately impoverished Bangladesh. He knew nothing about it but had heard an appeal on the radio for doctors and nurses to carry out relief work. He had also been inspired, so he told me, by Muggeridge's film, *Something Beautiful for God*.

He started working in Dacca for an Irish charity, Concern, but within weeks was openly voicing his horror at the general state of affairs in the city. It was not just 'the corruption, inhumanity, needless suffering, government hoarding and widespread pilfering', it was also the appalling treatment meted out to the Biharis, Muslims who had backed the defeated armies of West Pakistan in the recent civil war. From the start, Preger was not prepared to watch human suffering on this scale without letting the world know. He wrote a document for the London-based Minority Rights Group entitled 'The Situation in the Bihari Camps – by a doctor working in Bangladesh'. He also started firing off occasional angry pieces to the Catholic newspaper, the *Tablet*, as he was appalled at the West Bengal Church hierarchy for allowing such degradation on the scale of the Bihari camps to coexist with the beautifully dressed and well-nourished congregation he saw emerging from the Catholic Cathedral.

Preger met Mother Teresa for the first time when she came to Dacca to inspect a feeding programme run by one of her nuns. He had already seen, and been inspired by, the work of individual nuns and priests and he was overwhelmed by Mother Teresa herself. 'I believe that she and her nuns have hold of an absolute mystical truth and the longer I work here, the more apparent does this become,' he wrote to a Catholic priest friend at the time.[24] Based at the Children's Hospital in Dacca, Preger continued helping the Missionaries of Charity there for another two years, mostly working with feeding programmes. By 1975 he had three jobs: he was medical officer at the dispensary of the Swiss welfare organisation, Terre des Hommes, he set up a clinic for the poor at Kamlapur railway station, and he helped organise a camp for destitute children with funds from the International Boys Town. Soon, he began to have differences with Mother Teresa. 'I had drawn up a list of projects I felt Mother Teresa and her sisters could undertake, such as extending the work, especially the medical work, within the refugee camps for Bihari Muslims, and she shot every one of them down because of political reasons, not wanting to antagonise the Bangladeshi government. There was widespread starvation and disease in the camps, smallpox and tetanus especially, and the mothers were frightened to go to the hospitals because they'd fought on the losing side. Women and children were the principal victims.'[25]

Then in 1977 Preger uncovered rumours (entirely unconnected with

Mother Teresa) that Bangladeshi babies were being sold to the affluent West. At first reluctant to believe the allegations, once he obtained hard evidence of a kidnapping ring that was supplying babies for prostitution, pornography and worse, he knew he had to fight. Further checks revealed that two babies Mother Teresa had sent for adoption went unknown to her to adoptive families who simply did not exist.[26] His involvement led to his deportation from Bangladesh and, arguably, to many of his subsequent troubles with authorities. But Preger has never been one to compromise with truth or justice. 'I just can't see this as stepping outside the world of medicine, because you are supposed to be working as a medical officer. Well, with these poor people, losing their children is one of the biggest afflictions that could possibly happen to them. My view was that if there was something I could do, then I should do it.'[27]

Preger fought on for two years before finally accepting deportation back to England rather than paying a bribe to keep quiet. But within a few months he had moved abroad again, to Calcutta this time, working partly as a lay volunteer with Mother Teresa's Brothers of Charity and at the same time setting up a makeshift clinic for destitutes under the flyover near Calcutta's enormous Howrah Bridge. Increasingly, he worked on his own as his suggestions for improving the Missionaries of Charity operation went unheeded. In particular, knowing the highly infectious nature of the disease, he urged the separation of the tubercular and the non-tubercular patients. 'The tubercular patients were not simply walking among the others, they were eating together and using the same utensils. I begged Mother for a separate ward so that they would not transmit the disease, but it never happened.'[28]

It was not long before he was in trouble with the authorities again. The Calcutta Municipal Development Authority decided that the area where he was working should be redeveloped; they put up high railings making it impossible for the hundreds of destitutes who used to squat there to remain. At the same time the priest of St Thomas' Church in Middleton Row offered Preger the gate lodge of his presbytery garden for the stocking of medicines and patients' records. This was not only extremely convenient, because Preger's room at the YMCA was close by, but enabled him to take a dramatic step by giving these destitutes an identity, often for the first time. Preger and an assistant now started making a card index of each patient, including their names, as much medical history as was available and some rudimentary form of address such as 'under Howrah Bridge North', or 'the foot of third lamppost'. As Jack Preger's assistant at the time, Frances Meigh, who had first worked for Mother Teresa, put it: 'Mother Teresa did not keep records; but we found that their having their name on a record was a start, a beginning for that individual, the nearest perhaps that many would ever come to an official acknowledgement of their identity.'[29]

Not surprisingly the poor and needy in and around Middleton Row thought this was Preger's new base and, as word quickly grew, more and more started dropping in for medical attention and food. Rapidly, Middleton Row became the new Jack Preger Street Clinic. Although everything was locked away and the street returned to normal at night, the other residents of this smart area did not at all appreciate having a pavement clinic run by an English doctor in their midst. Nor did the parish priest at St Thomas', who reminded Preger that the storeroom was just that and was not to be used as a clinic. He threatened that gas meters were about to be installed in the gate lodge and said that patients there would pose an unacceptable risk. Much to the anger of the Church Corporation and local residents alike, Preger simply moved a few yards down the road.

And so once again Jack Preger, a most courteous and softly spoken man, found himself doing battle, this time in India but on behalf of the same sick and dispossessed people he had tried to help in Dacca. In September 1980 he received his first 'Quit India' order. Naturally he fought, but it took another ten years before Calcutta Rescue, Preger's social welfare charity which runs two street clinics, a mobile clinic, two basic education centres and a vocational training centre for poor and destitute people in and around Calcutta, was granted minimal formal recognition in West Bengal. The organisation is still not recognised under the FCRA (Foreign Currency Regulation Act), which would enable it to bring in foreign contributions without asking for permission each time and without having to account for every rupee in advance and if anything is left over make a fresh account for that. During those ten years, Preger suffered continual harassment from the authorities, had his mail regularly intercepted and opened, and faced court proceedings which resulted in almost two weeks in prison, an experience which left him seriously ill for at least four months. His position has still, at the time of writing, not been regularised by the Indian authorities.

One reason given to Preger by Calcutta police for not letting him stay was that he was a missionary worker, long mistrusted by many Hindus, afraid that foreign funds might be used to encourage conversions. Another fear was that urban charity work attracts more beggars to the towns and away from the villages. Yet both of these concerns could equally or better apply to Mother Teresa, but she has not been harassed in the same way. There is, however, a third reason unique to him. The West Bengal authorities did not appreciate someone like Jack Preger advertising to the rest of the world the total inadequacy of existing healthcare provisions. Mother Teresa never criticised those in power, and distanced herself from Preger throughout his years of difficulty, which he understood 'was for very good political reasons. If they got mixed up with trouble-makers like me there would be trouble for them too.'[30] As the Minister for Health for West Bengal, Prasanta Sur, stated: 'There is no problem in Calcutta and no need for Dr Preger to stay.'[31]

It was not only Indians who felt this way. Mark Tully, the distinguished BBC reporter, interviewed Preger for BBC Television in February 1982 as Preger faced the prospect of deportation or imprisonment. Tully put it to me in 1995 that few Londoners would be pleased to have an Indian doctor, who was an illegal immigrant, setting up a street clinic along the Embankment, for example. Where was the difference? Incongruously, the interview between Preger and Tully took place in the garden of Calcutta's resplendent Oberoi Hotel, by the swimming pool, and immediately got off to a bad start.

'You have had three orders to leave India, no less, you have broken the law in this way by refusing to accept these orders. You have broken the law ... why don't you leave?' Tully asked.

'They have my passport. If I agree to leave they will give me my passport. They are looking for a way out,' Preger replied. Preger went on to accuse the West Bengal government of wishing to conceal the existing conditions in the slums, to which Tully responded: 'But Mother Teresa's people work there...'

'Indian sisters only,' said Preger. 'Go in with drugs. A bag of drugs with pills labelled "For Fever – take three times a day." They may be aspirin, and cause a haemorrhage, they could need something quite different.'

Tully: 'So are you then doing better work with your untrained staff and with limited funds and resources than Mother Teresa? They, the people that you are treating, what they need is a complete scheme, what you are doing is almost an irrelevance.'

Preger: 'My schemes are rejected. But land has been given to Mother Teresa that could be used for these people.'

Tully: 'You need help from the government. Why do you insist on staying? Why don't you give up?'

Preger: 'My position seems hopeless, but it's not a reason to give up — it's the work itself that has the merit.'*

Throughout the 1980s, Preger continued to battle with the Indian authorities while operating Calcutta Rescue on an informal basis, waiting for it to be registered so that it could receive foreign contributions. Several films were made about him, one of which made it very clear that Jack Preger was no saint in his dealings with his own family, who had suffered deeply through his total commitment to the Indian and Bangladeshi poor. But, in his laid-back way, he radiates charm and inspires devotion among his followers just as much as Mother Teresa. Beth Holgate, producer of a documentary about him in 1991,† declared: 'He is the most impressive man I've ever met, not in looks but for his sheer honesty and refusal to compromise or let go and complete denial of material wealth. He has a fundamental belief in the right of the individual and he's interested in that man's gangrene leg and what he can do about it. He is not interested in the man's soul or in the numbers of those treated.'[32]

In 1993 the British government honoured Jack Preger with an MBE for services to the poor, and the Royal College of Surgeons in Dublin awarded him a special medal. He has tried to play down his differences with Mother Teresa because there are sometimes emergencies when,

---

* Jack Preger recalls being asked to redo parts of the interview so that his unflattering remarks about Mother Teresa could be removed. Mark Tully, although he remembers the occasion and has not changed his views about the relative value of Preger versus Mother Teresa in Calcutta, does not remember such a remake. The BBC has no archival material referring to the piece. Only Frances Meigh, Jack's assistant at the time, took a verbatim transcript which shows the original comments, not an edited final version.

† BBC1 Everyman, *Confessions of a Reluctant Saint*, 8 December 1991.

even though his organisation will pay for hospital treatment, he might need Mother Teresa's homes to accept a patient for whom there is no bed or whom no hospital will accept. 'On these occasions it is best not to tell the Missionary of Charity sisters that the patient has come from Jack Preger's,' explains one of his volunteer workers. Someone other than Preger has to write the referral notes in this case, maintaining the fiction that the patient was found lying outside a church, for example. Preger gave me a copy of a biography about him published in 1991 and pointed out a hand-typed correction slip which stated that a reference to his 'coming to blows with Mother Teresa' was without foundation. 'Meetings with Mother Teresa were rarely held and were always conducted politely,' the correction stated.

And yet Preger is scathing about the response of Sister Luke to a question from a top orthopaedic surgeon visiting Kalighat: ' "What do you do for pain?" "We pray for them," she said. Sister Luke once told me that, since most of the patients lived like dogs on the street, they were better off dead.'[33] And he is still deeply disturbed by practices which are encouraging the spread of tuberculosis. Preger showed me a letter from a forty-one-year-old tuberculosis patient who has 'no hope to live any more', together with his discharge note from the brothers at Nabo Jeevan. 'It is quite impossible for an ordinary person to buy these drugs. He has been discharged into a vacuum to become infectious and die and this sort of case is happening thousands of times over.'

Preger has good reason to be concerned about tuberculosis. Recently the WHO warned that a drug-resistant form of tuberculosis, in which body tissue takes on the appearance of cheese, is poised to kill tens of millions of people across the world. The new strain of the disease is airborne and therefore extremely contagious, 'an AIDS epidemic with wings', as a WHO spokesman put it to me. These drug-resistant strains are emerging because many infected people who are among the world's poorest and most ignorant are not completing curses of antibiotics. If patients abandon their treatment halfway through the six-month course the bacilli survive and develop immunity. According to Dr Joel Almeida, medical officer for the WHO Global Tuberculosis programme: 'If the multi-drug-resistant strain becomes predominant we will be back in pre-antibiotic days. All we will be able to do is pray and send people off to sanitoria like we did in the last century.'

Of course, it is difficult for NGOs to keep track of patients who think they are better and stop their course of drugs, especially if no records are kept. But governments and private practitioners are bad offenders too if they simply dole out drugs without being able to follow up and ensure the course is completed. However, there is a form of treatment known as DOTS (Directly Observed Treatments Short Course) which WHO has been advocating for the last twenty or so years in which health workers or others ensure that patients complete their antibiotic courses. Sometimes the line of responsibility involves a café owner being contracted to oversee the patient if he can give out the pills with a daily cup of coffee or a newsagent who sees a patient on a regular basis; sometimes a volunteer will go into the home and ensure the drugs are taken for the full six months, removing the onus from the patient coming to a clinic when he thinks he is better. In places where DOTS has been tried (these include Bangladesh, Nepal, Mozambique, New York City and China, where cure rates have doubled since the strategy was implemented), the results have been spectacular. Calcutta is one of the worst-affected cities in the world with at least 60,000 tuberculosis patients and a vast additional number who have unknowingly inhaled the bacteria and have yet to show symptoms.

The problem facing those trying to eradicate tuberculosis clearly is not medical – the medicines exist, are cheap and effective – but political. Tuberculosis has to be recognised not just as the leading cause of death for people with HIV but as a cause of needless death, an infection that need not kill, but which is killing more people than AIDS. 'The challenge is that people should be demanding good tuberculosis treatment of their governments,' the WHO spokesman told me. 'But many of the larger charities are not putting themselves in a position to help. We really need Mother Teresa to be raising her voice on this issue and to provide a moral conscience to the world to take the drugs that exist off the shelf and use them in an effective way. It is a political challenge.'[34] But it is one which Mother Teresa has not taken up.

As both Robin Fox and David Baum pointed out, the way forward for tuberculosis has little to do with building big new hospitals. Fox said: 'For tuberculosis you need diagnosis and treatment long before the patient reaches the bedridden stages and the best way to organise that is by a system of centres of decreasing sophistication going out into the community. For example, you need a simple laboratory and simple X-ray facilities with outlying peak-time clinics in the villages run by a nurse and medical assistants who can refer to a central clinic if necessary.' There may not be anything exciting about this but it echoes Baum's view that the real need is small-scale and rural.

Tuberculosis and AIDS are a dual epidemic, each antagonising the other, and the resurgence of this virulent strain of tuberculosis will thrust the window wide open for AIDS in India. Despite a ten-year AIDS prevention programme which included the use of old drawings from the Kama Sutra to 'advertise' monogamy, India has more HIV-infected individuals than any other country in the world – more than three million – and by the year 2005 will surpass the entire African continent in number of infections. 'But the seriousness does not seem to have sunk in yet,' according to an article in the medical journal *Nature Medicine*, 'as ignorance, apathy, corruption and lack of commitment at all levels are still the most powerful allies of the galloping AIDS virus.' Shiv Lal, project director of India's National Aids Control Organisation (NACO), admitted: 'We are in trouble. From high-risk groups the virus has gone to the general public.'[35] A major contributing factor in the spread of HIV is the Indian government's own half-hearted policy which does not allow distribution of condoms in prisons, needles to injectable-drug users or free drugs to AIDS patients. The country's semi-puritanical attitude to selling condoms has not helped either.

Yet while India is discovering much about the sexual proclivities of its males – there was a myth that HIV in India is spread mainly through heterosexual sex, but it is now clear that the country has a sizeable number of gays and at least one out of every hundred AIDS cases is known to be related to homosexual sex – there are also profound implications in the account for the kind of care Mother Teresa is able to offer. Because AIDS can be transmitted from mother to baby and is over-represented in areas of extreme poverty, and because babies who may not appear infected actually do have HIV but endure a long gestation during infancy and toddlerhood, this will mean a terrible new layer of disease and mortality to be dealt with. 'If tackled head-on with a high-tech approach it will mop up all the money the country doesn't have. It is a desperate – although I don't like to use the word – prospect,' said one doctor.

I had been told by those close to Mother Teresa that the problem of

AIDS in India was of deep and constant concern to her and that, as she was preparing to open by Christmas 1995 the first specifically AIDS-related home in India – she has several in the US and Haiti – this would be the most fruitful topic of conversation for me when I was to meet her. Mother Teresa told me she understood that soon India would have the highest incidence of AIDS in the world. 'But there is no medicine for it. It comes from the mothers and babies are born with it,' she told me. 'What can be done?' I asked. 'Nothing. It's God's will,' she replied. 'They must die in peace with God.' I tried to suggest that medical research might one day provide a cure, but she demurred: 'It is man's way. That's all we can do. We will spend the day praying.'[36] If her comments seem unduly negative, it is worth remembering how indecisive the Indian government has been. For example, only one-third of a US$87 million loan from the World Bank to fight AIDS has been used, although the five-year-plan programme ends in March 1997. And basic AIDS research has been a very low priority in India.

Mother Teresa's response to both the tuberculosis and the AIDS crisis is, like so much else of hers, paradoxical; far from taking the line that this was a self-inflicted gay plague that she would have nothing to do with, she has been in the forefront of those trying to help AIDS sufferers die with peace, love and dignity. The homes may be spartan, without televisions and other luxuries, or without the best medical care. But they represent a response to a crisis for which she has won praise. On the other hand, the crisis will continue and deteriorate dramatically unless the causes are addressed. In the case of AIDS this means educating the people about sex in general and teaching them to wear condoms in particular. It is unprotected sex which has caused the virus to spread so fast, and if anyone has the power to do good anywhere, surely it is better to prevent someone becoming ill than to help them die once they are ill.

Even if a large-scale modern hospital is beyond the abilities, or charism,* of the Missionaries of Charity and is best left to the Birlas, for example, who have built the magnificent Heart Research Centre on National Library Avenue, many Indian doctors could be used

* A charism is, literally, a grace or a talent, given by God; for Catholic nuns it means the particular focus of their Congregation's work.

imaginatively by Mother Teresa. Dr Manorama Bhargava MD, Professor and Head of the Department of Haematology at Delhi's prestigious All India Institute of Medical Sciences, was emphatic that new hospitals, possibly small fifty-bed ones, were desperately needed in India. 'Most of the medical profession knows only too well that God does not always decide – medical science has a role to play in saving life. The image of Mother Teresa is such these days that she could phone any doctor and say "I want to open a new hospital specialising in whatever, would you give some time free to work there?" and it would be very hard to refuse. Any doctor in India would feel that. But she hasn't done it.'[37]

Why was I uncomfortable with much of what I saw of the Missionaries of Charity's operation in India? I did not like the voyeuristic aspect that anyone could walk in off the street and watch people die. Nor did I feel it was right that I was shown tiny babies, 2lb or less, probably aborted foetuses, in intensive care yet in conditions that were far from sterile. I did back away but was ushered back in by my guide, proud of the achievement in saving them. I have seen only three of Mother Teresa's orphanages in Delhi, Calcutta and Albania, but the lack of even the most basic stimulation in all three was heart-rending. Worst of all, in Calcutta, there were cupboards full of toys, but one volunteer I met, an American teacher in her sixties, said she had great difficulty finding anything other than religious tracts to read to them.

But is it fair to criticise Mother Teresa for what she is not doing rather than praising her for what she is? Mother Teresa has always insisted she is running neither a medical nor a social but a religious order. Should she then be dabbling in anything to do with medicine? One or two of the sisters happen to be doctors, but no effort is made to send others for medical training, and even if a doctor joins the Missionaries of Charity, Mother Teresa will not promise to use her as a doctor. Putting a new gloss on the biblical parable of the talents, she once described to a helper the importance of using one's talents in whatever field; if trained as a doctor then use that talent to the full – but not at the Missionaries of Charity. Mark Tully, who knows India as well as any foreigner, believes that her uniqueness derives from the fact that she has not let herself become just another medical order, of which there are many in the country. The Catholic head of an international charity, who has long-standing experience doing similar work, has come to a different conclusion: 'I don't think in this work you can be an amateur. There are occasions when you can only give love and comfort, but if you can give more then it's your duty.'[38]

Almost all official biographies of Mother Teresa tell the story of how she started by washing the body of a woman infested with maggots; Navin Chawla, the Indian civil servant who became her friend and biographer, comments: 'Mother was to tell me on several occasions, "If we did not believe that this was the body of Christ we would never be able to do this work ... It is Christ we touch in the broken bodies of the starving and the destitute." '[39] 'Touch them, wash them, feed them,' Mother Teresa urges many a volunteer. 'Give Christ to the world, don't keep him to yourself, and in doing so use your hands.'[40] The ability to touch, with its wider implications, is especially important in India where the concept of 'untouchability' is so real. This is the true missionary spirit in action. It is more important to touch than to cure.

When I talked to Mary Cox, a Co-Worker for more than a dozen years who recently became a mature volunteer, about her experiences of working at Kalighat, she explained to me how massaging with oil was extremely important for an Indian, and touching bodies was part and parcel of the profound vision of Christianity which attracted so many young people. Wearing gloves was anathema for the work they were doing. I asked her if, as a mother of six (one of whom has been a Mother Teresa volunteer), she had not been tempted to wear surgical gloves as a safety precaution. No, she assured me, she had felt secure in the knowledge that a number of people were praying for her. 'Because I'm a mother and therefore used to touching bodies I wasn't frightened. All I came home with was scabies, nits and an intestinal worm.'

And yet, with the increase in HIV, AIDS and the drug-resistant tuberculosis, is it fair to expose naive, nineteen-year-olds, there to do penance for past privilege, to these risks in the belief that it is Christ's body they are touching? I was interested to see, when I went to Kalighat, a framed, handwritten message, almost too high on the wall to read, about when it was appropriate to use gloves and when to wash immediately if you came into contact with bodily fluids. It was, I was told by a young English girl, a new notice. 'But there are never any gloves around,' she added, as she handed me a filthy apron with yesterday's used tissues in the pocket. On another wall, another volunteer was painstakingly painting in bold, three-dimensional letters, the message Mother Teresa really wanted to get across: 'Let my hands heal your broken body.'

CHAPTER TEN

THEOLOGY

In the recent film *Dead Man Walking*, based on a true story concerning an American sister, Helen Prejean, there is a striking scene at the beginning when a male prison chaplain scorns the nun sitting before him: 'But you are not wearing a habit.' Sister Helen spent twenty years as a cloistered nun before deciding that there was a better way for her to make a contribution to the disadvantaged of New Orleans, 'that there was another way of loving people than loving just one man,' and this involved some painful decisions about where and how to live. It was, she admits, a struggle to come to terms with the real world. But one of the ways forward, if she was to be of genuine service, was to wear the clothes of the real world.

That she and other sisters like her were faced with these difficult, often agonising choices was a result of the Second Vatican Council of 1962–5. Pope John XXIII called the world's bishops to Rome for a conference which lasted four years and became a dramatic watershed in the history of the Roman Catholic Church. The Pope's aim was to modernise the Church in general and religious groups in particular – as he put it, 'by opening the windows and letting in the fresh air'.

There were several initiatives resulting from Vatican II which affected nuns, or women religious, many of whom belonged to age-old groups which had been painfully out of sync for several hundred years. All were called upon to renew themselves. This renewal took various forms but the intention was clear: convents should become more democratic and open in their lifestyle, times of prayer should be more flexible and less formal, and distinctions of rank and position, including the use of the term Mother, were no longer necessary. Before Vatican II the arrangements in most convents were strictly hierarchical; this encouraged the idea of charismatic leadership but left little scope for individuality. A provincial superior, that is the head of an order in one country, would enjoy tremendous power and this power was reinforced in all sorts of ways. One English sister recalled for me her memories of joining a convent more than twenty years ago: 'There was one door for the Superior and one for the rest of us, and she always had a special silver spoon in her tea and the freshest mustard. A large number of congregations, the so-called top-drawer communities, had two tiers of entry, choir and lay sister. If you were educated you became a novice who became a teacher and then a Mother. Those who were not educated could still enter and be called sister but would do domestic work and keep the boarding schools running, for example. The two were quite different. The system was based on a Jesuit way of life and it endorsed hierarchy. At its best it made successful use of very gifted people, but it could lead to an abuse of power.'[1]

One of the most obvious ways for vowed women to demonstrate that they were taking a new look at their role in the community was to dispense with impractical habits, often seen as a barrier to intimacy with those they were trying to help, or even a status symbol. Allowing sisters to choose their own clothes, within certain obvious limits, is today considered important because it allows not merely individuality to flower but with it the talents of that person to reach their full potential. The converse, where anonymity is encouraged, may help to retain the purity of a particular image but is now recognised as a potentially dangerous and damaging factor in restricting the inner growth of a personality not fully developed. It also enforces the submission of will which the Second Vatican Council sought to free.

Thus the freedom implicit in choosing one's own clothes is neither trivial nor merely symbolic. In Mother Teresa's case, the decision to retain a uniform (which is not a habit) is, of course, practical and is one applauded by Pope John Paul II, who has shown himself a strong advocate of nuns retaining a religious habit. Immediately after becoming Pope he insisted on traditional attire for nuns and has not deviated from this view. But it is also symptomatic of a much wider approach to the nuns in her charge. The pronouncements of Vatican II concerning a nun's way of life seemed to have little resonance for her work in India. Mother Teresa's formative years were between 1920 and 1940; by the time she left the convent in 1946 the major theological decisions in her life had been taken, her vision was clear, and she stuck to it with a singlemindedness that achieved what often appeared impossible and a doggedness that brooked no opposition from male priests. This was not a feminist response; Mother Teresa was the first to recognise that she needed priests to say mass, and her opposition to women priests has always been absolute. She frequently took the opportunity to reiterate her belief in the sanctity of Mary as the handmaiden of the Lord and her special role in the Christian panoply. 'No one could have been a better priest than Our Lady,' is Mother Teresa's often stated view.

Everything about the way of life for a Missionary of Charity fortifies an ideal of caring femininity, the traditional female role of submitting to men and suppressing one's own will, epitomised so beautifully by Audrey Hepburn in the 1959 film, The Nun's Story. This image, of a white woman in a habit ministering to the needs of the world's unfortunates, is the one so beloved by the Western media. The terminology used by Mother Teresa reinforces this, as she and her sisters each see themselves as the 'Spouse of Christ crucified'. She has described the relationship as a love similar to that of a wife for a husband but more extreme, and once responded to a comment that she must be married to have such wisdom about love in relationships by saying: 'Yes I am, but sometimes I find it difficult to smile at Him because He can be so demanding.'[2] Many nuns of the late twentieth century find the description of themselves as a Bride of Christ not merely outdated but ludicrous. As Clifford Longley wrote: 'Fifty years ago a nun in a religious order was expected to understand her vow of perpetual virginity as a kind of mystical marriage to Jesus Christ ... it was utterly chaste – impure thoughts were a serious sin – but not without an intensely romantic effect in a young woman's imagination. Final profession of vows was often performed as a kind of marriage ceremony with the "bride" in white.'[3] The American novel Mariette in Ecstasy by Ron Hansen* graphically demonstrates where this can lead

* Picador, 1996.

when the young girl in a turn-of-the-century convent suffers stigmata whenever she contemplates Christ.

Nonetheless, Mother Teresa herself wields as much power and authority as any man she deals with and has never been shy of telling priests not to intervene in the internal affairs of her House. 'Some priests would like me to change things,' she once told Father Eduard Le Joly, her spiritual adviser. 'For example, they have told me we ought to have curtains in the communal rooms. I do not want them; the poor we serve have none. Most of the nuns come from peasant homes, where there are none either. They ought not to have more comfortable lives here than they had in their own homes.'[4]

She has also been emphatic about not needing advice as to what she teaches her nuns. That the Missionaries of Charity do not have televisions may not come as a surprise; there is, after all, little time for leisure. Odder, perhaps, is the absence of newspapers and other reading material in all their homes around the world. For those who have to face the sordid problems of everyday life, a powerful case can be made for the importance of being well informed. Mother Teresa believes it is a question of trusting in the Holy Spirit and praying, and then you do not need newspapers to inform yourself. To do the work of a Mother Teresa nun calls for total simplicity and trust. A Missionary of Charity has access to only a few books each year and these are usually works of old-fashioned piety such as the 1950 volume Christ – the Life of the Monk by Abbot Marmion, or Seeds of the Desert by Brother Charles de Foucauld. 'It is good to study and read the works of the saints and other holy people,' said Mother Teresa. 'But we find that God teaches us all we need to learn through our actions and our work.'[5]

Sister Dolores, in charge at Kalighat when I visited in 1995, expanded on the same theme: 'We do try and take the time for spiritual reading; I love to read the works of the saints, which have been helpful, and anything on our blessed Mother, Our Lady – she is the best of mothers. But really I don't need to read many books because I am being taught all the time by others.'[6] As a former Missionary of Charity explained it to me: 'Mother Teresa does not believe her sisters should be more educated than those they are trying to serve.'

Mother Teresa herself expressed her views quite clearly during an interview with Vatican Radio in 1980 when she explained that, for her, faith was something to be lived rather than talked about. Her interviewer, Sean Patrick Lovett, was told: 'If you accept faith as a gift you don't want to know why. Once you start questioning then you don't like what you see. Her point was "ours is not to reason why". Not surprisingly, Mother Teresa does not want nuns with a university degree because she believes that too much thinking makes the mind clouded and confused.'[7] Yet as Sister Lavinia Byrne of the IBVM commented: 'Of all the work that women can do, teaching is that which most transforms society because it shows children how to be enquiring.' There is a proud history of education among women religious which Mother Teresa was quite clearly turning her back on, which explains why Loreto could never have accommodated her. Lavinia Byrne considers it 'a great shame for us that she left the IBVM. If she'd stayed we could have given each other those bits that we are now lacking ... We could have given her our heads, that kind of professionalism that goes with being more politically motivated and highly educated.'[8] The archives of religious congregations are full of stories of strong-minded women who challenged bishops, confronted popes or contested the norms of society. Most of all, women's religious life has been significant in the education of other women. The American writer Joan Chittister OSB says: 'Feminism, the consciousness of the graced and gracing nature of women despite the subordinating role definitions to which they were subject, is one of the gifts of religious life across time.'[9]

I dwelt on this point with a priest who knows Mother Teresa well and who has worked on the education of her novices. In the first place he suggested, 'You have to respect the decisions of the sisters on education because they would be reflecting on this on a regular basis and would have a good feel for the needs as well as being sensitive to what Mother would want.' Anyone who is interested in joining the Missionaries of Charity first stays as a lay person for two to three weeks on a come-and-see basis. At this point she gets the feel of a convent and the work and the sisters will be weighing her up, too. She then enters an aspirancy for six months, followed by a postulancy for up to a year, and then a two-year noviciate before taking simple vows, which are renewed annually. In the sixth year the girl will have one year of tertianship, then take her four final vows for life. 'Mostly it is obvious whether or not a girl is suitable for this life,' my informant explained. 'You hope the person themselves will leave if she is not.'

During those years a trainee sister, who wears only white without the blue border, will not be taught nearly as much theology and scripture as in other congregations. 'They will have the rudiments of Church history and the teaching of the faith and some understanding at a basic level of the sacraments. The emphasis is on the particular life of a Missionary of Charity. What is it about Mother's charism? They will be reading Mother's letter to the sisters. But from early on in their formation they will also go outside to do apostolic work to give them an early introduction to the life of the poor by working among them.' He insisted that the balance was just about right. 'You must not give them too much theology because an awful lot of Western theological reasoning is counter-productive because it is questioning the fundamentals. Take the ordination of women – people love to discuss it but it's a useless discussion because it's not getting anywhere and would end up confusing the young sisters. But also it's getting in the way and not allowing you to be hands-on in your work.'[10]

In spite of these reassurances from someone who knows the Congregation at first hand, it still seemed strange to me for an order founded in the middle of the twentieth century to eschew educational priorities. Even a Jesuit priest who spent five months living and working with the brothers and sisters of Mother Teresa is not happy with the arrangements. 'On the spiritual side also there are only two priests to look after the needs of the Mother House in Calcutta, where some 300 Sisters receive their formation. Is this a weakness? In our view it is a serious one. In the most intimate centre of their being, on the spiritual and professional level, these souls fired with love remain weak and small.'[11]

One of the Vatican's experts in canon law has doubts too. 'I think it is an indication of why she needed to leave Loreto ... The whole experience of Mother Teresa is the experience of a foundress being called to something new and different that necessitated a break. I think she really had a new charism,' explained the Vatican source, who preferred to remain anonymous. 'However, I would have a concern about the education of her sisters,' she went on. 'I would say that everybody who is going into religious life today needs a very solid scriptural foundation that includes a fair amount of theology and liturgical formation in order to live as members of the Church – public representatives of the Church. It's what you'd want for every member of the Church and certainly for those in religious foundations. Whether some of the sisters should be trained as nurses or social workers, I don't know that for sure in the Indian context. But if the sisters are going to run a home for dying AIDS patients, maybe some of them need to be practical nurses, at least in terms of medication and care,' she said.

'I have a concern for, and documents from this office call for, a very solid religious formation for all religious that includes human, spiritual, pastoral and then, according to the charism, a professional training. We accent the whole sphere of the human psychological development on which you build and root a spiritual life. The work of Mother Teresa's sisters is extremely hard and the lifestyle does not take advantage of modern conveniences, and I think in the long run a person has to have physical, psychological, emotional and spiritual strength to remain as they begin – a generous, joyful, dedicated person giving their spiritual selves. A curious piece of it is, and we can't remove the fact, that Mother Teresa herself is educated.' Not simply is she educated, but she travels frequently and has access on a regular basis to some of the world's most powerful leaders and opinion-formers.

It soon became evident to me that this was no dry academic discussion about the values of education for today's woman. There was a deeper concern behind the careful Vatican phrasings and this was about depression or even breakdown. 'I have a tendency to think that there is a physical and psychic drain in the kind of work they do among the extremely poor, the hard physical and, perhaps humanly speaking, unrewarding work. I think a minimum of privacy and free time, especially as a woman gets older, begins to take its toll if you get physically drained and there is nothing that re-enervates you. Certain kinds of prayer life can restore you ... silence is a zone of privacy; if it's silent it can be rejuvenating but if the prayer time is busy, for me it would be very difficult,' the source suggested. 'If spiritual formation does not continue to grow it needs very deep roots of faith, psychologically speaking, or depression comes, and it's much harder to live through it and come out of it.'

Not surprisingly there are no figures available for the numbers of women who leave the Order as a result of breakdown or depression, but one former Missionary of Charity who spent nearly twenty years before disentangling herself with great difficulty and sadness within the last decade told me: 'As I left, other people were beginning to leave but it was never to be mentioned and often it was unnecessary to leave, had there been more open discussion.' This English-speaking sister told me of the wealth of repressed talent and the many difficulties which she encountered throughout those years. 'When you're younger you think you can conquer everything, but by your mid-thirties you do start to question and that's where the support is lacking. There was someone in the group when I was in charge of a community abroad who was forty-two and I could see that she was not very well and should see a doctor. I contacted a hospital run by nuns and sent her along. She was clinically depressed. When Mother Teresa found out, she was not pleased and asked why she had been sent to a psychiatrist. The woman was sent back to India instead.'[12]

The 'busy' prayer time, that is the old idea where everyone prays together and says the same thing, may be comforting to some younger, less educated sisters, but it causes problems for many of the older, more thinking nuns. The idea that 'when the bell rings you drop tools and go' was a considerable stumbling-block for the former Missionary of Charity. 'For example, when I was in Africa feeding a hungry child, if that bell rang I would have to go and follow that. It was a big struggle because if you're speaking about Christ in people, why leave that Christ to find another Christ if He is everywhere?' Because this young woman tried to argue, however constructively, over these points she was always considered a rebel. And yet, from the age of eight, she had always wanted to work with the poor. After her first year at university she left to join the Missionaries of Charity. 'I think I felt very much called. In hindsight, I realise now that other congregations would say, "Finish your studies and have some experience. Don't decide when you're so young." But Mother Teresa doesn't think along those lines.' A senior nun in this country informed me she had personal experience of other young students feeling drawn to the Missionaries of Charity while still at college and being told: 'If God is calling you, you will know it, so come now.'[13] I was also told about a beautiful Scandinavian girl who wanted to be one of Mother Teresa's nuns and thereby broke her father's heart. When the father went to remonstrate with Mother Teresa, saying he thought this career would be quite wrong for his daughter, Mother Teresa replied: 'Why shouldn't God have the finest?'[14]

The English-speaking sister, who agonised for years before leaving, found much that was appealing about the sisters being contemplatives in action. 'They have lots going for them; they really do have a very simple lifestyle and they are where people need them. I know it's very difficult otherwise to go and live in a poor area, which, as a group, they can do.' But in the end she found that prayer was not and never could be a substitute for work and that Mother Teresa's adhesion to a pre-Vatican II lifestyle created an institutional and hierarchical atmosphere that was a barrier to the work. 'I could never write letters other than once a month and at Christmas and Easter, and then only to family members. Letters are opened and intercepted and when I complained I was just told, "This is the way we do it." Of course it was a question of trust and one's own commitment, but the trust seemed to be one way only.' This blind obedience, which the Second Vatican Council tried to reshape more than thirty years ago, is not of today. As the writer Paul Johnson commented recently, in a different context: 'I have known many members of religious orders and talked to them about their vows. They have all told me that vows of chastity and poverty were fairly easy to keep, and became easier ... much more difficult were vows of obedience – to obey without protest foolish orders from superiors who were manifestly not their intellectual equals. That, if anything, became more oppressive as they got older.'[15]

The ex-nun who spoke to me believes that the old-fashioned style of rigid obedience was part of the founding ethos. 'As many of Mother Teresa's first followers were schoolgirls from Loreto, the pupil–teacher relationship was continued. The schoolgirls have never really grown up. It is a big institution with some very good women but no one who can be Mother Teresa's best friend.' In this context she sees why the term Mother, an old notion which quite clearly expresses both childishness, dependence and an acceptance of not thinking for oneself, has persisted. It is a term few, if any, religious use any more.

When this woman eventually set in motion the formalities required if she were to leave the community, she encountered an aspect of the Congregation she had been unaware of. 'It was made very difficult for me to leave but I had the support of my family in Europe. Asians can't always draw upon that.' She applied first for a leave of absence, the legal requirement to enable her to go through a process of discernment. 'But I was never given that formal letter – Mother Teresa told me: you are either with us or against us, and I had to seek advice from a canon lawyer.' Eventually this sister acquired her necessary permissions, helped by the fact that her family was well connected in the local Church hierarchy, and was released from her vows. But when she started to study and took a small job to support herself she received another letter from Mother Teresa. 'She told me that as I had taken a vow to the poorest of the poor I should not be earning money. I was even visited by one of her people who told me to put my sari back on. I was bombarded by the feeling that I was divorcing.

'Eventually, I had to decide, "Am I prepared really to suffer with Christ and one day things will evolve with this Congregation, because there are some wonderful women there?" In the end I felt they never would and I had to leave.' Of course, one of the reasons Mother Teresa has so many young girls flocking to join her is the security of not having to make decisions such as the ones this intelligent woman wrestled with. The black-and-white nature of her existence is very appealing to those of immature mind who would find the challenge of taking decisions much more difficult. The greater freedom offered by Vatican II has not resulted in an increase in the number of nuns. This is partly because the modern world gives women so many opportunities for caring, independent lives without taking permanent vows. In fact, there has been a dramatic drop in the number of vocations throughout the West, especially in the US where by 1990 numbers were down by half from a record high of nearly one million nuns in 1970. Only in the third world are vocations keeping pace. With choice comes responsibility, and in order to make a responsible choice there must be an educational base. It is all of a piece. Young women who decide to join a congregation which does not offer the same degree of certainty will need to find much deeper resources within themselves. 'You have to be able to live freely as a responsible individual from the depths within you. Now that the structures have gone, you have to find those structures within yourself; it's a much deeper call. I find it more satisfying,' explained another sister, living in a more open community.

The austerity, too, can be very appealing and many of the world's idealistic young are attracted to Mother Teresa rather than to one of the bloated international charities precisely because of the genuinely radical lifestyle combined with the simple message that God's love is infinite. 'Be a carrier of God's Love,' Mother Teresa herself lectures novices in formation in Calcutta. 'If you don't have the zeal, then pack up and go home – no need to stay.'[16] It is impossible to know how many girls do pack up and go and whether the Missionaries of Charity in fact lose more entrants – and faster – than other orders. But several superiors from other orders think they do.[17]

It is a question of balance. To Margaret Shepherd, a Sister of Sion, it is crucial to be realistic as well as idealistic. For her, taking out a radiator from a house where the sisters live is of little benefit to those she is trying to help; worse it is 'patronising to the poor ... We are learning from the poor, the way we should respond to the poor is that we are in this together. Some of us are just emotionally poor or poor in education. Of course you can deprive yourself but I have had the opportunities of a good education, therefore I'm a rich person; we must recognise that and not play at being poor. You can live alongside the poor but you must also be realistic.'[18]

In all the talk of 'inculturation' that is so fashionable, the discussions usually focus on Western religious going to the third world and adapting to a more simple lifestyle they find exists there. But in Mother Teresa's case the problem is reversed. To what extent should the Missionaries of Charity inculturate when they work in the West? 'Is it contrary to their poverty to use a washing machine in the US? If they have a shelter for street women in the US, should they be content with making sure they're housed and have meals or should they also have skills and knowledge of social service agencies to get them into job training or to get them psychological training so that they might become productive, independent citizens?' were all questions posed by my Vatican source. 'It's my opinion that it's a better thing to do with someone if people are going to live another twenty years. The question is, do the Missionaries of Charity have other options, at least in some countries?'[19]

The rigorous attitude to austerity made news headlines when a former convent was prepared for the sisters with much local generosity in San Francisco. When Mother Teresa came, invited by the local Bishop, to inaugurate the house, she was extremely negative and said it was too big and too elegant. As a result, the mattresses, carpets and some other pieces of furniture were all thrown out of the window into the street below and a boiler installed to give hot and cold water was discarded. One of the sisters who was there at the time felt distinctly uncomfortable about the way it was managed. 'There are ways to do this other than in front of the TV cameras, especially when people have made sacrifices for you. It could have been done more discreetly.' There are stories of occasions when the sisters have been inundated with a glut of fruit, such as the tomatoes given to the sisters in the Rome noviciate. As everyone in the neighbourhood had grown their own the Superior decided that the sisters could preserve some to eat during the winter. 'When Mother came to visit and saw the canned tomatoes, she was very displeased. Missionaries of Charity do not store things but must rely only on God's providence.'[20]

One of the most austere groups of religious women are the Poor Clares, an 800-year-old order founded by St Clare, an Italian girl who became a disciple of St Francis of Assisi and formed her own Order. They still wear a floor-length brown serge habit and lead an utterly simple life of prayer and have the same faith that God's Providence will feed them as do the Missionaries of Charity. 'But it is not a blind faith ... I'm suspicious if people have total certitude. We have a part to play in it,' one Poor Clare explained to me. As many people come to them with a wide range of problems they insist that you must understand the modern world in order to pray for it. The novice director at a Poor Clare convent I visited explained to me that many of the novices they take these days are in their thirties and often have a university degree. The novices are sent for psychological assessment at a professional centre to see if they will have the mental fitness for such a life before joining. 'We encourage people to feed their minds, especially on the wider things of life including cultural matters. We have televisions, newspapers and radios because we feel it's very important to know what is going on in order to deal with it. It is an embracing of the world and ... an attempt to see God present in everything. We own nothing and we live a life of poverty, but we don't go in for austerity for austerity's sake.'

This novice director explained to me that in her community obedience is not a matter of the Abbess telling the sisters what to do or not do. 'It's a listening process and we're trying to discern God's will the whole time. I think it's quite infantile to be told do this or do that, because sometimes you are faced with two quite good ways of dealing with a problem. Rigid uniformity does not help because we are all so different.'

Part of a Poor Clare's work is not dissimilar from that of the Samaritans in England. People call them in distress and the sisters try to offer support and advice. 'We try to be with them and pray with them and enter into people's agony.' But this is skilled work and the Poor Clares attend regular counselling courses to update their knowledge. 'God will help you, but he expects you to use your minds too.' My informant was painfully aware of life's complications. 'I think we are all struggling in the mess of being in the human life ... sometimes you think it would be wonderful not to have to cope with all this neurotic behaviour. But that's the human condition, isn't it, and the impossibility of giving simple answers.' She and her colleagues are frequently faced with acute moral dilemmas, especially where AIDS and the use of condoms, forbidden by the Roman Catholic Church, are concerned. 'If preserving life is the highest moral value,' this quiet, thinking nun said to me, 'to say to people who are in love and living together that they must not protect themselves [by wearing a condom] against a life-threatening disease doesn't make sense.' It was clear to me that austerity for a deeply committed woman like this had little to do with whether she had a comfortable bed and enough to eat but consisted in not living cosily with her conscience. The constant search for the right answer was often uncomfortable and far more so than sleeping on a hard bed or being without television. But she and others like her understood that they were living at the cutting edge of the Church and society, or, as Joan Chittister put it, becoming the 'searing presence' of God's spirit in the world.

The need for professionalism in the 1990s was brought home even more acutely by another well-educated sister who had been in Romania just after 1989 when the full horror of deposed dictator Nicolae Ceauşescu's regime became apparent and the world was shocked by pictures of hundreds of abandoned and grotesquely handicapped orphans left in crumbling institutions to die or starve. She knew that there was a group of Missionaries of Charity working near by and went to visit. 'There was one English, one Polish and one Indian sister caring for abandoned babies, old people with special needs and very severely handicapped children all together in one house. None had professional training, nor even any preparation for working there. The English Missionary of Charity was finding the children very aggressive and very difficult and she couldn't cope. Yes, of course there were urgent needs in Romania but you can't go in and paper over the cracks. There was a time when we would have done that, but not any more. Every one of our younger sisters will be trained in something and stretched as a woman. We've learned from experience that the development of the human person is important for sanctity just as much as good faith.'

Sister Teresa Brittain was saddened by the tension she found at this Missionaries of Charity house, where the sisters were having difficulty communicating with each other and were very disillusioned by the ghastly situation. 'I asked them how they could mix such different needs together and the sister-in-charge told me, "I know it's not adequate. I don't really know what to do but I know this is not right." These sisters were virtually on the edge of a nervous breakdown and there seemed to be almost no human care. I don't find it impressive when people are so worn out and it goes against normal common sense.'[21]

I found echoes of this story talking to other aid workers. One English-speaking Catholic working in Latin America told me of a very disturbing situation she had personally encountered. 'I was taken to the Missionaries of Charity home in Jamaica by the Archbishop of Kingston to see the welfare work and in my opinion the conditions were not acceptable nor dignified.' There was one situation in particular that appalled her. An elderly married couple, in their seventies or eighties, were separated and had to sleep in separate dormitories. They begged to be allowed to be together. 'The wife was blind and she said to the Archbishop, "Please can you at least give me my own clothes back." She was crying all the time and plucking at her petticoat. But the sister told her that they did not have time to sort out clothes; everyone's clothes were taken and washed and she would have to wear whatever she was handed out. When I asked if some way could be found for the couple to share a room, I was told by one senior sister, "They are well past that age." ' What left an impression on this aid worker were the conditions of squalor and poor human relations, not the high standard of care she had expected to be offered by the Missionaries of Charity.[22]

But if the externals of Mother Teresa's Order are firmly rooted in the pre-1960s, so is her theology. Many Catholic schoolchildren were traditionally taught the catechism, 'Of what must I take most care, my body or my soul? Answer: My soul.' 'But we've moved on from that to a more holistic theology,' one sister explained to me. The soul–body dichotomy, or the concept of dualism, belongs to an old part of Catholic theology which has given the body a lower value than the soul, equated fleshly desires with negative and sinful aspects of humanity, and glorified suffering. Modern theologians try to counteract this dualism and do not glorify suffering but recognise it as an evil with no good in itself. Only if one can find a purpose in it can suffering be transformed into something worthwhile. As Sister Teresa Brittain put it: 'The old theology says you must bear your suffering here because you will be rewarded in heaven. Nowadays you work for the kingdom of heaven here and now and you don't wait for death. Liberal theologians say we must take suffering people down from the Cross, not go on hammering nails in because they'll be holier at the end of it.'

Clifford Longley was finally persuaded to join the fray over Mother Teresa because of the latent problems resulting from this dichotomised thought, which he detected as persisting in the Missionaries of Charity. 'It was the closest I'd come to putting any misgivings I might have about Mother Teresa in public,' he told me. Appearing in the wake of the *Lancet* criticisms and just a few days after Hitchens' attack on her political attitudes, his article attracted considerable attention. Longley wrote in the *Daily Telegraph* of the danger that too much female passivity and subordination in an effort to create a mystical union with the divine could slide into a complete rejection of humanity.

In attributing all that is good to God and all that is bad to the flesh – the will, self, ego and all their affections and passions – it soon starts to resemble Manichean dualism.

This is seriously at odds with the insights of psychology and psychiatry, not to mention the parable of the talents. This implies that differences between people are God-given and that individuality is to be cultivated rather than suppressed. It is not by emptying a person of all that is human in order to make way for the divine that sanctity is achieved; it is by the fulfilment of all that is human, bringing the human to its peak, Langley argued. He pointed out that such attitudes had deep implications for attitudes to suffering and to death. It is not just a sentimental word of comfort to say that the prayers of the dying are especially dear to God. They will soon be with Him in heaven and God is with all who suffer.

But it would be unhealthy to take the dying as a model for the living or to make suffering a goal. There is no doubt that Mother Teresa reveres the dying and those who have seen her in action are intensely moved by it. What must be asked, however, is whether she is in this respect free of all the Manichean dualism that had crept into the devotional life of religious sisters before the pendulum started to swing the other way? Are the dying treated as precious – even unconsciously – because they are about to be released from the flesh? And does this alter how they are treated?[23]

'I am on my way to Heaven,' reads the sign at the entrance to the morgue of the Home for the Dying. But as Mother Teresa explained in her 1995 book, *A Simple Path*, 'Anyone is capable of going to Heaven. Heaven is our home. People ask me about death and whether I look forward to it and I answer "Of course, because I am going home ... in Heaven we shall be able to love Him with our whole heart and our soul because we only surrender our body in death – our heart and our soul live forever."' In a letter to Co-Workers in Lent 1996 she said: 'We look forward to rising with Jesus, but each one of us must go through pain, sorrow, suffering, sickness and death. Because of the promise of the Resurrection we do not have to be afraid. We can accept all suffering as a gift of God. We may shed a few tears but inside we will be at peace and have a deep sense of joy.'[24] Many Catholics may share Mother Teresa's belief that suffering need not be pointless if it can be used as a powerful link through prayer. Indeed, Pope John Paul II has also said that suffering can be noble and necessary. But what she says sometimes goes beyond this. 'Suffering is a gift because it helps you to share in the suffering of Christ,' she said in a 1988 filmed interview.[25] She went on to give an example of a woman she once met who was in desperate pain in the final stages of cancer. She tried to comfort her by saying that the agony was a sign that she had become very close to God and was sharing the pain of Christ on the cross. 'So close that Jesus is kissing you – it's very beautiful.' 'Then please tell him to stop kissing me,' the woman replied, as recounted by Mother Teresa herself.

Explaining the importance of the Sick and Suffering Co-Workers, Mother Teresa said: 'You cannot go out to work, so I do the working and you do the suffering. I have a person who does that for me, she has had many operations already. She offers every operation for me, while I go running about the place for her. She is in terrible pain but she offers everything for me. We have an understanding that we share everything together. That is the bond. She, with suffering, I with work and prayers. Beautiful. Every sister has a sick person praying for her.' Navin Chawla, to whom she gave this explanation, responded: 'So you get extra strength and you give that to your work.' 'Yes, yes, and they get extra strength from our prayers, from our work, from the sacrifices we make. Beautiful.'[26]

In her care for the dying, Mother Teresa offers traditional solace which is, in essence, little different from the medieval hospices run by religious orders for pilgrims or ancient sanctuaries for the poor. In the nineteenth century groups of Roman Catholic sisters again started working to help the dying and Mother Mary Aikenhead,* founder of the Irish Sisters of Charity who started St Joseph's Hospice in Hackney in 1905, was of key importance to the modern hospice movement. And yet ask any group of schoolchildren, as I have done, who in the world has done most to transform care for the dying. You will, assuredly, be told Mother Teresa – not Dame Cicely Saunders or Sister Frances Dominica, for example, both deeply religious women who have pushed out boundaries dramatically in care for the dying, or even Elizabeth Kubler-Ross, the prolific Catholic writer on dying and hospice care. Why?

Cicely Saunders was born in 1918 to an upper-middle-class English family, went to Oxford and then trained as a nurse when the Second World War broke out. Because of recurrent back trouble she could not practise as a nurse but studied to become an almoner. It was at this time that she became a devout evangelical Christian and longed to know what she could do with her life in response to her exciting conversion. She is a warm person who has always responded emotion-

---

* Mother Mary Aikenhead made her noviceship at the Bar Convent in York, along with Frances Teresa Bull.

ally to people and in the autumn of 1947, while working in a part of St Thomas' Hospital that specialised in cancer patients, she met the man who was to become the catalyst for her work. David Tasma, an agnostic Polish Jew, escaped from the Warsaw ghetto before the 1943 uprising and had no relations in this country when he fell ill with terminal cancer. Cicely was appointed his medical social worker, and although the pair were to spend little time together, and came from widely different backgrounds and religions, they developed a deeply loving relationship. When David died he left her £500 'to be a window in your home' and, as they had often talked about the need for better care for the dying, with it planted the seed for starting a hospice where terminally ill patients could be offered not simply more skilful and continuous pain relief but spiritual, emotional and social help too. It took her another nineteen years to build.

Saunders decided to train as a doctor, qualifying at almost thirty-nine, and then in 1958 went to work at St Joseph's Hospice, in Hackney, East London, where she listened to patients and clarified ideas from her days as a volunteer sister at St Luke's, a home for the dying in central London. It was a period of dramatic changes in the medical profession. There were several new drugs becoming available in the 1950s and early 1960s – tranquillisers, synthetic steroids and anti-depressants as well as the increasing use of antibiotics and life-saving surgery – and Dr Saunders had learnt from her earlier work the importance of giving drugs regularly, by mouth if possible, without inducing a comatose state. 'As medical students we had all been taught to say "Try and hold on a bit longer," yet one of the big myths was that regular giving causes addiction. Not having routine pain relief is like a switchback that sends you wildly up and down.' By the 1960s life expectancy had risen considerably, death from infectious diseases was rare and, in addition, death and dying were slowly becoming words that could be openly talked about. Almost for the first time, an ageing population openly faced the questions of how, when and where they would die. It was in this atmosphere that the Voluntary Euthanasia Movement developed, from the 1960s onwards, as one response to the awareness of the dreadful conditions of elderly cancer sufferers in particular. The hospice movement grew up alongside as another response concerned to ensure death with dignity.

In June 1967 St Christopher's Hospice finally opened in South-east

London. Cicely had worked for at least seven years planning it in detail and raising the money. The central idea was a combination of deeply rooted spirituality with the very best care that medicine could provide. This includes blood transfusions, chemotherapy, intravenous drips and, perhaps most important, the comfort of efficiency. But it is symptom control only; anything more interventionist or high-tech will necessitate the patient returning to hospital. Although the religious basis of the hospice permeates her whole approach, she learnt from David Tasma that her own belief in Christ is not necessary for everyone else. Once she was convinced that Tasma had found his own route to God, 'I never felt I could worry about him ... nor indeed about anyone else who dies in the world without apparently any knowledge of Christ.' There is a chapel at St Christopher's but the 1992 Mission Statement of St Christopher's does not even use the word 'Christian'; instead it talks of people searching for faith and meaning in their own lives. From Dame Cicely, there may be some sadness that the hospice is no longer as Christian as when it opened, 'but the world isn't either and we're part of the world and Christianity is better for being battered'.[27]

St Christopher's has had an enormous influence on care for the terminally ill throughout the world. Since the 1980s it has hosted a series of international conferences, sometimes with representatives from as many as thirty-eight countries present, where the ideas they have developed can be shared throughout the world. In addition they have up to 3,000 professional visitors a year – health administrators, doctors, nurses and academics – for a day, a week or a month. From the start it has been recognised as an educational centre, an information service and an administrative unit in addition to its pioneering hospice role. But Dame Cicely insists that the message is 'These are the basic principles ... interpret them in your own setting and culture. That's why hospice and palliative care has spread around the world and we've learnt from each other.'

Dr Luzito de Souza, head of the gastro-intestinal unit at the Tata Memorial Hospital in Bombay and pioneer of the first Indian hospice, was frank about his debt to Dame Cicely and St Christopher's. Speaking at St Christopher's first international conference in 1980, he referred to the problems specific to all developing countries: hunger and poverty as well as physical pain. In India one in eight people will get cancer and 80 per cent will seek treatment when it is too late; so palliative care becomes the only humane option. 'It is bad enough to be old and feeble. But to be old, sick with advanced cancer and poor and hungry with nobody to care for you is often the height of human suffering.' In November 1986, after much fund-raising abroad, and sufficient funds invested to cover running costs, the Shanti Avedna Ashram opened with one ward of ten beds. By 1992, it had fifty beds, each with a sea view, and was able to care for up to 500 patients annually. Families were encouraged to help and there are facilities for families to stay. A sister hospice has been opened in Goa and plans are proceeding for others.[28]

Dame Cicely is a forthright and determined personality. Tall, with steel-grey hair, she could easily dominate any gathering at which she was present but has chosen to surround herself with others of equal stature and has steadfastly refused to let any cult of personality develop. Of course, she has not denied the recognition she so justly deserves, such as the Templeton Award for progress in religion with its £90,000 prize in 1982. But, according to those who know her, she really *does* believe that St Christopher's and the care of the dying is more important than she is. She gave short shrift to someone trying to proclaim a Saunders Day and has refused permission for any hospices to be called Cicely Saunders Hospices, 'because, I'm afraid I have to say it, I didn't want to be made a cult figure like Mother Teresa ... We never set out to have a string of homes, we set out to be a one-off and encourage others to follow.'[29] When someone from the National Hospice Organisation in America wanted to dedicate a book he was writing to Elizabeth Kubler-Ross, Mother Teresa and Cicely, the first two obligingly sent photographs of themselves. Cicely sent a photo of St Christopher's with the note: 'The whole community has done this, not me.' Tourists who read about St Christopher's in their guidebooks – and anyone working in the field will tell you that death and dying does have a romantic fascination – are politely refused entry.

Dame Cicely has been, above all, dedicated to relieving pain. 'If you're battered by physical pain it is very difficult to pay attention to spiritual matters, therefore it is enormously important to give patients freedom from breathlessness as much as to have space to be themselves and meet with their families. They must fulfil what potential they have at the end of their lives in physical ease. There is an amazing degree of rehabilitation in personal relationships and a search for the deepest being, a spiritual quest. Most people don't talk in religious language these days but if you know at a subconscious level that you're dying, it is a summing-up period. It's good to have your bags packed even if you don't know where you are going.' But is it possible to go on a spiritual journey if you are shrouded in pain? Yes, she believes it is. 'But the only pain that is easy to bear should be your own. Never say, offer up your pain to God. I think that's dreadful. To say to someone else, offer up your pain to God instead of giving them pain relief is the antithesis of Christian caring. The deepest suffering is often to wish you'd done more. I don't see suffering as having a deliberate purpose except that it brings people down to the most basic level. My feeling for suffering is simply to try and relieve it. Turning the argument on its head, we don't say let us see what this pain is going to do for them. We say, let us see what it is that we can do for them to take the pain away and what they can do then. That may be full of courage, endurance and beauty. I think more new things happen after the relief of pain.'[30]

Cicely Saunders is aware that dying people may have a heightened spirituality 'because you are left with the more essential person', but at the same time insists that death is an outrage. 'A dying person may have a look of peace but it is not a smile, it is simply the muscles relaxing. Death can be sentimental if you say that. And few dying people change their religions or make dramatic conversions. But there is a quiet acceptance as people come to terms with things and they may say things like "Oh well, perhaps it's all right."' Above all, she insists that the focus at St Christopher's and at the many other hospices which have modelled themselves on it is not on death. 'Hospice is about living until you die and it may be longer and better than you expect.'[31] She added: 'People here are choosing life, they are choosing life up until they die. Mother Teresa is choosing death much more than we are.'

Mother Teresa, on the significance of death, has said: 'For me that is the greatest development of the human life, to die in peace and in dignity, for that's for eternity.'[32] Few of those who die in Kalighat are Christian and, while the religious paraphernalia of the Home may be overtly Christian, Mother Teresa insists that, where the religion is known, Muslim or Hindu funeral rites are correctly observed. She has even said, when asked about whether she converts those in her care, that she wants to convert Hindus to be better Hindus, Muslims to be better Muslims as well as Christians to be better Christians. She has also said, 'the special aim of the society is to labour at the conversion and sanctification of the poor in the slums ... to labour at the conversion and sanctification of the poor in the slums involves hard, ceaseless toiling, without results, without counting the cost ... to convert and sanctify is the work of God, but God has chosen the M.C.s in his great mercy to help Him in His own work. It is a special grace granted to M.C.s without any merit of theirs, to carry the light of Christ into the dark holes of the slums.'[33] I have been told on at least three separate occasions of patients at Kalighat having rosary beads put around their necks regardless of whether they wanted them[34] and about baptisms in her institutions. 'Of course they happen. For those who feel some sympathy towards Christianity this can be very comforting and for those who don't, what harm will it do?' was one explanation I was offered. Another volunteer, working as a potential entrant to the Order, recounted how a young girl dying in agony had begged to be baptised. 'So I took some flowers out of their water and used that ... and said the right words. I was told never to mention it and I never thought it mattered.'[35]

Broadly speaking, that was the view I took myself. Throughout the research for this book I continued to believe, as I had explained initially to the priest who interviewed me, that there were many routes to what I thought of as God and the externals of a person's religion did not, it seemed to me, matter much. It was only when I was in Rome, chatting in the pleasant surroundings of a modern convent to a group of Catholic sisters from different countries about my research so far, that I found myself articulating this view. One of them sharply took me to task. 'As a Jew, Anne, conversion is something you should get worked up about, because it's been happening to the poor old Jews for centuries.' This nun was a member of the Sisters of Sion, a group founded in 1842 by a Jew who converted to Christianity hoping to convert other Jews, but whose charism today has changed radically and now calls for the sisters to give witness to the links binding Jews and Christians. I walked back to my hotel in the centre of Rome, through the park and down the Janiculum Hill, wondering if my attempt at objectivity was futile.

*

There are today many people involved in care for the dying each with something special to give. It is far beyond the scope of this book to mention them all nor is it my intention to suggest them as necessarily appropriate models for India. But in order to set Mother Teresa and her work in some sort of context it is important to see what else is being achieved. In Liverpool Father Frank O'Leary has overseen the establishment of a Catholic hospice where the rooms are built around a central chapel, Christocentric, an atmosphere of cheerfulness is pervasive, family, friends and pets are encouraged, medical standards are high and there is a modern hydrotherapy pool for patients' use. Father O'Leary visited Mother Teresa's home in Calcutta in 1962 and insists it was her influence which made him dedicate his life to building this hospice which opened thirty years later, and encouraging a string of other similar hospices to which it is linked in South America. The Sue Ryder Foundation, with eighty homes throughout the world, including twenty-two in the UK, is another major force in the field of care for the disabled and dying, owing much to the religious vision, determination and energy of its eponymous founder. Bernadette Cleary is founder of the Rainbow Trust, one of the smallest and most recently established hospice groups, with two homes for children. Size is irrelevant; there is a clearly recognised need that those with life-threatening and terminal illnesses need specialised care which is life oriented and pain relieving, focuses on the needs of the whole person, physical and spiritual, and on his family, as well continuing to offer support to them even after the death.

In 1978, Sister Frances Dominica, who was then the Superior General of the Anglican Society of All Saints and a registered sick children's nurse, found herself giving temporary respite care to friends whose child Helen was suddenly found to have a brain tumour. Although the tumour was removed, Helen's brain suffered severe irreversible damage. She was, at two and a half, left totally helpless, unable to speak, sit up or control her movements. Helen House, the first children's hospice in the world, was born from this tragedy as Sister Frances realised the enormous unmet need for parents, children and their families.

A hospital is an inappropriate setting for a very sick child. What was needed was a loving, supportive environment where pain could be controlled or prevented as well as unpleasant symptoms which can cause acute distress and anxiety. Both Sister Frances and Dame Cicely hope that as many of their patients as possible will continue to live at home, coming to the hospice only for short stays or possibly at the end of their lives. The aim is for each child to die gently and free of pain, perhaps in the arms of his or her parents, perhaps lying in a large bed with them, affirming to the end that the child belongs to the family. Helen House is small – it can only take eight children at any one time – and each child has his or her own bedroom. Parents may choose to sleep in the same room as their child or to use one of the flats. The team of people which looks after the children includes nurses, teachers, a nursery nurse, social worker, physiotherapist, play therapist, chaplain and others. There is also a team of bereavement counsellors as the role of the hospice does not end with the death of the patient, and there are close links with the Sisters of the Society of All Saints, Sister Frances' Community. Sister Frances admits that this sort of work tends to draw people who have a strong faith because it makes the sadness endurable. 'But I never ask if people believe in God, I feel God can take care of that himself.'

Helen House, which opened in Oxford in November 1982, has provided a shining example of hospice care for children which has been widely copied. There are now ten similar homes in the UK and one in Canada; three in Australia are planned, all taking different names according to local initiatives. Sister Frances has enabled these homes to mushroom because she has been prepared to question and is refreshingly honest in her admission that she has no explanation for the deaths of innocent children. 'As time goes by,' she told me, one sunny day at Helen House, 'I realise I understand the meaning of suffering less and less, but I know that God is there in the midst of it. His presence does not take away pain or distress, but he gives families the strength, courage, grace or love to cope with it. These explanations are a long way from saying that is why the child is ill, or that your lives have been changed because of the death of this little person, and all the traditional explanations given to children – such as Jesus needing another little angel – don't add up to enough either. You cannot explain why a young person should suffer and die.'

Sister Frances told me the story of a child who was dying of cancer being comforted that everything would be all right because Jesus had suffered on the cross, only to be reprimanded by the child: 'Jesus hung for three hours and I've been ill like this for five years.' She has wrestled with the problem. 'I think that even if I had stood at the foot of the cross I would have found it harrowing ... never beautiful. Perhaps that's the main difference between me and Mother Teresa. You can't get sentimental or religious about death and there is a danger of that. It is horrific. It is agony to see the pain the relatives suffer ... however profound their faith, there is still the agony and hell of separation to be faced. But you must stay with the question, why, why, why, and the only answer I think is God saying, "Here am I in the midst and you'd better stay in the midst too ... No human being has the answers and we betray our fellow humans who are suffering if we say there is an answer.'[36]

Palliative medicine is a very new speciality. It was recognised in November 1987 as a sub-speciality of General Internal Medicine by the Royal College of Physicians and some doctors in the field are keen to ensure that it does not just develop into 'symptomology', but goes beyond this to create conditions where healing at a deep personal level may occur for the individual patient. Perhaps, in recognising the creative potential of the darkness that is suffering, Mother Teresa has something to say to the modern hospice movement. It is a question of emphasis, which requires many other factors in place; but her contribution to the debate is not helped by the fact that the English she speaks is the convent language she learnt at Rathfarnham in 1928. Dr M. Kearney, consultant in Palliative Medicine at Our Lady's Hospice in Dublin, wrote, 'Symptom control alone is not enough. Symptom control is only the beginning ... I no longer subscribe to the view that the suffering associated with the dying process is without meaning or value. While I agree that we have to do all we can to reverse and relieve this suffering, there will be many missed opportunities unless we simultaneously find ways to enable that patient to discover something of immense value which I believe lies hidden in the depths of that experience.'[37] He concluded: 'While there is an abusive and useless dimension to illness, pain and suffering, which needs to be removed if at all possible, there is also potential in such experience ... something essential for that particular individual's healing at that moment in time.'

There is no more fundamental problem for twentieth-century religion than explaining why the innocent suffer. How can post-Holocaust theologians of any religion talk of a just God when millions were exterminated in death camps during the Second World War? Some Jewish religious thinkers, who surely have as much reason as any to ponder this point, have concluded that the only way to make life bearable when we cannot find answers is to recognise that some answers are beyond us. After all, the biblical story of Job, who questions why an innocent man should suffer, leads to the conclusion that 'God demands a change in perspective on the part of man, an acknowledgement of the limits of human knowledge and ultimately of man's insignificance in the scope of the universe'.[38] This position, demanding trust and faith in the face of tragedies we cannot comprehend, might not be so different from Mother Teresa's – after all Judaeo-Christian teaching is that life is a gift of God to be held in trust – were it not that contemporary Jewish theologians go beyond this to emphasise that faith alone is not enough. 'The only viable explanation is that the Holocaust and all evil pose a challenge to us all. When confronted by evil we must oppose it without compromise, without temporising, without hesitation ... Only the absolute conviction that he who saves one life saves the entire world can offer meaning in the face of an absolute evil. The certainty that evil challenges us to total and uncompromising moral action is rooted in the imperative to mend the world through resistance to evil ... Although we cannot ultimately explain why evil persists we can agree on the human imperative to actively resist it.'[39]

Dr Robin Fox wrote in the Lancet that Mother Teresa's approach was 'clearly separate from the hospice movement – I know which I prefer.' What makes his chilling conclusion so desperately sad is that for many in India there is not yet a choice. Some brave spirits are already working to change that.

CHAPTER ELEVEN

NUMBERS

Korça is an interesting, relatively cosmopolitan town in Southern Albania with rich historical associations dating from the fifteenth century. At nearly 3,000 feet above sea level, below the Morava mountains, it is extremely cold in winter. The Greek frontier is a thirty-minute drive away and, although during the communist regime Korça was cut off from all outside contacts, today the links with Greece could hardly be closer. Almost every family has a relative working across the border and the Orthodox Church is flourishing. A major exodus from Korça to the United States in the 1930s marked the onset of a decline, yet the pretty, balconied houses tell you that this was once a prosperous town with a vibrant culture; it was heavily involved in the Albanian nationalist movement and boasted the first girls' school in the country and the first school to use the Albanian language in 1887.

In post-communist Albania, Korça has become a battleground between the religions. In the centre of town is one of the oldest mosques in the country, now closed to the public but undergoing extensive restoration paid for by the Turkish government. The official was keen to show me, the privileged foreigner, the delicately painted interior. A short stroll away is a magnificent new Orthodox church where I, along with 500 jostling others, stood during a packed Sunday morning service in the crypt to hear Archbishop Giannolatos, the highest-ranking Greek Orthodox priest in Albania, some glorious singing and an organ accompaniment. A little further out of town I visited a large, bright new building erected by Seventh Day Adventists, which is not simply a church but also a community centre offering free education and some social services as well. As I walked back from there, I was accosted in the street by an American Protestant evangelical, a former banker, who learnt in a dream that he must come to Albania to do God's work and assumed I must be a missionary too. What other purpose would I have for coming to Korça?

I was there because pre-war Korça had sustained a small Catholic community, believed to be the result of an early-twentieth-century French influx. But their church, like many others in the country, was destroyed in 1955 and houses were built on the site. Catholicism was almost wiped out but for a few secret believers, like the woman who kept her prayer book hidden in a woodshed for thirty-five years. Then, after the fateful meeting with Mrs Hoxha, Mother Teresa's Missionaries of Charity were allowed into Albania and Catholicism was slowly re-established. A group of sisters opened a home in Korça in 1991 and Father Gary Walsh, a charismatic Canadian working in Calcutta, was asked by Mother Teresa to be their English-speaking chaplain. Under his tutelage the fledgling Catholic community was, by August 1993, able to celebrate mass in a brand-new building, situated in a pine wood opposite the sisters' house. The sculptor who created the bold figure of Christ above the altar was previously noted for his communist memorials. Young people in Korça, who have almost nothing to do outside school hours and few places to meet, have joined the Church in large numbers and some of them are already garbed in the plain white high-collared shirt and black skirt that indicates they are contemplating a future as a Missionary of Charity. Mother Teresa has visited this community several times to encourage and give her blessing.*

When Father Gary took a sabbatical she hand-picked his successor, Father Tedi Hochstatter, an Illinois priest who had previously been in Northern Albania working with her sisters and had overseen the opening of the Missionaries of Charity's eighth home in Albania, in

* Nonetheless, it would be unfair to accuse Catholic authorities of encouraging the rush to conversion in Albania which came with the first euphoria over religious freedom. The Papal Nuncio insists on written parental permission before a pre-confirmation instruction period of at least six months can begin. It is much easier to become a member of one of the other Protestant sects or groups.

the isolated mountain region of Dukagjin. In December 1995 Father Tedi decided to take the fourth vow of whole-hearted free service to the poorest of the poor and became, in a unique arrangement, what he calls an SMC, a Special Missionary of Charity. Before taking this decision he spent some time in Rome with Mother Teresa and had an audience with Pope John Paul II. The Pope presented him with a rosary and then, a moment later, with another rosary. A little confused, Father Tedi informed the Pope that he had already given him a rosary, which prompted the response, 'For Albania, I give double.'

For, in spite of the slight air of faded prosperity in Korça, relative to the rest of the country the needs are still acute. When I visited, electricity and water were both in short supply along with fresh food of any kind, including milk, fruit and vegetables. There was considerable malnutrition and vitamin deficiency; sanitary arrangements were un-hygienic as many people have no proper toilet, let alone sufficient cleaning materials. Children frequently suffer from burns yet open wounds are often bandaged with nothing more than dirty bits of rag – and there are neither facilities nor drugs nor trained personnel for cancer patients to be given adequate painkillers. Sisters from the Little Company of Mary, who came to Korça almost two years after the Missionaries of Charity, did what they could by training local doctors and nurses, and in four years raised an impressive £250,000 to build a new health centre in Korça, completed in October 1996, and intended to be staffed and run by native Albanians. The sisters organised a fund-raising drive through a newly created charity, SOS Albania, and creatively set to organising sponsored football events and slimming marathons. The European Community also pledged £150,000 towards the centre's running costs. A key aspect of the health centre was the education room intended for seminars and workshops so that ordinary Albanians would be equipped to improve their own lives.

Before it was finished the local population had to manage with a couple of dilapidated old hospitals full of cockroaches, mice and dampness, where conditions were often freezing cold because there was little or no fuel. In addition, there was a system of ambulances described to me as 'like a country doctor's little room where there might be some sterile gauze, lotions, a stethoscope and some scales, if lucky'. The terrifying-looking main hospital, now derelict, functioned for years sometimes with nothing more than herbs to offer its patients.

The Little Company of Mary sisters, all of whom are trained nurses, did their best to arrange occasional visas for sick children to be treated abroad alongside several other humanitarian agencies. But in April 1997, following civil war in Albania, the LCM nuns were forced to leave, having seen their new hospital all but destroyed by rampaging gangs, and Korça returned to misery.

In this morass of insufficiency what can the Missionaries of Charity do? They hand out old clothes, spectacles and food, but no longer medicines. They tried this when they first arrived in the early chaos of post-democracy but, without a trained pharmacist or nurse among them, nor anyone who spoke Albanian, this was not a success. According to sisters from the Little Company of Mary, who took over, the scheme was soon scrapped once it was realised that many were simply selling on the drugs while those who were desperately in need, dying of cancer at home, were too ill to stand in line and collect them. Some brands of morphine, handed out with the best of intentions to alleviate cancer pain, were a particular problem if, for example, they were designed to be given twice a day, twelve-hourly, but were in fact being taken four-hourly, through inadequate explanation, causing extreme nausea. The Little Company of Mary sisters helped train local pharmacists and handed over the job as quickly as possible. Today, the chief role of the Missionaries of Charity in Korça is running a children's home and teaching the faith in the outlying villages. This may involve some of the sisters spending many weeks living in the hills with families who once had ancient, now tenuous, connections to Catholicism.

Sister Lourdes, a gentle and pretty girl from Peru, showed me around the Missionaries of Charity children's home in Korça, where some twenty-three children, from nought to seven, many of whom have parents, are looked after. Some are abandoned in hospital after birth, others are handed over by the police if their mothers are prostitutes and several are so handicapped that their parents cannot cope with them. Babies are often left in their care in order that their parents can go to Greece to earn money. The orphanage, a much larger, state-run building where most of the children will end up, lowers over them next door. Families are large in Korça and this means many children are abandoned and end up in the orphanage. When they grow too old for this institution they are transferred to the home for mentally handicapped, where for lack of proper stimulation they become like their companions. According to a report by the Little Company of Mary sisters: 'In Albania there is obviously no form of family planning and the living conditions of the people do not help. In one of the villages we saw a place where as many as nine people, including three young children, lived, cooked and slept all in one room ... The birth rate is high and infant and maternal mortality is also high especially in the outlying villages which are isolated and inaccessible particularly in winter. The suicide rate is high as well.'[1]

It was quite evident to me, as the children clung to Sister Lourdes and somehow she conjured smiles from their tortured faces, that she had shown them unimagined love and compassion. When I commented on this to her she replied: 'You see, love is such a power, that's why we don't need qualified nurses.' (A cynic might have replied, 'Is that why they don't need books too?' My husband, reading aloud from the only picture book available, in a language totally incomprehensible to the children, was tugged incessantly to 'read' it again and again and again.) The babies' demands, some of whom were so malnourished they needed hourly feeding, were enormous and the Missionaries of Charity spend much of the day washing clothes and sheets by hand in huge vats with poles, passing the heavy wet bundles from one tub to another. Sister Lourdes admitted: 'We could not possibly have all the children who need our care, there are so many. So we choose the poorest of the poor. But it's very, very painful to have to choose.'

There was one two-year-old girl who seemed particularly attached to Sister Lourdes. I asked why she was there. 'It is a wonderful story,' Sister Lourdes began. 'She came here because her father is a very, very poor man who drinks and forces the lady to get pregnant, so she had many abortions. Before now, in communist times, they know how to do that. But we go and visit them and talk to them and they want us to look after the child because the mother cannot cope. Then a few months ago we visit them again and the lady tells me that the man has come home drunk again and forced her to get pregnant again. But we persuaded her not to have another abortion and promised her we would take the new baby and in return the little child will leave us and go home. So in a week or so the family is coming to bring me the new baby and take the older child away. It is a wonderful story because in communist times they would have an abortion. This time, they will sign a paper agreeing not to visit the new baby and once it is agreed she can be adopted.'

The story disturbed me for a number of reasons. But the baffled sister misinterpreted my silence as condemnation of the husband. 'Even though he's drunk he loves her,' she insisted. 'We have two families like that.' In fact, I was wondering what sort of value scale made the Missionaries of Charity show so much more concern for the child not yet born than for the three unhappy family members already struggling in the world. Why, when the problems surrounding them are so complex, do they persist in seeing life in such black-and-white terms: either adoption or abortion? No one would wish to condemn this mother to a vicious cycle of rape and abortion. But there are other options, and counselling or educating the woman in contraception or women's rights must be among them. These require time, which a Missionary of Charity who spends hours stirring washing in vats or teaching the rudiments of a religion to an uneducated mountainous tribe does not have, as well as a level of professional training which the Order does not believe in. But adopting a child, especially one brought unwanted into the world, is not a simple alternative.

Back in London, I recounted the story to Jim Richards, director of the Catholic Children's Society in Britain, who has spent the last thirty years dealing with difficult child welfare cases. 'It displays such crass ignorance of the last fifty years' experience,' he said. 'We were saying that nonsense in the fifties – that is "Leave the baby with us and you start your life anew." We now know you simply can't say that.' Richards' concerns were for both the child and mother. He explained: 'It is bad childcare to move a child at two ... you shouldn't start caring for children if you can't see it through. We must learn the lessons of the past. If the chain is broken there can be serious difficulties later on and usually are.' Then he told me of a seventy-year-old mother, not an unusual case, who had just made contact with her fifty-year-old child. 'She came to us and said: "Every morning since, when I wake up I think of him." We now know how mothers who have given up children for adoption without adequate counselling grieve and suffer a much higher rate of mental-health problems.'[2]

The Catholic Children's Society employs nuns on its staff from a variety of international orders, but they all have professional quali-fications across a wide range, including child psychologists, nursery nurses, counsellors, teachers, family therapists and social workers. Far from condoning abortion, Richards explained: 'The issue here is counselling skills. We have many young women who come to us pregnant and say what shall I do – have an abortion, keep the child or give it up for adoption? – and we will explain to them the difficulties with each of the options, which they must explore. For example mothers who have abortions may suffer depression later and you need to know that, but we also say if you decide to keep the child there will be problems too. We can tell them what we have found in our experience or what the latest research has shown, but we can only do that because of a depth of knowledge. How else can you guide a mother in such a difficult situation?' Again I turned to the Good Samaritan. Surely Mother Teresa was, like him, doing something rather than passing by on the other side of the road? 'The Good Samaritan did not set up a way station and an institution to help everybody in need who fell by the wayside. Once he'd done that he would have had to have thought about "How do I treat them?" He would have to have got that knowledge. Mother Teresa has set up a large institution and in so doing she cannot deny the knowledge that is available and must have a sense of humility that there are other people there and other sources of knowledge that she could bring in.' One way to avoid institutionalising the children, which need not be complicated or expensive, might be that the women who all wanted to go to Greece to earn better money could combine and take turns to provide childcare cover.

Jim Richards was careful to point out that he does not know Mother Teresa personally, and her adoption procedures do not have any overlap with his organisation. But he urged me to read *Love Is Not Enough* by the childcare expert Bruno Bettelheim, to give me an understanding of the tangle of issues in human growth and development, especially when dealing with other people's children. Inter-country adoption adds to the many hazards of an already difficult procedure. Anyone who has children for adoption is responsible for complying with the Hague Convention (May 1993) on the Protection of Children in Respect of Inter-country Adoption, as well as the 1987 UN Convention on the Rights of the Child, which tries to ensure that if children cannot be kept with their family of origin every effort is made to place them with their wider birth families wherever possible. The Hague document recognises that inter-country adoption may offer the advantage of a permanent family to care for a child for whom a suitable family cannot be found in her or his country of origin but sets up many checks and balances. It requires, among other things, that the parents have been counselled as necessary and duly informed of the effects of their consent, that the consent has not been induced by payment or compensation of any kind and that the consent of the mother has been given only after the birth of the child. In addition, the child (depending on his or her age and maturity) must be counselled and duly informed of the effects of the adoption, as must the prospective adoptive parents. It requires that accreditation to carry out inter-country adoption shall be granted only to bodies 'directed and staffed by persons qualified by their ethical standards and by training or experience to work in the field of inter-country adoption'.

Jim Richards knows only too well the complexities involved in each and every adoption. Mother Teresa sees only the utter simplicity of giving unwanted babies to childless couples. For her, difficulties exist only if you allow them to, which of course has a certain appeal. It enables her to get things done. Her clarity of vision and refusal to allow obstacles to impede her is a major reason for her success. When I discussed adoption with Sister Margaret Mary, one of her longest-serving allies in Calcutta, I was told, predictably: 'We are fighting abortion with adoption. There are so many babies and so many couples waiting – in Belgium alone there are two thousand parents waiting, but it's not fast enough.' Sister Margery, sitting in the adoption office of the Missionaries of Charity, confirmed that Switzerland, Belgium and Italy were the favoured locations. The nuns do not arrange UK adoptions 'because the paperwork would be too great and it would take too long. So far, we have no shortage of Catholic families.' Sister Margery told me that the birth mother can change her mind up to three months after signing the papers. 'Once they go abroad there is no turning back,' she added.

Given Britain's large Indian population it might seem strange that more Indian children are not adopted into families here, where they would not be deprived of their religious, racial and cultural heritage. Jim Richards again: 'People who tell you that Asian families are not into adoption are quite wrong. There are some strands of Asian culture where it might be difficult – if for example a child is born as the subject of a rape – but you will even find people who will adopt within that culture. There is a huge Asian population in this country and it could even be that they have relatives here.'

A spokeswoman at the Society for Indian Children's Welfare in Calcutta explained to me that the rules are different for the Missionaries of Charity and the many other adoption agencies in the city who will be granted a licence from the central government for foreign adoptions only if 50 per cent of their babies go to Indian couples, of whom she assured me these days there was no shortage. 'We have a waiting list of Indian families as the joint family system is dying out and more couples are living alone and making their own decisions.' She said that this licence was to be renewed annually, but that Mother Teresa has a special arrangement which means that her licence lasts three to four years.

Although international and transracial adoption has long been the subject of controversy – especially in Britain, where some politically correct local authorities have insisted on keeping black children separated from white parents and vice versa to ensure ethnic consciousness – current thinking on both transracial and inter-country adoption is more positive. One recent study finds no correlation between self-esteem and racial or ethnic identity and even suggests that transracial placement might help in the process of blending and sharing.[3] Could it be that, intuitively, Mother Teresa has got it right?

The beautiful Belgian girl who showed me around Shishu Bhavan certainly thinks so. She was an abandoned baby herself, brought up by the Missionaries of Charity until the age of four, when she went to a family in Belgium where she acquired an elder brother and much else besides. She is now a qualified nurse and this is the second time she has returned to Calcutta to help as a volunteer in the building where she began her life. She proudly showed me her photograph album with snaps of her comfortable home, loving parents and a party they had recently given for her. 'I was very angry a few years ago about my real identity and wanted to know who my birth parents were. I found out that they came from Madras, but now they are both dead and I don't feel they are my parents, just my Belgian family and Sister Charmian.'

It is hard not to describe Sister Charmian in emotional terms. She is gentle, sweet and utterly devoted to her charges at Shishu Bhavan. She told me with disarming honesty how she does her best to get together a small file for each child but that the information available on abandoned babies is often very slight. If she spent more time searching for records she would have less time with the babies. This work is what she has always dreamt of doing ever since she was a child in Kerala. 'When I was fifteen years old I read a newspaper article about the work Mother Teresa was doing for children and I ran away from home to join her. My parents were heartbroken. They were so worried about how I would manage because I was not used to washing my own clothes. I had had a very comfortable life. I'm now forty and it's okay, my parents can come to see me here. I have been with the Missionaries of Charity now in this home for eighteen years and sent nearly 4,000 babies for adoption. But even though this was what I most wanted I couldn't choose where to go. I never go out because something might happen. I just sleep from 3.30 a.m. for a few hours.' Would she be any better at her job with professional training? She believes not, that she has learnt all she needs to know for her job from experience.

Although there may be a huge demand for healthy babies in the Western world it is harder to place physically handicapped children. Yet Mother Teresa has even found a channel for these and the French, Swiss and Canadians have been particularly generous in providing homes for physically handicapped children from Missionaries of Charity homes. Navin Chawla, in his book about Mother Teresa, has provided a moving account of some of the Swiss families who have adopted severely handicapped children, some of them suffering from polio, others severely thalassaemic. One child had no hips and no legs and his hands turn backwards. Specialists fitted his torso into a base from which artificial legs protruded. According to Chawla, this child now lived in a 'unique family with an army of handicapped children where it mattered very little. What came across was the child's beauty, serenity and lively personality. It was as pleasurable to see him manoeuvre himself deftly up the spiral staircase to his room as it was to watch him take his first hesitant steps.'

Heart-rending though many individual cases are (and saintly though many of the adoptive parents are), that is exactly all they are. It is hard to resist the conclusion that if more attention had been paid to the mother's own health and nourishment many of these children might have been born without their disabilities. Adoption is no more a panacea for unwanted pregnancies than is abortion.

Attitudes towards abortion can be seen as the touchstone of a modern, civilised society; abortion is the issue on which Mother Teresa has willingly nailed her blue and white sari. In the last few years, abortion has become an increasingly political issue in many countries; in America, people who claim to be pro-life nonetheless commit murder – of those with different views – in the name of opposition to abortion. It is the ethical drama with which every woman of childbearing age has to grapple and many spend much time agonising over their reproductive responsibilities and duties. In the developed world it is almost impossible to give birth without having undergone various screening procedures, the purpose of which is to allow a termination if a gross abnormality is discovered. Few women who undergo an abortion do so other than as a desperate last resort, although they may be more vociferous about wanting the right to it. The Roman Catholic Church, and this is the position Mother Teresa has followed, has set itself against all abortions, believing that a fertilised embryo is a human being from the moment of conception and its right to life is absolute.* But most religions teach that human life is sacred; at issue is when 'life' becomes transformed into human life. In addition, many within the Catholic Church, as well as anti-abortionists from other religions, do recognise the validity of exceptions such as when the mother's life is in danger, when pregnancy is the result of rape (especially of a teenager) or when the child would be born with serious birth defects, for example without a cerebral cortex. The Pope and Mother Teresa do not allow for any exception, believing this would destroy their entire case.

It is all too easy to dismiss other people's religious beliefs as superstition; yet a belief system can prove helpful and, in an age of hitherto unbelievable technological possibilities, perhaps we need moral and ethical guidance more than ever before. But this is also an age which has seen some of the most barbarous inhumanity of man to man and, in comparison with this, it is a gross insult to all women to

---

* The 1992 Catechism of the Catholic Church states: 'Human life must be respected and protected absolutely from the moment of conception ... Since it must be treated from conception as a person, the embryo must be defended in its integrity, cared for, and healed as far as possible like any other human being.'

describe them as wilful killers or potential murderers for contemplating an abortion.

In her Nobel Prize-winning speech in 1979 Mother Teresa said:

> We are talking of peace, but I feel that the greatest destroyer of peace today is abortion. Because it is a direct war, a direct killing – direct murder by the mother herself. And we read in the scripture, for God says very clearly: 'Even if a mother could forget her child – I will not forget you – I have carved you in the palm of my hand.' We are all carved in the palm of His hand, so close to Him. That unborn child has been carved in the hand of God and that is what strikes me most, the beginning of that sentence that even if a mother could forget, something impossible, but even if she could forget – I will not forget you.
>
> And today, the greatest means – the greatest destroyer of peace is abortion. And we who are standing here – our parents wanted us. We would not be here if our parents would do that to us. Our children we want them, we love them but what of the millions? Many people are very, very concerned with the children of India, with the children of Africa, where quite a number die maybe of malnutrition and hunger and so on, but millions are dying deliberately by the will of the mother. And that is what is the greatest destroyer of peace today. Because if a mother can kill her own child – what is left but for me to kill you and you to kill me? – there is nothing in between.

She has said the same thing on many subsequent occasions. Yet it requires a spectacular leap of the imagination, it seems to me, to argue that a mother who submits to an abortion is encouraging 'me to kill you and you to kill me'.

In the summer of 1996, while I was researching this chapter, the abortion debate in Britain was dramatically refuelled by the news that one mother, married and middle-class, had opted for the selective termination of one twin, while another mother, who did not have the full-time support of a partner, and became pregnant with eight babies after undergoing fertility treatment, was advised that only selective abortion could save any of them. She refused the advice and in the event they all died. The media had a field day deciding which of the two mothers was the more, or less, responsible.

Under the 1967 Abortion Act in the UK, revised in 1990, a woman can obtain a legal termination if she is not more than twenty-four weeks' pregnant and if two doctors feel that continuing the pregnancy would be damaging to her physical and mental health. But today there is serious concern about how these conditions have been interpreted and whether, if what we now have is abortion on demand, that was the intention of the Act; whether it is beneficial to society in the long term. Discussion has shifted from concern about the consequences the event can have on the life of a woman to concern about the foetus. Doctors and lawyers are arguing about exactly when the foetus can first feel pain, with new research pointing in different directions. The most avid pro-lifers – an unsuitable name since those who favour the right to an abortion cannot possibly all be dubbed anti-life – have always insisted this is from the first moment of conception, while others say only when the brain and other organs have developed to the point where it can live the intellectual and spiritual life of a human being. Professor Lord Winston, one of the foremost British doctors involved in fertility research, believes that 'an invisible fertilised egg with only limited development potential is seen to have a different moral status from a formed foetus'.[4] His view would seem to have the weight of medical and legal tradition behind it, because abortion and murder have long been seen as different crimes differently punished. This is a distinction which has some basis, according to Clifford Longley, who nonetheless holds that abortion is always wrong. 'Doctors believe that between a fifth and a half of all pregnancies are terminated spontaneously in the early stages. Nobody regards this as a massive loss of human life that must be resisted by every means known to medical science as they surely would if similar numbers of children were dying shortly after they were born.'[5]

Meanwhile, the anti-abortionists appear to have seized the initiative away from those who call themselves 'pro-choice' – an equally absurd name since the value of 'choice', so obviously selfish when pitted against the sanctity of life, has never been upheld by Western philosophers as a worthy life goal. Paul Johnson believes that, once the public understands the ugly reality of what he terms the abortion industry, legal abortion at will could be ended. Writing in violently emotive terms, he recently argued that doctors in the West, operating under the laws legalising abortion, have now killed more living creatures than Hitler, Stalin and Mao Tse-tung put together. 'In our hearts we know, just as ordinary Germans knew in the early 1940s, that something horrible is going on amongst us, on a colossal scale.' William Rees-Mogg reiterated the same argument in *The Times*, but went a stage further by referring neither to a foetus nor to an unborn child. Lord Rees-Mogg talked of babies. He wrote: 'The Supreme Court has been responsible for a veritable genocide of American infants, comparable in number to the deaths for which Stalin, Hitler or Mao were responsible. Five times as many American babies have died as a result of *Roe* v. *Wade* [the US case which led to the legalising of abortion] as Jews were killed in the Holocaust.'

The comparison makes me shudder, and I am not alone. To terminate a pregnancy may not be praiseworthy, but drawing a parallel between the motives of an anguished mother and a brutal dictator who indulged his lust for violence by viciously attempting to eliminate a race seems to me entirely inappropriate. I wonder, what is the point of such a comparison? Even those who are convinced that the sanctity of life begins from the moment of conception do not normally need to bolster their arguments by referring to a foetus or newly fertilised embryo as an infant or baby. And why are there so many abortions in the US? Might it be because the access to services and advice about contraception is poor and because the climate of opinion does not encourage young people to come for help before they have a crisis? According to Marianne Haslegrave, director of the Commonwealth Medical Association, 'Middle America is opposed to contraceptive advice in schools because it still believes in an ideal – that children should not be sexually active. The reality is different.* They are, and without access to information or contraceptive services, they are turning to abortion.' In the Netherlands, where the government has for two decades provided free contraceptive services and basic sex education in schools and where all consultations with patients over the age of twelve must by law be confidential, the total pregnancy rate among thirteen- to fifteen-year-olds has dropped to 1.3 per thousand compared to 9.1 per thousand in the UK. Similarly the abortion rate, for girls under twenty is, in the Netherlands, about one-tenth of that in the UK.

---

* Those who doubt the veracity of this might be interested in the following figures for one family-planning advice centre in London during six months of 1991: 153 under-sixteen-year-olds visited the centre, 135 girls and 18 boys of whom 120 were already sexually active and the others wished to discuss the options. Of the sexually active group, fifty-one came for a pregnancy test and thirty-two came for emergency contraception, after the event.

India was, in 1952, the first country in the world to establish a National Family Planning Programme and, in 1971, one of the first to provide legalised access to safe abortion. Yet the results have been disappointing. Twenty-five years on, the Medical Termination of Pregnancy Act legislation has meant little for a majority of the country's women. World Health Organisation figures estimate that more than 20,000 Indian women die in unsafe abortions every year. Of the fifteen million illegal abortions that take place worldwide each year, four million, the highest for any country, take place in India. A 1995 Ford Foundation study put the figure even higher, at nearly seven million, which means that for every legal termination there are ten or eleven illegal ones. The study also put the spotlight on the 15,000–20,000 abortion-related deaths annually, 'a submerged iceberg of abortion-related morbidity largely ignored so far', according to Rami Chhabra, the Delhi-based writer and international consultant on population, health and women's issues who authored the report. 'Abortion is one of the most neglected public health issues in India – and women are paying a terrible price,' she said. 'Abortion was responsible for 5% of deaths in mid-80s but is now the cause of 15%. Doctors call it the double death syndrome, the mother along with the unborn child.'

As Chhabra points out, in most Western industrialised countries about half of abortions are being obtained by young, unmarried women seeking to delay the first birth. But in most developing countries abortion is most common among married women with two or more children. 'Thus the nature of the problem is radically different. Abortion is, therefore, not seen as a wilful assertion of sexual autonomy, but the woeful consequence of the lack of it; and, of effective, accessible and acceptable contraceptive services.'[6] There is a vast unmet need for contraception, evidenced by the enormous number of abortions in India, legal and illegal, which continue to occur in spite of a huge official family-planning programme and the strenuous efforts by NGOs to promote and provide family-planning services. Those who have been unable to use contraception resort to horrifyingly crude measures to induce an abortion such as a near lethal wooden stick with cotton wool at one end, twigs with rags soaked in arsenious oxide, arsenic sulphide and red lead, boiling water combined with acidic solutions, abdominal massage which cracks the foetus out by force, turpentine, cantharide oil, potassium permanganate tablets, roots and leaf veins of local creepers smeared with opium or savin, a concoction in oil form to promote menstrual flow which leads to death from intestinal infection.

This grisly list provides only too graphic proof that Indian women are in desperate need of, but failing to find, adequate advice on family planning. I have spoken to family-planning experts in London, Delhi and Calcutta who all tell me the same thing: that, as long as women remain uneducated about contraception, abortions, legal or illegal, will continue unabated. Those who wish to abolish abortion, and I do not know any woman who would not like to see the need for it reduced, must first tackle contraception and its twin, education.

The position of the Roman Catholic Church on birth control was set out in Pope Paul VI's encyclical *Humanae Vitae* (1968), which banned all artificial contraception on the ground that 'each and every marriage act must remain open to the transmission of life'. Mother Teresa has said on numerous occasions that she would never allow a family which had practised contraception to adopt one of the orphans cared for by the Missionaries of Charity. The starkness of the pronouncement has shocked many, including Catholics. Frances Kissling, president of the Washington-based organisation Catholics for a Free Choice, told me she was 'appalled' by her comments at the February 1995 Washington Prayer Breakfast. 'She baldly stated that she will not give a child for adoption to a couple that uses contraception because they cannot love freely and unconditionally. It has long been her practice to deny babies to US couples because she wants to create a demand for babies in the US that will help make abortion illegal here.'[7]

The Presidential Prayer Breakfast, which started out in a small, predominantly Protestant way during the Second World War, has grown to become one of the social highlights of the Washington year. It is held in the largest hotel ballroom in the capital, the Hilton, which caters for 2,000 guests, and is broadcast across the nation. Anyone with any political connections or social ambitions is there and in 1995 Mother Teresa, as the star guest, ensured a particularly high demand for tickets from those hoping to hear some of the wonderful stories about the work she has done worldwide.

After the expensively clad guests had munched their way through the breakfast, declined as usual by Mother Teresa, she climbed the podium to speak. She then addressed the audience for some forty-five minutes, approximately twenty minutes longer than agreed, which sent the organisers into a flurry as there were six speakers to get through, including readings from the Old and New Testament by judges and senators, and the schedule was tight. But throughout the forty-five minutes there was no discussion of her work, other than peripherally, as she chose to talk entirely about her opposition to contraception and abortion. President Clinton and his wife Hillary, vociferously in favour of a woman's right to both these, sat, like many others in the audience, stony-faced.

One observer recalled: 'She started off by explaining that "as I am the pencil of God, I know what God likes and does not like. He does not like abortion and contraception." She was extremely militant in tone and took the view that anyone who thinks differently was damned. This is not a great mind at work and there is something offensive to anyone who thinks differently. It was awful because she was a guest of a different-thinking President and Hillary's pro-choice views are well known.' This guest at the breakfast, a senior member of the Washington establishment, commented: 'Many others in the audience clearly felt that this was arrogance to the point of rudeness, but there were also some, I know, who felt a deep appreciation of what she was saying.'[8] Arguably, such courage to speak in the face of known opponents of her views is a clear display by Mother Teresa that her spiritual inner life matters more than anything else to her; worldly reactions are of no concern. Is this flawed saintliness, perfect saintliness or just difficult saintliness that knows no compromises?

But why has Mother Teresa singled out families who have practised contraception as unfit to adopt when perhaps they were doing so to screen for a life-threatening or painful genetic disorder yet longed to care for children who needed a loving home? Why has she not said instead that no family which has a known record of violence, such as the Albanian one I was told about, be allowed to adopt? Why has she not said that only families which can provide a suitable cultural and ethnic background, such as called for by the UN Convention on Human Rights, be allowed to adopt?

One of the major problems faced by millions of women in the developing world is the risk of contracting a sexually transmitted disease (STD) if they have unprotected sex with an infected partner. Condoms in this case are not merely a form of contraception but may be the only barrier preventing them from contracting a deadly disease, or becoming infertile, the outcome of many STDs. An infertile woman is of little worth in many such countries and she has lost her basic right to reproduce. For Mother Teresa to select only those families who have used contraception, which many would argue is a responsible way to behave in countries already struggling to feed, clothe, educate and look after their existing populations, as unfit to adopt seems unduly blinkered to many of her friends and critics alike. The linkage is flawed because it appears she is spinning children's lives on the wheel of dogma rather than looking at the needs of the children themselves.

Mother Teresa told Malcolm Muggeridge that there could never be too many children in India because God always provides. 'He provides for the flowers and the birds and for everything in the world that he has created. And those little children are his life. There can never be enough.' Charming though that is, it somehow misses the point. Of course, once children exist everything must be done to look after them. But, sadly, there is not always the provision for them and those who worry about a world where there may be too many children are looking at ways to prevent those not yet born from entering the world. Ten years after this comment Mother Teresa admitted to a *Newsweek* reporter that overpopulation was a serious problem. Her solution, which was natural family planning, involves either counting beads or temperature taking with graphs in order to ascertain the time of the month when a woman can have sexual intercourse without the risk of pregnancy. Graphs are obviously out of the question for illiterate women and most Indian females over the age of seven are illiterate – 61 per cent nationally in 1991, but in several northern states female illiteracy is higher than 75 per cent. Other methods of natural family planning recommended by the Missionaries of Charity include abstinence; 'but how many men can practise that? We're not all Mahatma Gandhi,' retorted one family-planning expert. Mother Teresa says that her sisters are trained in teaching natural family planning to the poor. 'And the best teachers are those who have taken vows of chastity. They can inspire others by the sacrifice they make for their love of all humanity.'[9] Clearly, however, natural birth control has a high failure rate and relies on the relationship with the partner. It has little relevance for prostitutes.

I visited a clinic in the heart of Calcutta's red-light district, Bowbazar, which helps to improve the health and social welfare of Calcutta's sex workers and their children, run by Dr Biral Mullick, a large, kind-hearted gynaecologist. The clinic is funded by the Humanity Association, one of India's oldest NGOs founded in 1924 by Dr Mullick's father under the guidance of Mahatma Gandhi with the initial intent of eradicating untouchability. Over the years the Humanity Association has provided a wide array of educational, health and social services in West Bengal and in 1979 helped establish the Indian Rural Medical Association to train rural health workers. But today Dr Mullick's work centres on an outreach programme for commercial sex workers which involves organising small classes for prostitutes on basic literacy and health awareness about AIDS and other STDs as well as an educational and activity-based programme for their children. More than 60 per cent of his patients are scheduled caste and all treatment is free.

Dr Mullick worked alongside Mother Teresa in the middle 1950s, collecting clothes and supplies for her organisation. 'But when she understood that we were promoting family planning she was very angry and disassociated herself from us,' he told me. Dr Mullick is sceptical of the success of Mother Teresa's natural family-planning methods as many girls come to him for an abortion saying that they tried to use the method they had been taught by the Missionaries of Charity. Some of these girls are extremely young and Dr Mullick himself has had to give an abortion to a ten-year-old girl. Sex education for men and women is the most important aspect of the Humanity Association's work and they have pioneered a programme which, by recruiting women from among the commercial sex workers to train as teachers, incorporates role-modelling and peer education.

There is widespread but not universal agreement that India's biggest problem is its ever-increasing population, notwithstanding the valiant efforts of successive governments and NGOs. The population growth is mostly explained by the sharp decline in the death rate while the birth rate has decreased only slightly. Today, the population of India is almost 1,000 million – 949.6 million in 1996 – with an estimated doubling time of thirty-seven years. India will soon overtake China as the most populous country in the world. The high rate of population growth has consistently tended to nullify the benefits of growth in the

Indian economy (3.5 per cent per decade since 1951) and made it difficult to bring about improvements in living standards. In the three decades since 1965 population control has therefore been treated as a national priority and a multi-pronged approach to family planning was evolved which by 1985–6 was costing a massive Rs 651 crore (£186 million) annually. Some 513,000 nurses, midwives, health visitors and health guides are employed to help implement the policies.

Initially, the contraceptives offered were the conventional ones: condoms, diaphragms, jellies and foam tablets; in 1956 sterilisation was introduced and then the IUD (intra-uterine device). By 1966, while officially promoting a free choice of methods, special emphasis was laid on sterilisation with high cash incentives given. But this policy had to be abandoned after Mrs Gandhi's brash younger son Sanjay, during the 1975 Emergency, encouraged forced sterilisations.

Why have the family-planning associations in India not had more success in getting their message about contraception across? According to Mrs Sudha Tewari, managing director of the Parivar Seva Sanstha, which runs the popular Marie Stopes clinics, the scandal of the forced sterilisation programme left many politicians scared to take up the issue 'for the sake of their own political skins'. Her organisation gets only 5 per cent of its budget from the government; the rest they have to raise themselves. 'The government budget for family planning may appear high but it is spent on maintaining the administrative infrastructure, not on the NGOs in the field who could be much more productive, and many women live too far away from any facilities. Family-planning advice is meant to be free but the availability is not always there. Sometimes women have to travel for two or three days to reach a clinic. According to a 1994 government survey, 20 per cent of families want no more children but nonetheless are not practising family planning because they cannot access help.'

Mrs Tewari is pessimistic about the future. 'The whole system is breaking down because of overpopulation, roads, transportation, schools, hospitals, everything, and it all has an effect on the environment; we sometimes go for five or six hours without water.' In addition, lack of contraception was having a disastrous effect on the health of Indian women, 40 per cent of whom live below the poverty line, and on the health of babies. 'Too many children are born when the mother is too young or too old. Indian women are very self-sacrificing and will give away the last scrap of food rather than have any herself. But if the women are undernourished the babies are born with a negative start, physical disabilities and an underdeveloped brain.' In India the child mortality rate is 85 per thousand live births but even more disastrous are the annual 450 maternal deaths per hundred thousand, which the Cairo International Conference on Population and Development (ICPD) 1994 has said should be reduced to 75 per hundred thousand. In the UK the figure is 3 or 4 per hundred thousand. 'At the moment I don't see how we can achieve that,' Mrs Tewari said. She is convinced that if measures are not taken in the remaining years of this century which allow for the population to be informed, to be concerned and to choose, there will have to be coercion in the next.

Mother Teresa has often been criticised for her lack of sensitivity in opposing contraception in a host country whose government is trying desperately to reduce the population and for declaring as fervently as she does that there can never be too many children. Of course, no one is seriously arguing that in India, where only 2 per cent of the population is Christian, rural Indian women are not using contraception because they have heard Mother Teresa oppose it, and in any case Muslims and Hindus too have religious misgivings about abortions and some forms of contraception. Many Indian parents in rural areas still see a high fertility rate as an insurance against high infant mortality. For poor people, children are an asset; by seven or eight they can contribute to family life by collecting firewood, tending animals and watching younger children, which frees the adults to earn money outside the house. But Mrs Tewari insists: 'Mother Teresa's pronouncements do have a significant if indirect influence ... What she says affects our funding, and NGO funding generally, and policy decisions at a wider international level and so this does filter down to affect the rural person indirectly ... For six years from 1985 to 1991 we suffered because America under the Republicans cut funds to countries and organisations which allowed abortion. Oh definitely, Mother Teresa has an influence.'[10]

Clearly if poor rural women are to get access to quality advice on reproductive health many far-reaching changes in their lives are required, all of which need funding. One of the most dramatically thought-provoking occasions for me in India in 1995 was a specially convened meeting of a women's group some three hours outside Calcutta in South 24 Parganas, the southern part of West Bengal. It was a difficult journey. After two days of torrential rain continuously flooding the tracks across the paddy fields some of them had become impassable. Nonetheless we abandoned the car, changed to an auto-rickshaw, and when that became impossible walked through the mud to our destination, a bamboo- and straw-thatched building with a mud floor and beautifully stencilled walls. As soon as I entered, some 200 women from fifteen scattered villages burst into spontaneous song: 'We must solve our own problems, we will prepare our daughters,' they rejoiced. One by one they stood up and told me, through an interpreter, about the huge strides they were making in their lives, learning about money and their legal rights and ensuring that their daughters would have the same education as their sons. Their hair gleaming, their saris gorgeous, and smiling through their pan-stained teeth, they told me how they had rescued one ill-treated wife from her in-laws, another from a drunken husband. One woman explained that the worst problem they had all faced was getting their husbands' agreement to attend self-help meetings in the first place. 'Before, no one was allowed into the home of another, now we go anywhere. We are not afraid and our granddaughters will not be exploited.' When they asked me the worst problem faced by women in my country nothing I could say seemed relevant; I was just thankful I did not have to make that long journey across the paddy fields every day of my life.

The women's meetings were started in 1985 by NISHTHA, an organisation helped by grants from Oxfam, Action Aid, Goal and other international funding agencies, whose aim was to make village women aware of their rights and status in society and to help them become economically self-dependent. By any standard the educational situation of Indian women as indicated by their literacy levels is appalling. The villagers in South 24 Parganas had no proper access to education and health services and were mostly subjected to centuries of superstition, fatalism and dependence on men. NISHTHA's ten-year health-education programme has resulted in 90 per cent immunisation of children in the project area and covered themes such as basic hygiene, locally available, cheap and nutritious food, common diseases, importance of weighing and food charts for children. All this is taught with a variety of different visual aids such as posters, flash cards and photographs. One course on offer takes women to the police station, post office and bank so that they are familiar with and not intimidated by these institutions. There is also advice on pre- and post-natal care but contraception and women's reproductive health are not specifically taught; the idea is that understanding of the importance of these will follow automatically and without coercion once the fundamentals of women's lives have changed. Where this has already happened, among India's urban middle classes, the birth rate is already falling rapidly. Valuable though the work of NISHTHA is, there are doubts whether India can afford to wait for a general increase in the standard of living to bring down the birth rate.

Robert McNamara, one of the world's most vociferous campaigners on the need to reduce global population, understands that first the status of women and especially their educational levels must be tackled. McNamara, who has been a long-standing champion of Mother Teresa, sees no contradiction between her stance on birth control and his insistence, stated unequivocally in New Delhi in 1992, when giving the Rajiv Gandhi Memorial Lecture, that 'the rapid growth of population is one of the greatest barriers to economic growth and social well being of [the people] of our member states. That was my view in 1968. It is my view today.' One of the problems outlined by McNamara in the lecture was the lack of adequate agricultural land. 'India is already at the margin of its cultivable land and the scope for expanding the irrigated area is much less than in the past. In sum, at the projected population levels, India is likely to face food-production problems similar to those which will confront other developing countries. As we move further and further into the future, the likelihood of meeting the Indian food requirements will become ever more doubtful.' He went on: 'A culture of poverty is being transmitted down the generations, sacrificing human resources and impeding social mobility. It is a disgrace that we in the developed countries as well as the elite within the developing nations permit such a situation to exist.'

Analysing what should be done, however, McNamara stated his view that 'population control' in India has been too narrowly identified with family planning. While stressing that the family-planning programmes may need strengthening, he said that an over-emphasis here had meant that India had failed to give adequate attention to other factors, which also affect fertility, such as early marriage and education. Early marriage in India was not only preventing a more rapid fertility decline, it was also putting the young brides at high risk of damage to their health from premature pregnancy and putting their infants at high risk of early death. 'It is difficult to exaggerate the importance of the links between education and the greater acceptance of contraception and lower infant mortality.'

There is, however, a lonely voice prepared to argue publicly that there are no adverse effects of population growth whatsoever. Lord Bauer, a professor of economics at London University, maintains that the so-called population explosion is a blessing and that the world's most densely populated countries such as Hong Kong, Singapore and Malaysia are among the most prosperous. Prosperity, he says, depends on people's conduct, not their numbers.[11] Peter Bauer argues that the 'problem' of population growth is an invented one for which remedies then have to be produced. One of these, of course, is contraception. 'But in societies where contraception is widely practised there will be many childless couples who take no interest in the future and this leads to instability and unhappiness.'[12] Bauer concedes that once women in developing countries are exposed to the Western media and Western contacts they will probably choose to have fewer children; he nonetheless thinks the debate about population growth has nothing to do with women's rights.

I think it has much to do with women's rights and children's rights, especially a woman's right to have control over her own fertility; a woman's right to be educated; a woman's right to have access to good healthcare; and, one of the most fundamental human rights, a woman's right to reproduce, not to mention a child's right to be fed and loved. Many poor rural women, and not only those in India, have none of these rights and for them the only readily available means of birth control is often an illegal and highly dangerous abortion. Not one of the family-planning counsellors I have spoken to endorses abortion as a method of contraception; they all see it as a last resort where information on contraception has failed.

Today the emphasis of the population debate has subtly changed to examine first and foremost the needs of women and children, rather than whether or not the world can sustain very high population levels, although if the West lowered consumption rates, improved distribution and put greater emphasis on sharing that would help too. Many women in India will go on having more children than they want, many of them dying or producing deformed children in the process, as long as the underlying problems of poverty, degradation and lack of education remain. It is now recognised that the economic, social and medical wellbeing of the whole country depends to a large degree on the health of women, and family planning is the essential link in various aspects of overall development goals. But family planning does not mean telling women how many children they must have. One counsellor explained to me her personal philosophy: 'Our advice may not be religious but it is very moral. I think it is moral not to harm people or to harm yourself either. I don't think it's moral to have unprotected sex and say if I get pregnant I'll have an abortion.'[13]

CHAPTER TWELVE

POLITICS

On Friday, 17 May 1996, immediately after national elections in India had returned the BJP party to power and the political horse-trading had begun in earnest, Mother Teresa called on the new Prime Minister, Atal Behari Vajpayee, at his private residence. She was accompanied by senior churchmen but no details of the conversation were released. While many deals and alliances were being frantically conducted behind the scenes it was her picture, greeting the new Prime Minister, which the Asian Age considered front-page material.

Mother Teresa has always insisted she does not involve herself in politics and in India, a country fiercely proud of its secularity, this matters. But at the same time she has maintained very close relations with both local and national politicians, many of whom have courted her. In Calcutta this started in the late 1950s with Dr B. C. Roy's initial endorsement of the unknown nun. But it continued long after 1967, when the communists gained control of West Bengal, as one of the most extraordinary political friendships of modern times took root. On closer inspection it is not extraordinary at all: both Mother Teresa and Jyoti Basu, leader of the CPI(M), the Marxist branch of the Communist Party of India in West Bengal, are supreme pragmatists. She may be emotionally opposed to communism and he intellectually opposed to religion but for twenty years each has played a significant part in maintaining the success of the other. Basu would like to persuade foreign capitals to invest in West Bengal. He makes regular trips abroad, especially to London and understands what a revered spiritual icon Mother Teresa is in the West.

Jyoti Basu was a doctor's son whose first education was at the hands of the Loreto nuns. He was then taught by Jesuits at Calcutta's prestigious St Xavier's College and, after university, went to London, where he read law. It was there that he first became influenced by communism, with a Western liberal tinge, and this led, on his return to India, to a spell in prison. The imprisonment completed the politicisation of Jyoti Basu, who has cultivated an image of brisk asceticism and self-control and has retained power in four elections during one of the most difficult periods in the state's history. He is neat and well preserved, appears humourless to the point of taciturnity, and does not look his age, eighty-four at the time of writing, almost the same as Mother Teresa. It is no coincidence that the experiences of his formative years were similar to hers. In giving Mother Teresa land grants he has gone out of his way to support her, he has publicly greeted her on birthdays and given her work public endorsement by opening new homes for her.

One of the biggest challenges faced by Basu's state government is of course Calcutta and its twelve million inhabitants. In 1961 the Calcutta Metropolitan Authority (CMA) was responsible for providing accommodation for about 77 per cent of the urban population of West Bengal. Spread over both banks of the Hooghly, Calcutta is still the dominant urban centre of a vast hinterland as well as the industrial heartland. About 90 per cent of India's jute-making capacity and 60 per cent of its rubber, footwear, wagon-building, tyre and tube industries are located in and around Calcutta. Throughout India there has been a general move away from the countryside towards the cities, as the desperate undertake the usually illusory search for jobs and wealth. Yet for many pavement or slum dwellers, however squalid their living conditions, life in a city is frequently better than starvation in a village, especially during the monsoon season. And so they keep on coming.

Calcutta has many problems common to all Indian cities, including insufficient road space, sewerage and drainage, frequent disruption of power supply, infighting among politicians and widespread corruption, as well as some which are uniquely its own, such as various influxes of refugees in their millions from neighbouring Bangladesh, which it has done its best bravely to absorb. But Basu, although criticised for not doing more – he could, for example, have located the tea industry outside the city or had some warehouses moved to North Bengal at the very least – has overseen both major land reforms and some rural development, as well as urban planning, in an attempt to lure people back to the countryside. While formally giving his allegiance to communist doctrine, in reality Basu 'has articulated a philosophy of socialism which is a complete confirmation of the central government's programme of liberalisation and economic reform', according to India's Ambassador to the UK since April 1991, Dr L. M. Singhvi.[1]

During Basu's stewardship the urban population within the CMA has been reduced to 64 per cent, with projections that it will be down to 50 per cent by 2021. Both the power and the traffic situations, while appalling by Western standards, have at least been checked and three innovative projects have been completed which are a tribute to Basu's determination to drag Calcutta into the twenty-first century. One is the Calcutta Metro system, the first in South Asia, even though the marshy ground on which the city was built was far from ideal for such a venture. It is nonetheless clean, efficient and cheap. The second is the new terminal building at Calcutta airport, which makes a dramatic impression on travellers prepared for the filth and squalor they have been told to expect there, and the third is a twin bridge over the Hooghly, the Vidyasagar Setu, which stands comparison to many contemporary landmark bridges. In addition, there is a big petrochemical plant with ancillary industries being created at Haldia, a hundred miles outside Calcutta, which could create employment for 100,000 to 150,000 people. The biggest project of all, to set up New Calcutta, a township between the airport and Salt Lake City, is the sort of visionary large-scale dream that could significantly relieve pressures on the old city. Still in the planning stages, New Calcutta should accommodate half a million people and play a key role in the regeneration of West Bengal in the next century. But these plans require a massive investment.

Why should Mother Teresa's ability to get on with, some would say use, a man like Jyoti Basu be criticised? She, and therefore her constituency, the poor, have derived enormous benefits: land, or buildings, have been given, publicity gained and potential difficulties smoothed. Of course, her canny ability to create good working relationships with powerful leaders, not all of whom are politicians, shows that she is not entirely 'otherworldly'. But arguably this world-liness enhances rather than diminishes her reputation. While I was in Calcutta there was a story running in the newspapers about a piece of land having been sold to Mother Teresa by someone who did not have a legal right to the land. Once it was established that the government owned the land and wanted Mother Teresa to move she refused and there was stalemate. Eventually the state government offered her another piece of land and a compromise was suggested whereby she would vacate one part of the land and forty-six families would be accommodated in two-storey structures somewhere else, for which the state would pay. This ability to negotiate is not a characteristic normally associated with a nun, but how lucky that the dispossessed have someone to speak for them. How important is it to renounce all contact with the material world in order to be considered saintly? Why be surprised, explains Sister Cyril, IBVM, a Loreto nun who runs the Rainbow day school in one of the most blighted areas of Calcutta, near Sealdah station, that she is 'a very powerful person? You can't be the founder of such a large congregation of sisters by being soft and gentle. Obviously there is a great deal of strength in her, a resilience, a great deal of shrewdness and wisdom, which is part of her whole set-up. She has very clear ideas on how her Congregation is to be for one, she does not want a Congregation that can easily be taken over by the rich or the highly sophisticated.'[2]

There was a time, not so long ago, when India treated foreign charities and missionaries with suspicion, believing that they were trying to exploit poverty or had a secret agenda, which was to convert. This distrust found voice in the 1976 Foreign Contributions Regulation Act (FCRA), which requires all charities wishing to receive foreign funds to be registered; this is to prevent foreign money being used to fund sectarian or terrorist activities. In effect it is a law which slows things down, provides more opportunities for bribes and is the bane of most charities. Once the organisation is registered it must be audited every six months. Many people question the wisdom of such a law since companies can in any case bring money into India through the Reserve Bank of India without going through the FCRA. Part of the antipathy towards Jack Preger, and the difficulty he has had in being officially registered, is simply explained by a dislike of foreigners stepping in to do what Indians feel they can do themselves. Both he and Mother Teresa have been criticised for encouraging ever more have-nots to Calcutta.

There is also a sense of dignity and self-respect among most Indians, a conviction that, free of their colonial past, they could resolve their own problems. As a former Foreign Minister of India, S. K. Singh, explained, foreign aid agencies often complicated matters. 'I've been in situations where outsiders came rushing in to help and one always found one was coping all right until the outsiders came and needed interpreters and cars and telegrams. One was spending too much time accepting their marginal help.'[3] Why, in the advertisements for Oxfam or Christian Aid, was it always an Indian or perhaps an African child with a glycerine tear in its eye, asked Singh, but never a Chinese or Indonesian, for example? Why was India the butt of all induced sympathy?

This feeling erupted in Calcutta during the making of the film City of Joy, when there were demonstrations led by the CPI(M), who resented the way the West portrayed their city as a hellhole while the hero of the film was a white man. For a time the Calcutta high court even had filming stopped on the grounds that it was 'against the honour and respect of the Indian people'. Uttpal Dutt, an actor, director and member of the CPI(M), said the portrayal had 'nothing to do with Calcutta as it is ... the poor are being treated as a commodity to be exploited and used'. Buddhader Bhattacharya, Information Minister in the CPI(M) government, was strongly opposed to the film being made claiming that it encouraged 'the political philosophy of those who think that anyone living in a third world country must be a beggar, consumptive, communist or prostitute'.

Roland Joffé, who directed the film, hit back at his critics, labelling them bureaucrats, blind to the poverty surrounding them and irritated when reminded of it. He accused the CPI(M) of being 'very confused in their politics towards poverty. They are Indian but colonised by Marxism, an outside force invented by a nineteenth-century Russian Jew living in London, honed in Russia. And it's a colonial movement because it was brought here by the British who claimed they were fighting colonialism. But they see it only in the way they are trained to see it and therefore it is not surprising when people bring a camera to bear on poverty which they claim they have got rid of.' Ian Smith,

Joffé's right-hand man, recognised the pain of a city that felt it was being exploited and misjudged by the world. 'Every image it threw up was of the black hole and Mother Teresa. It seemed to confirm in the eyes of the world the very thing Calcutta wanted to get away from: the stereotypes ... we were sticking our fingers right into the wounds,' Smith explained.[4]

Bengali views on Mother Teresa, as on everything else, cover the entire spectrum and one of the most endearing traits of the Bengali is his never-ending desire to talk, hence the proliferation of the coffee shops. Here he will tell you with pride about the flowering of the universities, the huge number of newspapers and booksellers and the traditions of his native Bengali literature, culture and cuisine, especially Bengali sweets, the production of which is a miniature work of art. At one extreme is Dr Aroup Chatterjee, the Calcutta doctor now living in London who had agitated for the film *Hell's Angel* to be made. But Chatterjee was deeply disappointed with this; it did not, he felt, approach the subject from the point of view of Calcutta, which was his concern. In October 1995 Chatterjee returned home to find out and record for himself what effect Mother Teresa had on those most in need. He positioned himself on Bridge Number Four, one of the bridges in Calcutta regularly scheduled for widening, which shelters several rows of slum dwellers on either side. To date, nothing has been done about widening the road space. Prem Dan, Mother Teresa's huge home, principally for the mentally handicapped, is in the shadow of these slums. Over a period of days Chatterjee took his video camera and talked to the largely Muslim slum dwellers about Mother Teresa. A month later he invited me to watch his film.

Fakir, a butcher who has lived for four years in a slum on Bridge Number Four, said, 'Mother Teresa, I've never heard of her ... Free food from Mother Teresa? You can't just queue up for that, you need a card. I can't get one.' Next, Chatterjee asked two men sitting against a wall very close to the building itself if they received food from Prem Dan. 'No,' they said. 'We hear that she helps people but it's a card problem. We don't know how you do it.' Chatterjee spoke to a tea-stall owner, to a man from Bihar who tans leather and to beggars, and the answers were all the same. No, they do not receive help from the Missionaries of Charity because you need a card. A van driver who had lived in the same slums for twenty years said, 'They've never helped us. They only help Christians. She has special provisions for Christians.'

When Chatterjee took his video camera to the streets of central Calcutta and asked beggars outside the Oberoi Hotel what they knew of Mother Teresa it was clear that misconceptions were rife. One leper insisted there was no use asking her for help as she wouldn't help people from Andhra Pradesh, while another in a wheelchair said Mother Teresa only helps people from Orissa. A dwarf, begging on the Lower Circular Road, insisted he had never heard of Mother Teresa even though he was almost outside the Mother House as he said it.

Chatterjee maintains that the attitudes of the desperate pavement and slum dwellers, who apparently have no knowledge of Mother Teresa, are vivid testimony to the inflated nature of the Teresan myth. I'm not so sure, although it is an interesting experiment since so often we hear the views of the expatriate Europeans and even of the middle-class Bengalis but rarely those of the poor themselves. The writer Amit Chaudhuri, who spends half the year in Calcutta, recalls a film about Mother Teresa in the early 1980s with 'a large number of affluent, admiring British people in it in close proximity to Mother Teresa and the latter smiling and saying more than once to the camera: "We must sell love" ... I couldn't see in what way, except the most superficial, these affluent and photogenic Europeans had anything to do with poor in Calcutta.'[4]

In any publicity concerning Mother Teresa the poor usually feature, speechless, surrounding her with an adoring gaze. The truth, as ever, is more complicated, as Dharani Ghosh, a senior columnist at the *Statesman*, explained to me. Ghosh is a kurta- and dhoti-wearing Bengali, proud of his Jesuit education in the city. These days he mostly writes book reviews of great erudition, but he laughs a lot as he peers through his thick bifocals and he, too, evidently loves Calcutta. He remembers a time when Mother Teresa was much more in evidence on Calcutta streets, and could be seen waiting at bus stops, walking along or talking to beggars. But these days, he concludes, she is overly protected by her sisters.

Ghosh says: 'Frankly speaking I've never seen anyone who actually died on the streets. It's just not part of the average Bengali's existence, yet the idea has captured the imagination of some and the rise of Mother Teresa in the public esteem has been at the expense of Calcutta.

I don't get offended by that, but I'm puzzled. By what standards is Calcutta being judged? I'm not saying Calcutta is a good city but if people are shocked at the squalor they should have screamed in the fifties and sixties or even forties when the first refugees came. Calcutta is a decent, well-planned city, no worse than Bombay or Delhi, and compared to them it has a very low crime rate. Also, the cost of living is not high, which is a good thing because you can live cheaply and cover the city by metro for five rupees – that's unthinkable in any other city.'

Ghosh believes that most Bengalis are indifferent to Mother Teresa. 'They don't care either way. They just take her for granted because she has been here such a long time ... they see her as a creation of the newspapers ... We must remember that Mother Teresa is not needed. Calcutta does not need Mother Teresa, or it needs everyone, including me!' Ghosh laughed. He explained that, first, one had to understand the Hindu attitude towards beggary. 'Everyone should be a beggar at some time. God wants you to beg and it is a necessity and therefore should not be evil, but the West will not grasp this. I don't think Mother Teresa understands that ... because when you give alms you should be humble. I get the impression she is "doing something" for the poor and therefore this makes her patronising and irrelevant to the Indian ethos.' The poverty problem was so vast that only the government could solve it and nothing Mother Teresa, or any individual, did could change it. 'Why is she always called Mother Teresa of Calcutta?' he pondered. 'This strange city will survive by itself.'[5]

Given this level of xenophobia, how has Mother Teresa by and large avoided criticism? According to Dr Singhvi, Mother Teresa is accepted because she is serving humanity in general, not India in particular: 'She has become one with India by participating in the universal ethos of sacrifice. She is of India in spirit.' He went on: 'I believe that wherever she worked she would have created an exemplary cloak of goodness and would have been received with gratitude, but India was one country where a sense of universalism is part of its heritage and cultural legacy.' Dr Singhvi insists that arguing about how many people Mother Teresa actually helps is beside the point. 'To quantify Mother Teresa's work is to belittle it ... to quantify it is a peculiar Western failing which really lets us into the void of statistics, which mean nothing.' Had she not been there, would the government have done more? He believes not, 'and even if it had, it would not have ennobled us. The government has social and economic responsibilities which she does not have; what she is doing is creating empathy with her fellow human beings.' That is the reason, Dr Singhvi believes, why Mother Teresa is the pride of Calcutta, part and parcel of the city, why the newspapers treat her as a celebrity who is both trusted and respected and, relishing the presence of a Nobel Laureate among them, mark her birthdays, increasingly, with photo-opportunities or special supplements.

There are those in Calcutta who believe that hers has been a comforting presence for any ruling body because she does not ask awkward questions of them. She accepts what she finds without criticism and is therefore not simply tolerated but welcomed as an endorsement, on the international stage, of what the government is doing. One of her former sisters described this as 'colluding with wealth' and said it was a major reason compelling her to leave the Order. 'Mother Teresa makes good friends with all the leaders but it's not doing anything except giving them credence ... The sisters are with the people at grass roots but if you're not taught how to grapple with the issues how can you fight them?'[7] Mother Teresa does not insist, as other charities do, that poverty must be eliminated. She believes there will always be poor people and they enable the Missionaries of Charity (and others) to demonstrate Christ's love. 'That is what we have been created for – to proclaim Christ's love, to proclaim his presence.' She has said repeatedly that hers is an organisation not of social workers but of women religious. When she talks about material poverty it is not to describe it as a ghastly state to be avoided and overcome but as a perfect state which the Missionaries of Charity should strive to attain; after all, 'Our Lord on the cross possessed nothing.' To become poor like Christ, that is to choose poverty, is the aim, rather than examining why there is poverty and looking at ways of overcoming it. 'The poor are great people and we owe them deep gratitude. If they did not accept us then we would not exist as Missionaries of Charity ... To be equal to the poor we choose to be poor, like them in everything except destitution. Each of us has given our word to God to follow Christ in poverty.'

Mother Teresa explained clearly what should be the vocation of those who choose to follow her when she recounted a conversation she once had with a missionary brother. 'This brother really loves the lepers,' she said. 'He came one day after he had had some difficulty with his superior. He said to me, "I love the lepers. I want to be with them. I want to work for them. My vocation is to be with the lepers." I said to him, "Brother, you are making a mistake. Your vocation is not to work for the lepers. Your vocation is to belong to Jesus. The work for the lepers is only your love for Christ in action and, therefore, it makes no difference to anyone as long as you are doing it to Him, as long as you are doing it with Him. That's all that matters. That is the completion of your vocation, of your belonging to Christ." '[8]

The italics are mine; I find the phrase nearly impossible to grapple with. Can she really have intended what the phrase appears to mean: that this man's loving work with the lepers makes no difference to anyone? A Jesuit I consulted for advice implored me to remember that English was not her native language, that she was not a theologian and that her very simplicity and faith that all good things come from God was what made things happen.

In reality the Missionaries of Charity are involved in social work, which to some observers may appear similar to that which many NGOs undertake. But her aims are quite different, and this has helped her relations with those in authority. Some NGO leaders, desperate to buy land in the slums which they complain the authorities won't sell them, look enviously at Mother Teresa's easy relationship with the government. Mother Teresa has Jyoti Basu eating out of her hand, they say. In West Bengal since 1989 there is an additional restriction on NGOs wishing to fund a project, a restriction not on the donor but on the recipient, where any proposal has to be cleared by the Social Welfare Fund of the West Bengal government. Some major charities, like the UK-based Oxfam, find it so hard to get their proposals accepted that they have almost given up working in West Bengal. 'It is highly subjective, personal and corrupt. Not all proposals are accepted and we are not comfortable with the ones that are,' an Oxfam worker in Calcutta told me. As a result Oxfam has almost no projects in West Bengal at the moment and has turned its attention to other states. Oxfam was, from 1959, one of the first major overseas development agencies to support the Missionaries of Charity. At first this was on a small scale, for example blankets were sent to the Home for the Dying and leprosy drugs and vitamins were bought. In the latter part of a

1960s Oxfam agreed to provide funds to buy new premises for a Home for Abandoned Children in Calcutta – a grant of £16,667 was approved in 1970–1, but suitable buildings could not be found at the time and the grant was cancelled when Mother Teresa made other arrangements and said she would not require its help.

In 1976–7 Oxfam once again became involved with the work of the Missionaries of Charity by supporting a number of their projects around the country. Mostly, their assistance involved maintaining the fabric of dilapidated buildings rapidly falling into disrepair, providing wire mosquito netting on nursery windows or fitting doors to cupboards. In 1977, Oxfam was asked to support a Home for the Dying and Destitute in Howrah established by the Missionary Brothers along similar lines to Mother Teresa's original home at Kalighat. Howrah Town is the crowded, dirty, commercial and manufacturing section of Calcutta. Its station is the main rail terminal for services from Calcutta to the rest of India and it inevitably attracts the poor, the beggars and the dying who hope to scrape an existence from the benevolence of the travellers who pass through in enormous numbers. The single-storey building at Kalighat can take up to 200 patients, many of whom are collected from Howrah station by Mother Teresa's sisters. The aim was to provide for the immediate physical needs of the people on the borderline of death. However, Brother Ferdinand, in requesting Oxfam's support, said that they could only accommodate forty patients at the present time since they lacked beds. They asked Oxfam to pay for fifty metal beds for the Howrah at a cost of £17 each.

Oxfam's field director for East India, while recommending that Oxfam agree to the request, nonetheless struck a cautionary note. 'This is a straightforward welfare and charity project in the tradition of the Missionaries of Charity. One may have reservations about the long-term usefulness of such projects and wonder whether the brothers' energy and dedication could not go into more constructive work. These thoughts tend to fade into insignificance, however, when one sees an old man who had been admitted to the home. His hands with which he has been trying to beg are covered in sores and pus and he is barely able to move his limbs. The brothers are carefully washing him. As Mother Teresa says, "What this man needs most in his last days or months is probably what he has never had before – love." '[9]

However, within the last six years, as the central government of

Narashimo Rao embarked on unprecedented policy reforms and economic liberalisation, foreign investment was, almost for the first time
since Independence, warmly welcomed and foreign charities increasingly seen as partners in projects. At the same time Indian authorities
began to recognise the need to make much bolder efforts themselves
to help the poor and needy and they started to look at NGOs in a far
more friendly manner. It has been estimated that there are perhaps
one million voluntary organisations in India; of these some 15,000
are development organisations registered under the FCRA as eligible
to receive foreign funds and an estimated 60,000 are NGOs involved
in developmental activity. This proliferation of NGO activity, which
covers an enormous variety of needs including health, education, art
and agriculture, has evolved largely since the late 1970s and early
1980s. It is, according to one expert, the jewel in India's crown and
has thrown up some talented leaders.

It is important to remember that the explosion of NGO activity did
not start until nearly thirty years after Mother Teresa began her labours.
In the late 1940s there were charitable organisations as well as other
orders of nuns doing good works, but no one who was looking at the
whole picture of the needs of Calcutta society. Mother Teresa was
responding to a crisis and, in a sense, that is what she has continued
to do. But for the first twenty years she was working with limited
resources and no international publicity. As the NGOs started to
mushroom they had the advantage of being able to specialise, to choose
a particular area of need and react according to current research. There
are some charity workers who believe it is only because of Mother
Teresa's pioneering work that these other organisations got going, that
Mother Teresa put Calcutta on the charity map and raised world
consciousness about the needs. Yet there are others who point out that
she is bucking the trend of current thinking among the NGOs, which
is aiming for self-help, empowerment and social transformation. She
is stuck in the time warp of the 1940s, which is welfare-oriented, still
sees a need for giving handouts and will never change the underlying
situation. More seriously, her work might even eclipse some of the
other charities if the West concludes that Calcutta is well taken care of
by Mother Teresa. They would be dramatically underestimating the
need.

There is an irony here as Indian leaders are still, and rightly so, extremely sensitive to any fund-raising activity that presents India only as a mosaic of problems. And yet that is unquestionably the effect not only of what Mother Teresa does but also of other charities, who argue that they are promoting developmental projects, but are only too aware that it is emotion, not long-term plans for bringing water, which makes people reach into their pockets. Their brochures are full of pictures of the starving and deprived. Charity does reinforce the idea of a problem in any country and it is very hard to present good ideas for raising money to help people in a positive light. One scheme which offers hope rather than misery as a reason for giving has resulted in the setting up of 580 village libraries throughout the country. Another idea called Barefoot Booksellers aims to encourage reading in the villages as well as providing rural employment.

There is no doubt that the publicity given to a Christian missionary organisation undertaking such widespread relief work acted as a spur to some Indians. Nina Singh, then wife of the former Minister for Defence, Research and Development, Arun Singh, and close friend of the Gandhi family, came to know Mother Teresa well when she lived in Calcutta and started to work for her first by teaching the novices English and then by arranging any small favour she could to help. Nina Singh had good contacts in the catering trade and persuaded a number of establishments that instead of regularly discarding towels, sheets and linen after a few months they should give them to Mother Teresa. 'I've been to various hotels and restaurants,' she told me, 'and when you talk to them about Mother Teresa there is a definite sense of guilt because she's not one of us and yet look how she's putting herself out for us, for our dying and for our lepers; therefore we must back her. It's only a question of asking. Soon after that I got a steel company to make all her cribs free.'[10]

Mother Teresa has three dramatic advantages over similar charities. In the first place she has a large pool of willing labour, which is free and which works long hours uncomplainingly. Secondly, since 1987 she has enjoyed free travel on Air India anywhere in the world, as do any of her sisters or escorts, upon request, and a free pass on the railways for herself and her sisters. No other charitable institution has been extended such facilities and, with large distances to cover, travel costs are a major inhibiting factor. Thirdly, she is given land or buildings with no government linkage. The paperwork required by other charities, often in triplicate, if they are given such gifts, is enormous and can take up months and use much money. Other charities therefore have much higher running costs. There is also her own charisma, personality, determination and leadership qualities; she can be very persuasive, as many donors to her cause attest, and inspires tremendous loyalty among her workers. Once she had reached the international arena her charisma stamped itself on the Western consciousness and the success became self-perpetuating. By the 1980s it was a well-established fact that if you gave money to Mother Teresa the media took notice of you but if you gave it to other organisations you got no publicity.

Even Milton McCann MBE, an Englishman who grew up in Calcutta and runs one of the most successful NGOs, is forced to admit: 'We are overshadowed here. When people think of Calcutta, they think of Mother Teresa. We can't help it but we get less money.' McCann, who was born in Rangoon in 1931, had always wanted to become a doctor, but after his father died his family could not afford the training and he went into industry instead. But the urge to do something, to alleviate the all-pervasive poverty surrounding him, did not go away and in 1968 he started visiting one of the worst slums in Calcutta with the idea of bringing up just a few destitute children and orphans. He continued for ten years teaching the children in a makeshift school building in the early morning and then going to his job while trying to raise money to develop the slums. Today he is secretary general of the Bengal Service Society (BSS) and of the Terre des Hommes (India) Society. He is responsible for about thirty projects in West Bengal and two in Orissa, which cover approximately 14,000 children. He has a staff of nearly a thousand, most of whom are paid employees, as this is a way of rehabilitating local people, although there are also some volunteers. Between them the staff maintain three crèches, seventeen dispensaries and four hospitals and feed many thousands of children every day. McCann's primary objective is to create independence, not dependence, to develop skills and promote self-sufficiency, to rehabilitate totally. One hundred thousand young people have passed out of his organisation to become self-supporting members of society. 'All our programmes are based on the concept of rehabilitation and no spoon-feeding is encouraged.'[11]

McCann is not a religious man, he never goes to church, but he is motivated by the deepest human understanding of the need for self-respect as well as love for his charges. His work occasionally overlaps with Mother Teresa's, whose dedication, he says, he greatly admires. If he has a patient with leprosy he will refer him to her and she in turn might send a child who needed specialist surgery to his hospital. But his motivation has more to do with social justice and breaking the cycle of poverty. As we drove past Prem Dan and saw beggars gathering he commented: 'If all you do is relief work you make more people beggars.'

When McCann started work in the dilapidated slum called Sapgachi, near the city garbage dump on the eastern fringe of Calcutta, he saw the vicious circle of poverty in action. It was arguably the worst slum in the city, a swampy marshland with no roads, no electricity and no sewerage systems. Ten thousand people struggled to live there in flimsy shacks, but in the monsoon season every year some died, some were left homeless and the rest lived among floating garbage, waterlogged lanes and hordes of mosquitoes and flies spreading their annual quota of disease and death. Every year the same story repeated itself. But in 1995 I saw in Sapgachi a clean village with schools, hospitals, training areas and a job-placement unit. The children, who fight for school places, have to pay 17 rupees a day for the privilege on the basis that they will only value what they are given if they make a token contribution. They are fed while there because McCann understands the importance of nutrition for mental development and says, realistically, it helps cut down on absenteeism: 'They won't miss a day if they know they'll be fed.' Sadly, the BSS can usually only take one child per family, unless the family is absolutely destitute, in the hope that that child will eventually be able to earn a living and support the rest of the family. The children I saw were as immaculately turned out as any from a top convent in the centre of town and took a huge pride in performance. My friend and I were treated to a brief, but unforgettable, display of their gymnastic and musical talents – and the children *are* talented – but almost more impressive was the devotion in their eyes as they greeted McCann. He has high standards for them now – 'Poor somersault,' he whispered to the coach at one point – and high hopes for their future. They will all leave school with a high-school certificate and often also a trade.

McCann today has to spend most of his time fund-raising. There is never enough money. He can no longer come to the slums and play games with the children as he used to. BSS was launched with a small gift from the Paul family of Calcutta and some money from the Canadian High Commissioner, who agreed to visit the proposed site when it was still a slum and was immediately bowled over by the effort McCann was making. He has had money from the Tata and Birla families as well as from the Swiss and the British governments. But as his projects spread and some earlier sources dry up he is constantly travelling and appealing for someone to give his children 'a chance to shine'.

Dr R. C. Biswas, director of the Cathedral Relief Services (CRS), follows much the same approach as McCann. 'Charity', he told me emphatically, 'is the oldest form of NGO work and it is outdated. People must be the custodian of their own development and once we have developed skills we gradually move out and they can do it themselves. I belong to the development stream and have a great faith in people who, though poor, can work out their own salvation. Charity just gives them a form of dependence.'

Notwithstanding its title, CRS, with offices in the shadow of the magnificent St Paul's Cathedral just across from the Maidan, is one of the most progressive NGOs in Calcutta. 'Relief is purely for emergency situations,' explained Dr Biswas. 'We began during the Bangladesh war and famine but once the refugee problem settled we saw there was much more to this than showing the poor to the world and lining up with a cane outside the Missionary of Charity gates to give them food. It is the same ones who come back to get more.'

Biswas himself lived in a bustee for twelve years while qualifying as a doctor, 'so I really do know the problems first hand'. For the last thirty years he has worked in development and believes fervently in a people's movement that goes well beyond 'just handing out'. Biswas has been responsible for training nearly a thousand volunteers who then organise people from within the bustees to organise themselves. 'You must pick them up, give them skills and then you have your force. The difference between us and Mother Teresa is that she uses outsiders, many of her nuns come from Kerala, but we go to the people themselves. For example a young girl who is married and lives in the slum; we pick her up and train her so that she can do something for herself. We are enablers, not a charity.'

CRS is currently working in fourteen slums of Calcutta, trying to act as a partnership. 'We don't build buildings and have no infrastructure but we find a community centre where we can have regular meetings and talks and we want to hear it from their mouths.' The total project offered by CRS includes three major components, health, education and training, with special emphasis on women's adult education, teaching them, for example, how to cook foods to sell to snack bars, as well as self-respect. It also runs a number of clinics and schools where, again, a nominal amount is charged 'because this gives people a right and a human dignity. We are trying to make men and women out of them. Then, if you don't like the teacher, you have a right to complain.' CRS treats 400 registered patients with tuberculosis and every Christmas organises an annual party and entertainment for patients and asks other groups in the city to contribute. 'The Missionaries of Charity used to give rations to us but recently when we approached them for this they told us to have our programme first and then send the patients along to queue up and "We will give them something." '[12] This is the charity Biswas so abhors.

CRS manages on 28 lakhs rupees (£48,000) annually, funded in thirds by Christian Aid in the UK, the German charity Bread for the World and by money raised locally by CRS, for example through selling advertisements in a programme bought at the annual inter-bustee school sports day held in the Cathedral grounds. It receives minimal government help. 'We have applied for money to finance programmes in schools on AIDS awareness but were refused. I know if I wanted to get a centre for AIDS patients I wouldn't get it. The government of Jyoti Basu knows it does them good to be seen to give buildings to the Missionaries of Charity ... but [Mother Teresa's] agenda is tiny compared with our work and projects ... She is not relevant to our times. We have to get through an enormous amount of work with very little money.' As with BSS, there is some overlap between the two charities in the medical sphere as the Missionaries of Charity sometimes refer patients to CRS clinics for diagnosis. 'But the Missionaries of Charity have access to drugs that we don't have access to and these drugs cost us 5 rupees for each capsule that we can't afford but still we give them what we have.'

Clearly all the NGOs desperately need money to fund their often imaginative and wide-ranging programmes and as they look at Mother

Teresa's organisation benefiting from well-organised teams of Co-Workers sending money from abroad as well as government concessions, it is easy for them to assume that, if only they had her resources, they could work wonders. But that does not necessarily mean that if the money did not go to her it would come to them. Without an open audit of Mother Teresa's accounts it is impossible to know exactly how much money she has. According to Monimoy Dasgupta, the reporter at the *Calcutta Telegraph* who has followed her most closely, this is now Rs 100 crore (£17.2 million). Over the years, there have been several large prize donations and the corporate sector in India has been generous too. Jet Airways gave 1 per cent of its revenue to Mother Teresa at one time and Tata Tea gave Rs 20 Lakhs (£34,500). This was followed by a decision to give one rupee per kilogram of tea sold in Calcutta from January to March 1994. However a shareholder of Tata Tea who attended the AGM of the company on 19 September 1994 objected to these payments to Mother Teresa since there had been no prior shareholder approval nor any reference made in the annual accounts. The latter omission caused a furore at the AGM but a company spokesman later explained that the donation was viewed from the point of view of promotion and was therefore debited to the general expenditure account.

Christopher Hitchens cites the testimony of a former Missionary of Charity who ended up working in an office Mother Teresa maintains in New York City. This nun was in charge of taking the money to the bank and estimates that there must have been $50 million in that bank account alone. It is widely assumed that there is also money kept at the Istituto per le Opere di Religione, the Vatican bank used as a clearing house by many Orders with international connections, to and from which Mother Teresa's sisters are often seen hurrying. One former Missionary of Charity I spoke to told me that if she, as a superior, were sent money for a specific project she would ensure it was used for that. 'But if it was sent generally for the poor I would send it to London or some money was sent to a bank in Rome,' the former sister told me. 'I think she is a very wealthy Congregation. Apart from money, they get given so many things.'

But this is largely money from European Christians and, although more progressive Catholics might give it instead to Cafod, the Catholic overseas agency which promotes human development and justice issues, it is highly unlikely that if they did not give it to her they would give it, for example, to the Ramakrishna Mission. This largely Hindu-funded organisation, which now has 130 branches in and outside India, was registered in 1909, twelve years after it was started by Swami Vivekenanda in 1897, and is involved in philanthropic and welfare activities of a non-proselytising nature. The Ramakrishna Mission is always to be found in times of emergency, such as floods or drought, offering relief service and often remaining for years until rehabilitation is achieved. The Mission also runs hospitals, schools and women's training and I saw a dramatic example of a slum rehousing project in Rambagan, North Calcutta, which it had undertaken. Most aid experts believe that Mother Teresa has not managed to tap into the really large Indian fortunes of a few Hindu families, although she has many volunteers from that stratum of society.

Rumer Godden thinks the latter is one of Mother Teresa's most notable achievements and that, far from eclipsing other charitable organisations, Mother Teresa's work has resulted in a quite new charitable activity among Indian society ladies. 'There is a great change now; they all say "I must go now, it's my leper day," and you'd never have heard this before.'[13] This is a sensitive issue. Mrs Chaudhuri, the elderly daughter of a wealthy Bengali family with a well-honed response to charity, clearly bridled when I discussed Godden's comments with her and she told me how one organisation she worked for, Nari Seva Sankar, had been involved in social work since the time of the Bengal famine; way before that, her grandmother had started the first school for girls in a small village in Bihar. In 1949 the Sarva Seva Sangh movement was formed along Gandhian principles with the intention of decentralising power, putting it back into the hands of the peasants and dispensing with private ownership of land.

Lady (Aruna) Paul, who has herself worked for Mother Teresa, admits that perhaps there were a few 'society women' who had nothing better to do and who got involved with Mother Teresa just to be seen there. But she also believes that a sense of charity is deeply ingrained in most Hindu families and is nothing new. 'You don't necessarily have to be wealthy to show charity. Our whole way of life is based on the idea that the needy are looked after naturally by the wealthy. Family retainers would be fed, clothed and cared for and if you employed a maidservant you were responsible for her welfare and her family's welfare and you would consider helping them out even at the cost of going without things yourselves. This attitude means that it is not necessary to have big charitable organisations and big balls.'

There is no doubt that the Hindu concept of charity differs greatly from the West's. In the first place, there is the belief in karma or acceptance of fate based on the idea that one's conditions in the present life have been determined by deeds in the past life. Although the ultimate aim is to break the cycle of birth and death through deepening spiritual insight or good works there was a tendency towards charitable inactivity on the ground that one's fate was preordained. Increasingly, Hindus accept that poverty is the result of economic circumstances and can be changed. Zerbanoo Gifford, author of a book on Asian philanthropy, believes the upper echelons of Indian society are spontaneously generous 'but maybe the criteria are different and if you keep going to the super-rich you may find them rather tired'.[14] The super-rich in India, including the industrial empires run by the Tata, Godrej and Birla families, for example, have an impressive history of charitable giving but have traditionally preferred large-scale projects such as founding hospitals, schools, business colleges or other institutions, which will bear their name in addition to many other small-scale donations which do not necessarily attract attention. However, as ties of caste and community diminish, the growing middle class, estimated at between two and three hundred million people, will find itself increasingly important in providing the charitable backbone of the NGOs. These new donors will need to be convinced, however, that they can have an impact, that the charity is well run and professional, and will expect to be shown accounts and details of where the money is spent. They will then become more committed and involved donors.

The Birla family in particular has a colossal and well-publicised reputation for charity: a university, a Hindu temple, an educational trust, a hospital, a museum and a planetarium are just some of the institutions they have funded. 'Oddly, not a single Birla rupee has yet gone in the direction of Mother Teresa and her sisters,' wrote Geoffrey Moorhouse in his book on Calcutta in 1971. 'And the Birlas have many, many rupees.' Yet by the 1990s that position was no longer tenable for such a prominent family. Today, various representatives of the Birla family give both time and money to Mother Teresa.

However, charitable donations are not finite and Mother Teresa's genius was in marketing herself and in understanding how to harness the power of publicity that came her way to find new sources of money. Other organisations might do well to emulate some of her ideas. She has reached the point now where if she needs architects, or almost any other kind of professional help, such services are offered free. Most of her professional advice today comes from Naresh Kumar, the international tennis player who represented his country at Wimbledon for twenty-one years before turning to a highly successful business career. Kumar, now in his late sixties, and his exquisite wife, Sunita are one of Calcutta's truly golden couples. He is a committee member of the Bengal Chamber of Commerce, vice-chairman of a leading furnace company and a personal friend of the artist M. F. Husein, whose series of paintings of Mother Teresa have been so popular and graced at least two of the most elegant homes I saw in India. The Kumars, devout Hindus, have been helping Mother Teresa since 1967, after their second son was born and Sunita decided she wanted to do something other than sit at home all day.

'Whenever Mother Teresa seeks my help, I consider it a privilege,' Kumar says. 'It's so easy to work for her ... you just ring people up and convey her wishes. Everyone does it for her free, no one dares charge.'[15] Kumar scans many official documents for her or helps her arrange building materials, whatever is the pressing need. He insists that although her accounts are looked at by an auditor there is no further need for openness. 'You can be 110 per cent sure that with Mother any money does not go to her or her sisters. In any case to whom should she account and why? I've been in business long enough to know what business accounts can be. Accounts mean very little. She has got above these things. Her mission is to look after the poor, that's her entire story.'

Not everyone takes such a relaxed view, especially after it was revealed in 1987 that Mother Teresa was the target of an international swindle. Gangs of well-organised thieves recognised an easy prey and began intercepting mail meant for the Missionaries of Charity, who only became aware of the loss after a US donor asked for a receipt for a donation. It was believed that the stolen money, which totalled almost £100,000 (or Rs 30 Lakhs, according to Dasgupta, which is greater) was being laundered in Singapore and Hong Kong. Lord Paul, whose family is heavily involved in a variety of businesses in Calcutta, is full of praise for her work with the sick but raises a cautious eyebrow at how her finances are handled. 'It's one thing to collect the money and do the job, but it's a tremendous amount of money and not enough back-up; you need a proper organisation for that amount ... to make sure it's not going astray.'[14] When Muggeridge interviewed Mother Teresa she was quite open about not keeping accounts. It was an important reason for not accepting grants from government, which would have required them.[15] Navin Chawla, twenty years on, sings the same song. 'Keeping accounts ... would mean that in the four hundred and sixty-eight houses of the Missionaries of Charity around the world, at least one sister would be distracted from her true work of comforting and helping the lonely, the afflicted and despairing.' But today Mother Teresa has had to submit to auditors for some of her funds as Indian law requires it; the bulk of her money is believed not to be kept in India.

Whatever else Mother Teresa wants the Kumars to do it is not to organise fund-raising activities. These stopped shortly after the Nobel award, partly to prevent any danger of the money being misused, but also because Mother Teresa prefers people to give directly, with no intermediary involved nor any obvious pressure brought to bear. 'If anyone wants to give it will come,' Sunita Kumar explained. Her husband cited an example of how he paid a visit to S. K. Birla not so long ago and told him how Mother Teresa was preparing a home in Tangra, a slum area in the north of Calcutta, for destitute women, many of whom had been in jail and upon release were being forced into prostitution, as well as some who were mentally retarded. According to the Kumars, Jyoti Basu had requested Mother to take on these women and house them. Would Birla like to participate in the new home, Naresh Kumar asked? 'Within five minutes he had written out a cheque on the spot for five hundred thousand rupees.'[18] With friends like the Kumars, who needs to fund-raise?

There is certainly a case to be made that by courting Indian politicians Mother Teresa has brought money, land and buildings into her Order. She is therefore very successful at what she set out to do. But I'm not sure that that makes her political — not quite. It seems to me that the political side of Mother Teresa is most clearly seen not in India itself but when she travels to other countries. In 1983 she flew to Spain on the eve of a major debate in the country about abortion, divorce and birth control to lend her support to the right-wing clerical forces opposing any secularisation of the new monarchy.

The following year, in the middle of a fiery American election campaign, she made an unexpected appearance at a New York meeting where she denounced abortion as murder and described Jesus as 'the little unborn child'. This was a particularly timely visit as the Democratic vice-presidential candidate, Mrs Geraldine Ferraro, was coming under heavy fire from the Archbishop of New York, John O'Connor, as well as from anti-abortionist activists for her acceptance of the right to choose an abortion in certain circumstances. In the event Ferraro was not elected. In 1988, as we have seen, Mother Teresa came to England with much the same message just before Parliament debated David Alton's abortion limiting Bill. This support, given to a number of 'pro-life' groups in the 1980s, was crucial, according to Marianne Haslegrave of the CMA. 'In the 1980s she helped the opposition become stronger because she has an aura about her; it helps if you can quote Mother Teresa because if you're meant to be a living saint and you do this sort of thing, it makes it much more difficult to combat the arguments. She is responsible for the politicisation, which I don't like.'

Mother Teresa has always had strong ties with Ireland and thirty or more of her nuns are Irish. But in the 1990s this too is a country agonising over secularisation, and issues such as abortion, divorce and whether condoms should be more widely available are right at the top of the political agenda. In August 1982, the year before a pro-life amendment referendum, she spoke at a news conference in Dublin organised by SPUC before addressing a Right to Life meeting in the National Stadium. Eleven years later, in June 1993, she addressed a crowd of around 50,000 at the Marian shrine in Knock, appealing to the Irish people not to allow abortion or divorce into the country. 'Let us promise Our Lady we will never, in any circumstances, allow a single abortion in this country,' Mother Teresa said. Shortly afterwards, sounding distinctly more liberal, the Archbishop of Tuam, Dr Joseph Cassidy, preached that anyone who is pro-life must also be pro-mother. He went on: 'There are situations in life where an expectant mother, for reasons unknown to us, is tempted to have recourse to abortion. In the circumstances in which she finds herself the temptation may prove too strong. While we uphold the right of the innocent to life, no one of us can afford to judge ... There are situations where a mother's life may be threatened by pregnancy and where she and her family are terrified lest she be taken from them. A mother's life is priceless in itself.'[19]

As many in the sunny crowd pushed forward and asked Mother Teresa to bless their rosary beads, a young woman approached, clasped the old nun's hands and said: 'I am expecting a baby in November so please pray for me.'

'I will pray that she will be a Missionary of Charity,' Mother Teresa replied, smiling.[20]

Two foreign trips in particular have brought Mother Teresa considerable criticism. In August 1980, following a conference in Guatemala, Mother Teresa visited Haiti, one of the world's poorest and most deprived countries, ruled for almost three despotic decades by the Duvalier dynasty. At the time of Mother Teresa's visit, not her first to the island, Jean-Claude Duvalier was President for Life, and his First Lady, a divorcee by the name of Michèle Bennett Duvalier, lavished millions of dollars on herself and was hated with a passion. But she promoted herself as defender of the poor and regularly toured health and education centres trying to raise money for the Michèle Bennett Duvalier Foundation.

Mother Teresa said, when she was in Haiti, that although she had met many kings, presidents and prime ministers, 'I have never seen the poor people being so familiar with their heads of state as they were with her. It was a beautiful lesson for me, I have learned something from you.'[21] This simple homily praising the couple was shown on state-run television for at least a week. A reporter for Newsweek challenged her on her way home by putting forward the view that the extreme poverty of such countries was the result of political oppression and that the only way to change such poverty was for the Roman Catholic Church to become more involved politically. 'I do not get involved in that sort of politics. Everything was peaceful in the parts of Guatemala that we visited,' she told him.[22] Having sidestepped that question, she was then asked for her opinion of liberation theology, the radical theology proclaimed by many clerics in Latin America, which emphasises an active engagement in social justice for human rights and sees itself as the correct interpretation of Vatican II. 'You cannot serve two masters,' Mother Teresa replied. 'Someone once asked me whether it is better to give fish or fishing rods to people who are hungry. But the people who come to me are sick and dying; they are so weak that they cannot even hold a rod. They must be given the fish first and maybe the rod will come later.'

In February 1994 the anger and the passion of the Haitian people – the majority of whom earn less than $150 a year – boiled over into revolution, forcing the loathed Duvalier couple to flee. But by then Mother Teresa had several homes in Haiti as well as the Haitian Légion d'Honneur.

In 1989, twenty years or so after her unsuccessful battles with the Albanian government for permission to visit her mother and sister before they died, and four years after the death of Enver Hoxha, Mother Teresa paid what the Albanian press called a 'private visit' to Albania at the invitation of the communist leader, Ramiz Alia. During the visit, from 14 to 17 August, Mother Teresa was taken to see a variety of health clinics and nursery centres. She spent time with Hoxha's widow, Nexhmije, and told her, according to the official government publication, that she was 'overjoyed at all the major transformations achieved in our country during the forty-five years of the people's power'.[23] When her hosts took her to the dazzlingly majestic Martyrs' Cemetery on the hillside above Tirana to admire the imposing statue of Mother Albania and its marble stairway among the pines, palms and cedars, Mother Teresa acquiesced in their plans by laying a bouquet of flowers on Hoxha's magnificent tombstone, then on the stepped platform next door to Mother Albania. She also, apparently, pressed a religious medal into Mrs Hoxha's palm.

In return, Mother Teresa was given what she most wanted: two houses where her sisters could start work among the poor and old of this tragic country. Her introduction to the Albanian people was under way. At first, officialdom described her simply as a well-known benefactress of Albanian origin, and many ordinary Albanians thought she was a wealthy expatriate returning to dispense money. But within a year or two she had become a national hero, praised by Muslims and Christians alike for her humanitarian work. Suddenly she featured on postage stamps and in school history books and now is often compared with the country's only other hero, Skanderbeg. For Albanians, Mother Teresa proclaims to the world that they can produce inspiring figures of world stature and is therefore of key importance in the battle to restore national pride. In 1995 there was even talk of her apparent, but unlikely, wish to be buried in the beautiful but benighted country, which would of course dramatically change the country's familiarity with tourism. Making Albania into a pilgrimage country might be the greatest gift Mother Teresa could give them.

However, knowing as she did at first hand through her mother's and sister's experiences the repressive and brutal nature of the regime under which Albanians suffered for forty years, what compromises did she have to reach with herself in order to place the wreath on Hoxha's grave and thus appear to condone his rule? Albanians themselves understand realpolitik only too well, and if this was the price of moving her sisters into a corner of Europe that had been denied Christianity for forty years it seemed to her a small price. 'Those who criticise Mother Teresa for showing respect are ignorant of her philosophy,' was the comment of the Albanian Catholic Bulletin. 'She is above all a Christian following in the footsteps of Jesus Christ. The heart of the Christian message is forgiveness and in Mother's own words "without forgiveness there can be no real love". To view her as a pawn in the government's game is to vastly underestimate this saintly woman, who is above politics, and her lack of bitterness sets an example to us all. Yes, the government used her for public relations but thereby opened the door to forces they were ill prepared to face.'[24]

'Above politics' does not strike quite the right note for me. Nor apparently does it do so for Jack Preger, who once said: 'The fact of the matter is that Mother Teresa is prepared to shake hands with any type of murderer who happens to be in political power. For example, when there was a diplomatic reception some two weeks after the coup in Bangladesh she was there lining up with the rest of the diplomatic corps and shaking hands with the new people in power – the very same people who had just murdered fifty of their opponents and will no doubt go on killing future opponents.'[25]

Five years after Mother Teresa's historic visit to Albania I was in Tirana. Apparently, Mother Teresa had been there again a few days before me to sort out a 'confusion' over the houses given to her in 1989 by Ramiz Alia. Alia himself had just been released from jail. The houses were privately owned in pre-communist times and, now that the communists had fallen, the owners, like many elsewhere in Eastern

Europe, were reclaiming not only their property, but lost rent as well. 'Mother Teresa is very pragmatic,' explained the Papal Nuncio, Monsignor Ivan Dias. 'She is trying to solve it but cannot accept that the Missionaries of Charity should give up [the houses] or should pay. As far as she is concerned, it is charity that must prevail, not justice. After all, the Catholic Church itself has not got back all its properties and there are some with illegal occupants we can't get rid of.'[26]

Clearly Mother Teresa does not consider the episode as tantamount to accepting stolen property, any more than she believes she accepted money from Charles Keating, the US multimillionaire financier sentenced to ten years for his part in a savings and loan fraud that will eventually cost American taxpayers $500 billion plus interest. And yet, according to Christopher Hitchens, 'Keating made donations (not out of his own pocket, of course) to Mother Teresa in the sum of one and a quarter million dollars. He also granted her the use of his private jet. In return, Mother Teresa allowed Keating to make use of her prestige on several important occasions and gave him a personalised crucifix which he took everywhere with him.'[27] When Keating was standing trial in 1992 Mother Teresa wrote to Judge Lance Ito begging for mercy because 'he has always been kind and generous to God's poor and always ready to help whenever there was a need'. At the same time she insisted, 'We do not mix up in Business or Politics or courts. Our work as Missionaries of Charity is to give wholehearted and free service to the poorest of the poor ... it is for this reason that I do not want to forget him now while he and his family are suffering.'[28]

Paul Turley, deputy district attorney for Los Angeles, who was one of the people who worked on Keating's prosecution, strongly believed that as Mother Teresa, by her own admission, was hazy about Keating's business and work, she should be given unambiguous details 'of the source of the money that Mr Keating gave to you and to suggest that you perform the moral and ethical act of returning the money to its rightful owners'. 'Mr Keating', he wrote to her, 'was convicted of defrauding seventeen individuals of more than $900,000. These seventeen persons were representative of 17,000 individuals from whom Mr Keating stole $252,000,000 ... The victims of Mr Keating's fraud come from a wide spectrum of society. Some were wealthy and well educated. Most were people of modest means and unfamiliar with high finance. One was a poor carpenter who did not speak English and had his life savings stolen by Mr Keating's fraud.' It was a most powerful letter, in which he urged Mother Teresa not simply to love mercy but also to do justice, as commanded by the biblical prophet Micah. He then asked Mother Teresa to do what Jesus would do if he were given the fruits of a crime; what Jesus would do if he were in possession of money that had been stolen; what Jesus would do if he were being exploited by a thief to ease his conscience. 'I submit that Jesus would promptly and unhesitatingly return the stolen money property to its rightful owners. You should do the same.'

To date, neither Mother Teresa nor anyone representing her has ever responded to Turley's letter,[29] proof for Hitchens that she is neither innocent nor unworldly. 'In her dealings with pelf, as in her transactions with power, Mother Teresa reigns in a kingdom that is very much of this world.'[30] But there is a twist to the tale. In April 1997 Keating's earlier state conviction was quashed on the grounds that Judge Lance Ito had given the jury 'flawed instructions'. The federal convictions fell because 14 of the 18 jurors knew or learnt details of the state case and conviction. At the time of writing Keating is not living under a conviction. However, his future is undetermined as his case is to be retried by the US Attorney's office in Los Angeles, although no trial date has yet been set.

Accepting for a moment the view of her detractors that here is no innocent abroad, would Mother Teresa necessarily be a better person for being at best innocent or unworldly, at worst politically naive? All Missionaries of Charity take, in addition to the three vows of poverty, chastity and obedience, a fourth vow of wholehearted and free service to the poorest of the poor. This vow, unique to them, emphatically means they are not in business to offer service to the rich and is Mother Teresa's explanation for not opening big new hospitals or educating her nuns to a higher level and all the rest. But while Mother Teresa may be excused for not knowing details of Keating's or Maxwell's business deal, it is not difficult to see that these men, as well as the many other politicians and their wives who regularly stop at the Mother House for a photocall with Mother Teresa, are exploiting both her and the poor for their own ends. Why has she, at the very least, not allowed herself the privilege of good advisers who could have told her that she was being manipulated? What else was she doing in the case of Maxwell, Keating or even Hillary and Chelsea Clinton who, while in India in March 1995, posed for photographs with a baby from Mother Teresa's orphanage, than offering a service to the rich and powerful?

The moral dilemmas today for anyone trying to raise money are both important and difficult. The University of Oxford, which has an ethical committee to examine the source of gifts when it considers that the money being offered could be tainted, nonetheless found itself in a dilemma recently when it was offered money from the Flick family to establish a chair at Oxford. In the end, Dr Gert Rudolf-Flick withdrew the endowment amid controversy over his father's connections with the Nazis. But among the voices who denounced the use of money to buy forgiveness there were plenty who believed that forgiveness should certainly start with the next generation.

Given the desperate drive for money, without which charities can do nothing, what questions can and do they ask? In Mother Teresa's case there would be no shortage of willing and qualified candidates prepared to form an *ad hoc* ethics committee, with the role of advising her not just on the provenance of gifts of money but also on who might be photographed with her. Mother Teresa had a small council of senior nuns but this comprised women who had made their lives within the religious order and who would be unlikely to have the authority to overrule her.

I have lost count of the number of times I have been told in the course of researching this book, 'So what if Mother Teresa's sort of help does not change society, surely there is room for both relief and developmental aid?' The people Mother Teresa helps are so weak they need to be given basic care and attention before they can do anything for themselves, the argument usually runs. But, again, that is to miss the point: those particular people may be beyond 'developing' but developmental projects aim to examine the source of the problem, to prevent more of those people needing the same sort of handout help. The argument pivots on whether Mother Teresa, because of her international standing, is potentially diverting funds from organisations which help alleviate the very problems she is trying to address. No one is saying we should not pick up people from the street, but shouldn't we as well as caring try to prevent these situations from recurring in the future? Mother Teresa does not address herself to that at all.

I put it to Roger Riddell, research fellow at the Overseas Development

Institute, that there was surely room for both types of aid. 'No, I don't think everyone would accept that. If you have a mushrooming of organisations which are solely and exclusively involved in relief and welfare and which draw a lot of money, then you are actually frustrating the efforts of those trying to solve the long-term problems. In Zaire, for example, you can argue strongly that the provision of aid, although intended to help the poor and needy, is *de facto* nurturing and supporting the regime.'[31]

Looking at the future role of charities and aid provision it is sobering to see that out of a total of US$65 billion of all aid worldwide, 94 per cent is government aid and a mere 6 per cent is raised by charities and similar organisations. Bearing this in mind, what Mother Teresa does or does not do, or what any other NGO does, can never fundamentally alter the position of the world's poor. What she does, she freely admits, may be only a drop in the ocean and I fully accept is no less valid for that. But perhaps it is time to assess more rationally where the money is going if after fifty years it remains only a drop. If co-operation between the Missionaries of Charity and other NGOs could be increased, the drops might even become a flow.

World aid has undergone dramatic changes in the last few years. Most of today's donors require accountability and professionalism; they might say: 'I want my money to help that problem; can you show me that you are more efficient at actually solving the problem than the next one?' In consequence, all NGOs are now looking more rigorously at the impact their money is having. One of the reasons development projects do not always work is because they require certain political conditions as well for the development to be sustainable. But should charities involve themselves in politics or has the world reached a point where NGOs can no longer remain neutral? By so doing they are supporting the status quo which is preventing change. Most Bengalis recognise that if the problems of Calcutta are ever to be solved this will require major government initiatives and an unbending will to see these through. The government is, of course, already the major provider of aid, but the real challenge is to make the system more efficient rather than drumming up more money. Following the 1996 elections in India it was estimated that 85 per cent of government money allocated for social development nationally was not actually getting there – the leaky bucket syndrome, as it is generally known.

This explains why many people prefer to give to smaller projects where they can see the particular school, clinic or art programme for which their funds are earmarked, or sponsor a particular child whom they might one day meet.

Perhaps some radical new ideas are required for the next millennium. The elimination of third world debt is not a new proposal and, with the burden of servicing the debt now reaching critical levels, is talked about more urgently. In Uganda for example the government spends £1.60 per person a year on healthcare and £19 per person on repayment of debt to Western countries. And yet so far the IMF has not been persuaded to use a small part of its gold reserves to cancel the debt of twenty of the poorest countries. More acceptable is the idea of micro credit. Mohammed Yunus, a former professor and banker in Bangladesh, believes the best way to eradicate world poverty is not to donate billions to fund large ventures but to give loans, often as little as £20, to the destitute, most of whom are women. Yunus has invented the idea of a rural bank which offers credit to the poor, thus allowing them to earn money, without being fleeced by middlemen, to repay the loan. The bank actively seeks out the most deprived section of Bangladeshi society – the landless, assetless, rural poor, often including beggars, illiterates and widows, yet claims a loan repayment rate of 99 per cent. Yunus started his Grameen Bank twenty years ago; today it has over two million borrowers and works in 35,000 villages through-out the country. Borrowers must form a group, which encourages repayment on loans: these are always for a year with interest fixed at 20 per cent – simple interest, not compounded. He identified a need and a means to solve it, discovering along the way that lending to women, who traditionally have the least economic opportunity in Bangladesh, was most beneficial to the whole family, and that women were more careful about their debts. Yunus believes that giving people credit unlocks their humanity. He estimates that, in 1996, thirty-six million of the world's poor have been helped through loans from his and similar banks. 'If we can reach 100 million, that will be a critical mass, the rest will be easy.'

Yunus adds: 'People say I am crazy, but no one can achieve anything without a dream. When you build a house you can't just assemble a bunch of bricks and mortar, you must first have the idea that it can be done. If one is going to make headway against poverty one cannot do business as usual. One must be revolutionary and think the unthink-able.'[32] Mother Teresa too had a dream, which she also has translated into reality. She provided a refuge of last resort for those who were dying when the alternative was to die alone on the street. And while I saw and was told of literally hundreds of groups, charities, organisations, community centres, which help babies, street children, prostitutes, young married women, tuberculosis sufferers, all those with potential life in front of them, when it comes to helping the aged, the insane, the doubly incontinent, the lepers and those on the extreme margins of society the name of Mother Teresa is impossible to avoid. But, after fifty years, the world of charity has moved on. Those who give are, by and large, no longer prepared to do so in the vague hope it does some good somewhere. They are more knowl-edgeable about the structures that keep people poor, more politically aware and more focused and efficient in their campaigning attempts to help the people they are trying to help.

CHAPTER THIRTEEN

EGO

On 4 February 1986 the world's two most revered living Catholics united in feeding the dying and destitute of Calcutta. Pope John Paul II went to Mother Teresa's Home for the Dying on the third day of his pilgrimage to India. After embracing the seventy-five-year-old missionary, cupping her veiled head in his hands and kissing her brow, he served dinner to those who could still eat and blessed those who could not. Then he went to visit the mortuary, marked the sign of the cross on the forehead of each corpse and sprinkled them with water. Calcutta was the Pope's first major port of call after his two-day state visit to Delhi, and he spent over an hour at Kalighat, the longest he had spent anywhere except when conducting mass, both indications of the importance he attached to Mother Teresa's mission.

In the evening, the Catholic and civic authorities organised a big reception at St Xavier's College to which all the city top brass were invited to participate in a mass and prayer service. Officially, the Pope was guest of honour, yet after the reception, when most of the guests had left, there was Mother Teresa with the military and police surrounding her, walking along the specially laid red carpet towards the exit. 'And they were all bowing, adulation is the only word I can think of, and everybody feeling so honoured she was there,' recounted Sister Cyril of the Rainbow School. Just then Mother Teresa called out to the Loreto nun, 'Sister, take a lift with me.' But Sister Cyril already had a jeep waiting for her, so she declined. 'But as we walked out together I noticed a Black Maria standing outside, the inside was completely carpeted and there was an armchair for Mother Teresa to sit in ... the inside was beautifully done up for her.'

Sister Cyril went on to say how this episode taught her the special kind of suffering God has devised for Mother Teresa. 'That she is such a very, very humble person, so totally given to God and to the poor, and yet she has to accept amiably, or amicably rather, the kind of adulation she gets from officialdom and from everybody in the city.'[1] This is the only explanation for Sister Cyril of the meaning of Mother Teresa. 'In our tradition, the Catholic tradition generally, anyone who is the founder of a religious order has to carry the cross very acutely, they have to suffer a lot. And I had often wondered about Mother Teresa because she seemed to get so much publicity and so much adulation from everybody. I often wondered because it seemed so different to the founders of every other congregation in the Catholic Church; each one had either been excommunicated or thrown out by their followers or had suffered a complete setback, a complete reversal of everything they thought God was calling them to. But it seems as if Mother Teresa has all the time been succeeding, succeeding, suc-ceeding with everybody loving her, offering adulation and so on.'

Mother Teresa insists that she does suffer constant humiliations, the relentless media exposure being the principal one. Referring to the coverage of the Nobel Peace Prize in Oslo in December 1979 she has often said: 'For that publicity alone, I should go straight to heaven.' Navin Chawla has written about her extreme discomfiture whenever she wins an award, which he insists has not lessened with time. When the Indian Prime Minister Narasimha Rao gave her yet another in the mid-1990s she said: 'This publicity, these lights, this also is a form of humiliation. I accept this, as I did the Nobel Prize, only as a recognition of the poor.'[2] But to the outside world it often seems to be as Sister Cyril described it, one long round of publicity and adulation. If it is so hateful, why does she allow a sign on a noticeboard at the children's home, Shishu Bhavan, which reads: 'Of all the nice things in the world, the nicest must be Mother'?[3] Why do the sides of her ambulances now read 'Mother Teresa's Missionaries of Charity', not just 'Mission-aries of Charity', as they used to? Is it possible constantly to deny one's own ego when presidents and prime ministers and other world leaders seek one out, when one's head features on medals and postage stamps and one of India's most famous painters, M. F. Husein, reproduces image after image? 'I am nothing,' says Mother Teresa constantly, 'nothing but a pencil in God's hands.' But how can a person, convinced that they have been chosen to do God's work on earth, also believe that they are nothing, unless that work has no value? Is it wise for any congregation to have so much publicity around one person? Is it possible that, in spite of all the world approbation, Mother Teresa could remain the humble nun of forty years ago?

Anyone who has had any dealings with Mother Teresa knows how extremely approachable she has been. She spoke to everyone who engaged her in conversation, blessed their rosary beads or signed a book and, for a brief moment, concentrated entirely on them. There was no formality, no appointment system, no dress code. Until prevented by ill health, she really did take her turn at cleaning the lavatories and scrubbing the cots. Hers was a very spartan bedroom, arguably the worst in the house as it was over the kitchen and, without a fan, extremely hot. Above all she answered her own telephone, which is more than one can say for many middle- or junior-ranking bureaucrats in any country, suffused with a sense of their own importance and the preciousness of their time. When Nina Singh, the government minister's wife and volunteer, had personal problems and her marriage foundered, Mother Teresa came and spent a whole day with her, holding her hand and praying. 'I asked her how she knew about all this,' Nina Singh recalled, 'and she said, "Do you think when a daughter is in pain and agony, doesn't a mother know?"' Mother Teresa then went to the house of the 'other woman' and asked to pray with her. 'This made me very angry with Mother and I told her so and shouted at her and said she had belittled herself. But she just smiled. There is something about her, as if only you exist for that moment, as if the pain is flowing out of your lips into her. She has so much time, she is never in a hurry.'[4]

There was another marriage Mother Teresa was desperately sad to see collapse. Princess Diana had first been introduced to Mother Teresa by the Indian Ambassador to Britain, Dr Singhvi, and there was an immediate rapport between the two women. Diana had already staked out her areas of interest – helping life's marginalised, particularly AIDS sufferers – and the pictures of Mother Teresa clasping Diana's hands captivated many in Britain who already surmised the Princess's own personal anguish. In addition, it was known that Diana's mother, Mrs

Shand-Kydd, was considering converting to Catholicism – she was received into the Church in 1994 – and there was speculation whether Diana, privately, might wish to follow. In 1989 Mother Teresa announced, before sharing a platform with the Princess at the 16th International Congress for the Family: 'I am coming to Britain to meet Princess Diana. I do not really have the time but I must be there ... Everywhere there is a need for giving and Diana has more influence over the British people than anybody else.' Mother Teresa went on: 'If she tells them how important it is to make their families strong they will listen, if she asks them to care for the poor, for the homeless, they will hear her. So I must speak to her while I have the chance.' To another reporter she added: 'For a start, I shall tell Diana that she and Charles should have more children. They should be setting an example sharing all their love with lots of children. Two is not enough – they should have five by now.'[5]

However, as the royal marriage foundered it was of course impossible for Diana to lecture others on the importance of strong and united families, but she had identified herself very closely with Mother Teresa's philosophy and was known to be a great admirer of the nun. In 1992, during an official visit to India with Prince Charles, she had pressed for a visit to the Missionaries of Charity in Calcutta but was unable to see Mother Teresa herself on that occasion as she was ill in Rome. The Princess spontaneously arranged for an unscheduled stopover in Rome, on her way back to London, so that she could see Mother Teresa personally. Diana's high-profile charity work and impassioned pleas on behalf of several underprivileged groups soon led the British media to start calling her Britain's answer to Mother Teresa.

One of the last full-length interviews Mother Teresa gave smoothly glided on to the subject of her relationship with the Princess, just before the divorce was announced in March 1996. Daphne Barak of *Ladies Home Journal* was granted an interview only after she agreed to spend time working with the nuns. Mother Teresa said of Princess Diana: 'Oh, she is like a daughter to me.' She was then asked about the break-up of her marriage and replied: 'I think it is a sad story. Diana is such a sad soul. She gives so much love but she needs to get it back. You know what? It is good that it is over. Nobody was happy anyhow.' Not surprisingly, the article sparked a controversy as the remark undermined Church teaching on divorce. Mother Teresa was then forced to issue a lengthy 'clarification' which emphasised that 'the teachings of Jesus Christ on the indissolubility of marriage ... have been the basis of my lifelong opposition to divorce. My love and fervent prayers are with the Royal Family at this difficult time ... The family that prays together stays together.'[6]

This unwelcome publicity for Mother Teresa – although it indicated her very human response in the first instance – could have been avoided if she had insisted on the interview being conducted by one of her senior sisters. But she was not good at delegating. There was back-up from the small group of elected councillors, but their chief function was to oversee the training of novices rather than to take over the role of the Superior General, even though they had to take decisions during the months while Mother Teresa travelled. Sharing power is always difficult with any foundress during her lifetime, doubly so in Mother Teresa's case given her energy, determination and drive and the perpetuation of the headmistress–pupil role. In addition, other people would have been deeply disappointed if she did not turn up in person. Sue Ryder faces the same problem, but insists that other people must accept as a fact of life that she could not possibly respond to all calls personally. Mother Teresa could have tackled this problem much earlier by insisting on sending other sisters to open houses or collect awards on her behalf and by developing the media's awareness of some of her other sisters.

In October 1994 she agreed to an eleven-page feature in the glossy magazine Hello!, for which she was presumably paid the same as some other Hello! interviewees. This can range from £2,000 to £10,000. Billed as 'an exclusive and deeply moving interview with the woman who has done so much to alleviate the suffering of the sick and poor', the piece has eight pictures, most of them close-ups of Mother Teresa herself. It would not have been difficult, at this stage of her life, for her to stipulate that her agreement was dependent on the writer and photographer making some of her other sisters better known. One might expect that the Catholic Media Office in London would have been involved in such a big feature in a British magazine, but they knew nothing about it. In fact they have virtually no contact with the Missionaries of Charity or Mother Teresa when she visits, and, to their bemusement, are often among the last to find out something connected with them. 'The way the media treats Mother Teresa in Britain is entirely without the input of the Catholic Media Office here. The sisters are very distinctly reluctant to deal with us, or the media generally,' a spokesman for the Office told me. 'Whenever the press rings me now, I refer them to Father Alexander Sherbrooke but I warn them that Bravington Road [where the sisters are based] is not media friendly. They are an autonomous organisation, outside our remit.'[7]

A Jesuit priest who worked for many years in a poor parish in Goa where Mother Teresa has a house, feels particularly strongly about the exclusive focus on Mother Teresa herself. He met her on two occasions some twenty years ago and found her 'a very domineering character with no humility at all when she began to demand a conveyance to reach her to Carembolim, a neighbour village'. Father Moreno de Souza, whose job for some time was to take care of the pilgrims who went to pay their respects to the relics of St Francis Xavier, always did this journey on foot. He was shocked after all the stories of sacrifice he had heard about her. Father de Souza could not understand why she had to be present personally whenever a new house was opened. 'Why are others unfit? Houses are opened in Europe including Russia, where Indian sisters are sent as humble workers or slaves at the service of the white skin. I consider this work undertaken in the West as a revival of slavery of times gone by.' He also felt deeply resentful of the way 'coloured people are made to worship her as a "living saint" – even pictures on calendars are printed depicting her as a "living saint". Yes, some intelligent brown-colour Catholics have protested in writing against this sort of blasphemy. Some priests have made her a "small goddess" in their sermons; she is always cited as a model to be imitated in the works of charities undertaken. Are there no other models in India?' Father de Souza considers 'the propaganda made in favour of Mother Teresa is an insult to our Indian religious sisters, who also work for the poor and the destitute but without any financial help'.[8]

Yet Sir Sigmund Sternberg, businessman and tireless worker for inter-faith dialogue, sympathises uncritically with Mother Teresa's response to prize-giving and award ceremonies. 'It is terribly important for her to come in person because that is the only way to bring people together and make such an occasion interesting,' he insisted. Sir Sigmund, the only Jewish Papal knight, believes fervently in the power of religion as a force for good and has spent years trying to promote understanding of other people's religions and the need for a religious dimension to life. For him, Mother Teresa has an extremely good product 'and there is no point in having a good product if you don't advertise it and market it'.[9]

Such commercial analogies are not wholly alien to Mother Teresa's way of thinking. In Calcutta she used to be greatly in demand to grace many occasions, from football matches to school prize-givings as guest of honour, her presence considered good PR for the city or the school. Her condition for attending a football match at Salt Lake City stadium recently was 300 bars of soap and 300 saris, a small price. However, the Rev. Noel Sen, Presbyter of St Paul's Cathedral in Calcutta, has misgivings about how this situation was allowed to escalate so that Mother Teresa became equated with some sort of mystical power. 'She can cause havoc,' he told me over a delicious tea of green curry sandwiches. When the principal of the United Missionary Girls High School, a Protestant foundation in Calcutta, invited her to attend the school's annual thanksgiving service in the cathedral she accepted and a place was duly kept for her. Perhaps it was the knowledge that she was attending which ensured that the magnificent cathedral, with its Burne-Jones west window, was overflowing. 'However, she came half an hour late at 5.15 when she should have come at a quarter to five. We were right in the middle of prayers but when she came and walked to the front amid the glare of TV cameras everyone got up and the service was completely interrupted and it made a mockery of the whole thing.' Noel Sen was not impressed by such a dramatic entrance, which detracted from the serious nature of a church service. It was not a good lesson to teach schoolgirls. He had another occasion to marvel at Mother Teresa's sense of her own centrality to events when Archbishop Robert Runcie came to visit Calcutta in 1986. 'Runcie had a very tight schedule and built into it was a visit to Kalighat. But Mother Teresa insisted that he see her children's home as well. I thought this was not possible but when I went off to check the lunch arrangements at the Bengal Club I came back to find Mother Teresa had hijacked him and arranged for him to visit Shishu Bhavan.'[10]

Paul Handley, editor of the Church Times, accompanied Archbishop Runcie on the visit and remembers how Mother Teresa's determination to show him her corner of Calcutta left the official party perpetually fighting the Calcutta traffic to keep other appointments. When they were at Kalighat she led the Archbishop to be introduced to every single patient, many of whom presumably had no idea what was going on, in the belief that each one was of worth. 'Once she had him there she announced: "Now we're going to my children's home." Suddenly, we were in her grip and there was no way of refusing,' Handley recalled.[11] At the children's home, which is on the other side of the city, the tour again involved meeting almost all the children and babies individually. Given that most of the rest of Runcie's trip was spent giving sermons, having high-level meetings or at press conferences, Mother Teresa was only too aware that what she provided would be a salient experience. She understood that much of the purpose of her Home for the Dying is the effect it has on visitors. She wanted the Archbishop and his party to see how leprosy patients and rickshaw drivers are treated in exactly the same way as world leaders – she employed neither a different language nor a different approach. This is not so much an indication of humility as a key part of the charisma and aura and an indication of her canny psychological insight.

Whether Mother Teresa forced the press to notice her or whether the press forced Mother Teresa into a role which she occupied under protest is, in a sense, unimportant at this point. She accepted the role, not altogether unwillingly or else she would have stopped it, and used the publicity to advance her cause. Many people, apart from the media, contributed to building up the myth. In India there is a long-standing reverence for deities, gurus and goddesses and a natural respect for holy people. Mother Teresa has certainly become a goddess in Indian eyes, as well as a living saint in Western terms, and while she has not absorbed anything from India that would modify her dogma it is probably true to say that there are certain virtues in Hindu spirituality, particularly the belief in karma, which suit her own beliefs, while the individualism and search for absolute freedom in the West strike a jarring, questioning note.

The ability to offer people the unerring certainty that you know best is a key element making for powerful spiritual leaders. Anthony Storr, an authority on gurus as spiritual leaders offering new paths to salvation, has identified a number of other traits, such as intolerance of criticism, a relationship between the guru and his followers based not on friendship but on dominance, the need for an enemy and a rallying call against that enemy, and the fervent certainty or per-suasiveness with which he proclaims his spiritual message to others.

Some of these characteristics might well be said to apply to Mother Teresa; the enemy in her case being abortion and the rallying call 'we are fighting abortion with adoption', although Storr was not specifically writing about her in his recent book, *Feet of Clay*. He points out that while there have been gurus whose holiness, lack of personal ambition and integrity are beyond question, most good people do their good deeds quietly, without hope of reward or public recognition. 'Genuine virtue is usually unobtrusive, although it may be perceived as something less admirable when exposed to the glare of publicity, as happened with Albert Schweitzer and Mother Teresa.'[12]

The effect of this deification can clearly be seen from the roughly eighteen trips which one branch of the YMCA in the UK has organised to India with groups of young people, who all have to raise the money to travel themselves. Part of the time out there is spent working, manually, on YMCA projects and part is spent volunteering with the Missionaries of Charity. The highlight of the trip, according to Glyn Evans, general secretary of Swansea YMCA and organiser of the trips, is always the meeting with Mother Teresa. 'It's a big thing for them to meet an international icon,' he explained. 'They all come away feeling their lives are changed because they realise the value of life and living to a greater extent and because material things matter so much less.' One volunteer commented on how guilty he felt after refusing to give one rupee to an old beggar and then spending 38 rupees on a drink for himself.

One year Glyn Evans took boys who were on probation accompanied by their probation officer. One was a constant offender who has not reoffended since, while another two have returned to Calcutta under their own steam to work. Why was it necessary to travel 5,000 miles to teach these boys the value of service to others when there are plenty of people in this country doing social work who could make use of extra labour? Evans accepted that it was partly the effect of travelling so far and having to raise the sponsorship money to do so, as well as the complete culture shock of seeing so much poverty and need alongside cheerfulness and gratitude, but above all it was because of Mother Teresa herself. 'The meeting was not compulsory but they all washed and put on a clean tee-shirt, which was a big thing for them, even though one of them had "chairman of the bullshitters' club" scrawled across,' Evans recalled. No one can remember much about the conversation, or if anything of significance was said, apart from the fact that Mother Teresa commented on their tattoos. 'But the effect of the meeting was that they revised their opinion of life in this country and decided it was not so bad after all.' Was it Mother Teresa's innate goodness that had this effect or was it that the media has created a figure of supra-normal proportions in an age devoid of heroes? These boys, some of whom were 'really difficult', were able to meet someone they believed was a living saint and came away feeling their lives had been touched by a force greater than anything they had yet encountered. Perhaps the true importance lay in what they would be able to tell others when they returned. Who is to say?

This belief that Mother Teresa is mandated by God is inevitably shared by all her sisters. They work with a sense of higher purpose so deeply ingrained that they perform often impossible tasks with complete trust in Divine Providence. It is a life of total surrender and, according to Mother Teresa, to accept is to be cut to pieces. 'Holiness', said Mother Teresa, 'is a simple duty for each one of us, especially for us who have been chosen. We have been chosen to belong to Christ.'[13]

What this means in practice is that temporal rules often seem unimportant to them. For example, a group of Missionaries of Charity in South London started running a summer play scheme for under-eights in Southall. When the authorities went to check this out – they discovered that it was not operating under all the required rules, such as fire regulations nor were the necessary screening processes for volunteers – to prevent, for example, paedophiles masquerading as helpers – being enforced. This was pointed out to the nuns, but the following year they ran the same play project but cut the time offered to just under two hours, which entitled them to evade the law. However well intended the scheme, the attitude revealed is one of utter confidence and certainty. There have been other occasions when Mother Teresa's sisters have met civic laws head-on. When a New York City official inspected one of Mother Teresa's homes in Greenwich Village, and, concerned about fire hygiene and garbage regulations, asked to examine the electrical wiring of her settlement, she reprimanded him saying: 'It's not your business how we do things here.'[14]

In 1992 Mother Teresa tried to open a refuge for the homeless in London, but Lambeth Council turned down her application to convert a disused magistrates' court on the ground that it would not have been of a high enough standard. Lambeth councillors said that her plan for a hostel for thirty-three men, which included a chapel, a dining room for up to eighty people and accommodation for twelve nuns, was rejected 'because it does not meet with contemporary standards for hostels'. A Missionary of Charity sister in London commented: 'We don't understand why we were turned down. The homeless are suffering on the streets and are longing for a warm bed. We have the money to open a home and can offer them food and a roof over their heads.'[15]

The confidence bred by such certainty can lead to isolation, however, which is rarely helpful. The Conference of Religious (COR) in Britain exists for the mutual support of provincials, both male and female. It is a national body with a national voice and can lobby for ways to alleviate poverty. It is allied to Church Action on Poverty and has a social justice desk that deals with the homeless, asylum seekers and refugee problems. The Missionaries of Charity are the only Congregation of women religious in this country – apart from one or two small orders which are not large enough to benefit – who are not members of the Conference of Religious. Sister Gabriel Robin, general secretary of the COR, explained to me the many advantages of membership. In the first place there is the inter-congregational formation programme, which aims to offer all women's congregations a high level of education over several years, and allows for considerable individual input. But Missionaries of Charity novices have never appeared at these; they run their own formation programme. 'Another positive aspect of the programme is the possibility of meeting people with other traditions, other charisms and other forms of spirituality and not feeling threatened in your own ... We see it as if they are working in isolation,' Sister Gabriel added. She believes that collaboration offers many opportunities for religious women concerned with social justice, whether they are helping with the elderly, immigrants, those with AIDS or council estate tenants. Failure to connect with other like-minded groups or qualified people means you lose out, she told me emphatically.*

---

* I was referred, although not by Sister Gabriel, to Can. 708 in the code of canon law, which states: 'Major superiors can usefully meet together in conferences and councils, so that by combined effort they may work to achieve more fully the purpose of each institute while respecting the autonomy, nature and spirit of each. They can also deal with affairs which are common to all and work to establish suitable co-ordination and co-operation with Episcopal conferences and with individual bishops.'

The Missionaries of Charity's sense of uniqueness and belief in God's purpose for them was noticed by other Catholic aid workers in Ethiopia at the height of the famine when everyone was dependent on troops airlifting them and their food supplies to the worst-hit areas. 'An informal queuing system was in operation whereby aid workers asked in advance for the favour of being transported there and back, but they often had the rather galling experience of being told yes and then sent off the plane when a group of Missionaries of Charity arrived, insisting that their need was greater, and jumped the queue. It was a not infrequent occurrence.'[16]

Many of those who have criticised Mother Teresa in the last decade have focused on the contrast between her own private medical care and the level of care offered in her homes as convincing proof of her solipsistic tendencies. It is a fact that Mother Teresa has received treatment at some of the world's top medical institutes, which have presumably benefited themselves from the valuable public exposure. And what leader wouldn't? For every criticism of her actions in this regard, an equal number of people believe that there is a sound indication of her practical common sense, her leadership qualities, her recognition that by staying alive she can do more good. Mother Teresa herself insists that when God wants her he will take her, in which case what is the use of medical care? A Jesuit I have discussed this with explained that, while she believes the hand of God is behind everything, that is not incompatible with accepting medical care if available since that too comes from God.

In April 1996, Mother Teresa fell and broke her collarbone, then in June she broke her foot, but she nonetheless continued travelling, albeit in a wheelchair, and came to Wales to open the 565th convent of her order. But three months later her long-standing heart trouble flared up, this time complicated by pneumonia and malaria. She was taken then into the Woodlands Nursing Home in Calcutta and put under heavy sedation in the intensive care unit. She remained stable for a few days but then, at the end of August, it appeared that the fever, which caused her fragile heart to stop beating every time her temperature rose, had too firm a grip. As soon as she was taken off the respirator she worsened immediately. Despite chloroquine for the malaria and thousands of prayers worldwide she was reportedly sinking fast. At one point she was even given the last rites as her heart apparently stopped for two minutes, but it was revived by electric shock. Sister Dolores explained: 'People who have never seen a bible are praying because they know it could save Mother.'

In early September, after regular chest physiotherapy, among other treatments, she was pronounced better and allowed to leave the nursing home. The doctors were astounded by her rapid recovery and remarked on her amazing resilience. When I discussed Mother Teresa's powers of recovery with her personal doctor in Rome he explained that her stimulus to live is of course very great but is not necessarily a religious force. He has seen many people with noble ideals, politicians as much as religious leaders, who have a similar fierce energy to carry on in the belief that they still have much to do; this can create a physical force. He explained that in his experience, and he has not seen Mother Teresa during her recent illness, Mother Teresa did not resist medical treatment on the ground that when her time is up God will take her. 'She is both obedient and brave. She has no fear of death,' Dr Vincenzo Bilotta said. 'When I told her she must not go to London she was disappointed but said obviously God wants me to remain in Rome, and she succumbed to what the doctors wanted.' She then cracked a joke about the fact that although medically speaking she had a bad heart, 'You know that my heart is good and to be good you have to spend a long time with doctors.'[17]

On 16 September 1996 she was back in hospital in Calcutta for a brain scan as she had fallen from her bed. Although this proved a false alarm, in late November she fell critically ill again. This time she was rushed to the gleamingly up-to-date BM Birla Heart Institute in Calcutta, where she had blockages removed from two arteries. One of the doctors who performed the angioplasty, Mother Teresa's third in five years, was Dr Patricia Aubnel, a cardiac surgeon from Los Angeles, who has treated Mother Teresa for more than twenty years. According to Dr Aubnel, Mother Teresa had asked to be sent home to be with her sisters. She said she wanted 'no special treatment and expected to die like those she had been serving most of her life'.[18] Another of her doctors in September had leaked to the press Mother Teresa's concerns about having expensive private healthcare treatment as she was worried that her hostile critics, 'especially Tariq Ali and Christopher Hitchens', might misconstrue her admission to the nursing home as 'a sign of affluence and taking undue advantage of popularity'.

Mother Teresa was quoted then as saying: 'If so many sisters can be cured inside the Missionaries of Charity, then why not me? I would like to be treated like any other sister. There is no need for special facilities because most Indians do not have proper medical facilities.'

The journalist who recounted this leak, Parnab Mukherjee, said Mother Teresa was adamant about this for a long time and agreed to be hospitalised only after hours of persuasion. However, we were not told who was doing the persuading nor why they felt it necessary to urge Mother Teresa against her own better instincts. The loudest *cri de coeur* came just hours before the latest angioplasty and was considered so dramatic that the Independent newspaper splashed its headline: 'Mother Teresa, I want to die'. Its story, which claimed that Mother Teresa had begged openly and repeatedly to go home to God, was based on an interview with Jim Towey, a former seminarian with her Order who had known her for eleven years and now heads a foundation in Florida dedicated to the dignity of the old and dying. Towey said that when he saw her after the September illness she told him she did not want to live any longer. 'She's helped so many people to die that she can accept mortality much better than her doctors. She didn't want to go into hospital [in September] and she doesn't want to be in hospital now.'[19]

Are Mother Teresa's apparently clearly expressed wishes being disregarded or has she been persuaded that her Order is not ready for her to leave them? Is this acceptance of private healthcare a weakness on Mother Teresa's part? Or does our criticism of her in this regard reveal the barrenness of spiritual thought among many of us in the West who are uncomfortable with the idea of having high moral icons in our midst because they remind us of our own failures and inability to improve the world – hence our search for the feet of clay? Why is it that moral rectitude and religious certitude strike a jarring note in late-twentieth-century society? There is a sense among many, particularly journalists, that any legend which has endured this long needs to be exposed, as happened to Albert Schweitzer. James Cameron, who had visited the doctor at Lambaréné in Gabon, accepted that while his original achievements were considerable and his sacrifices notable, 'yet his accomplishments were negligible; his mission an illusion; his hospital in the equatorial forest medically valueless or even dangerous, existing solely as a frame for his immeasurable ego; his own philosophical contribution to the advancement of Africa rather worse than negative'.[20] And yet Cameron was concerned that, in redressing the balance of uncritical devotion, there was a danger of destroying all the achievements of the young Schweitzer and ignoring the value that numbers of people were presumably deriving from the inspiration of the Schweitzer mystique.

For some, Mother Teresa is not just a symbol of religious good but a symbol of the expiation of the great guilt of colonialism – the original sin of the modern world. 'The steady stream of volunteers from the prosperous West, mainly young people ... come to assuage the hurts of the past perpetrated by their forefathers as much as to relieve the miseries of the present,' said Chidananda Dasgupta, the Bengali writer and film director. Yet, however much of a focus she provides to the illusion that the West comes to the aid of the East, I believe most people who revere Mother Teresa as a living saint do not do so from motives of colonial guilt. When I asked Robert Sarno SJ at the Congregation for the Causes of the Saints if there was any doubt about Mother Teresa's speedy canonisation he replied curtly: 'We don't discuss people who are very much alive. I don't know her personally and I wouldn't have anything to say about the process of canonisation for someone who is alive. We don't start the process until five years after the death.'[21]

This is correct, of course; a living saint in Catholic terms is an impossibility and Sarno was particularly reticent, I assume, since he is widely touted in Rome as being one of the sources for a recent, revealing book on the process of canonisation. But Mother Teresa herself is not coy when it comes to talking about saints and sainthood. One of the signs that struck me on a noticeboard in her orphanage in Delhi declared: 'Let me make saints for the Mother Church,' and many of her writings dwell on this.

'What is a saint but simply a resolute soul, a soul that uses power plus action? Wasn't this what St Paul meant when he said, "I can do all things in Him who strengthens me"? My sisters, I will not be satisfied if you are just good religious. I want to be able to offer God a perfect sacrifice. Only holiness perfects the gift.' ' "To resolve to be a saint" means I will despoil myself of all that is not God. I will strip my heart and empty it of all created things; I will live in poverty and detachment. I will renounce my will, my inclinations, my whims and fancies and offer myself as a willing slave to the will of God. Yes, my children, that is what I pray for daily for each one, that you may become a slave to the will of God.'[22] In this sense, Mother Teresa does see herself as a saint, or as someone who lives a life of such holiness that increasingly they become intensely aware of their own unworthiness, and she sees holiness or saintliness as a duty of all of us.

Fleur Cowles, the American author and socialite, had a revealing anecdote in her recent memoirs. She wrote: 'I held Mother Teresa's hand in mine, never forgetting for a moment that I held the hand of a saint. Tom, my husband, sitting close, asked: "Mother, why don't they make you a saint while you are alive? Why wait until you're dead?" Her face lifted and lit up in laughter. "Oh they're waiting for me to go up there first," she replied, the first finger of her right hand motioning in a twirling climb upwards above her head.'[23]

Fleur Cowles is right: most people today who call Mother Teresa a living saint see her as an everyday saint, a good person, one of heroic virtue even, who has given a voice to the poor and marginalised, and they see her as a true imitator of Christ, which is how the early Christians understood the meaning of the word. They are not thinking about sainthood in a technical sense, for which you have to be dead. Many people who meet her for the first time as well as those who know her well, talk about her radiance; what they really mean is not physical beauty but some special sort of grace, or charisma, which they perceive shining through her to inspire others. Ultimately, the way her life has touched others, particularly those in the West, will probably be judged a far greater achievement than anything she has done to change Calcutta. Hardly surprising, therefore, that the Albanians long for such a saint to be buried in their country. Although several countries have awarded Mother Teresa honorary citizenship she has identified herself most closely with India. Knowing how lovingly her Indian sisters would tend her grave, it would be extraordinary if anywhere other than Calcutta was her final earthly resting place.

Nonetheless, there are those who warn that Mother Teresa's formal declaration as a saint – the placing of her name in the canon, or list of saints – is not automatic. The procedure is lengthy, and arduous and, although the underlying values required are unchanging, it is difficult to predict precisely the emphasis of a future Papacy. For example, the cause for Padre Pio, the Capuchin friar from San Giovanni Rotondo in Italy, has already begun, but has not made the sort of headway most people expected for such a well-loved figure; apparently, he was said to have had a temper. Yet Padre Pio became a cult figure from 1918, when his hands manifested the stigmata in imitation of Christ's suffering, as his followers devoutly believed. The seemingly undeniable aspect is that the wounds never healed and Pio was obliged to wear gloves more often than not for the last fifty years of his life. Hardly any progress has been made in the cause of the martyred Archbishop Oscar Romero of San Salvador, gunned down at the altar in 1980 by soldiers who tried to silence his demands for social justice for the poor. That country's prosperous elite, strongly opposed to his canonisation, have so far had their way. Yet in the next century it could be that only those who have been activists for social justice will be considered worthy of the title saint.

In the early part of this century, it was the rule that fifty years had to pass since death before sainthood could be declared, although St Thérèse of Lisieux, Mother Teresa's namesake, created a modern record by taking only twenty-eight years. But much changed under John Paul II, who has speeded up the process in an effort to give the world a unified message about the strength of Catholicism. In 1988 alone, a busy year, he canonised 122 men and women and beatified many more. This compares to a total of fewer than 300 since 1234, when the Papacy was first given exclusive control of saint-making. Even though his preferred candidates are usually bland, pious, apolitical, male figures from several centuries ago, the process can still take decades if legal and scholarly arguments are involved, which include listening to the Devil's Advocate, a.k.a. the Promoter of the Faith, arguing his case with a spokesman for the cause. The fastest process so far is that of José Maria Escrivá de Balaguer, controversial founder of the secretive and sect-like organisation, Opus Dei, who died in 1975 and was beatified by John Paul II in 1992. Even Cardinal Basil Hume, not noted for his outspokenness, expressed concern over the recruiting methods of Opus Dei, yet the organisation had vast financial reserves to support their founder's cause and there is today real concern that only religious orders have the time, money and effort to promote candidates. Lay people, whose lives may carry a more relevant message for contemporary believers, in practice never qualify.

For the long process of canonisation does not come cheap; the Sisters of the Blessed Sacrament in the United States estimate that they spent more than £250,000 on getting their founder Katherine Drexel merely declared blessed in 1988. Not surprisingly, Dorothy Day, the American Catholic convert who founded the Catholic Workers, a group which, on behalf of the poor, does similar work to the Missionaries of Charity, will not be declared a saint partly because one of her granddaughters wrote to stem the tide towards her canonisation, saying: 'She was a humble person living as she felt the best way to improve on the world's ills – take all your moneys and energies that are being put into her canonisation and give it to the poor. That is how you'd show your love and respect for her.'[24]

Although the cause for Mother Teresa is likely to be well organised, with no shortage of financial resources, and modern communications will make it much easier to produce the necessary documentation much faster, there is a rising tide of Catholic opinion that believes Mother Teresa, although widely supported as a candidate for sainthood, deserves better than posthumously enduring 'a discredited trial by petty Vatican officialdom'[25] so that her relics may be invoked for their power. Peter Stanford, former editor of the Catholic Herald, wrote about the costs involved in canonisation: 'In the case of the Missionaries of Charity ... it will be a stark choice between opening a hospital or paying countless Vatican officials whose job it is to play God.'[26] Kenneth Woodward in his authoritative book, Making Saints, writes: 'The men who ultimately decide are working within a system which is deficient in the checks and balances expected of a profession. Too much room is left for subjective judgement, pressure and caprice ... The lack of professional procedures leaves the system open to the charge of manipulation.'[27] The Church's response is that whatever the defects of a system, if God wills it, it will happen, so ultimately it will produce the effect God wants and the saints God wants.

Like Mother Teresa, Opus Dei's Balaguer was openly talked of as a saint for years before his death and John Paul II was known to be a long-standing and devoted admirer. While it is unlikely to be John Paul II who presides over Mother Teresa's cause, she has been of key significance for his pontificate and the two have formed a close personal and ideological relationship based on much more than their shared Eastern European roots and coincidence of dates. Mother Teresa has been extremely important for this Pope partly because of the ongoing discussions about the position of women within the Church. Of necessity, there have always been too few women in positions of authority in the Catholic hierarchy, which made it increasingly valuable to have a woman reinforcing the doctrinal message. 'She is one of very few women in the top echelons of the Church who is very orthodox,' explained Marco Politi, Vatican expert at *La Repubblica*.

Given the impossibility, for him, of ordaining women as priests Pope John Paul II has needed to do everything else he can to boost what he calls women's special role and feminine genius, which enables them to give birth, raise children and care for others. John Paul II has said from the beginning of his pontificate that the Mother of Christ stood very near to Christ and is therefore closely connected to his redemption. 'Mother Teresa embodies for him,' said Politi, 'at an international level, both the feminine genius of all women and the special care for the third world, which is increasingly important as the West and the industrial world is slipping more towards materialism and industrialism.'

Politi and others insist that Pope John Paul II is no misogynist, but his refusal to countenance women priests has caused difficulties. Women in religious orders – twice as numerous as men – are the infantry of the Catholic Church, yet many of them are silent dissenters. They may be neither loud nor aggressive in their criticism of his orthodoxy, but critical they are. I have met several myself. Often they work in hospitals or schools, with old people or drug users, or in other areas of social need, and many of them are known to be opposed to the Pope's unyielding position on contraception.* In this context it is hardly surprising that the Vatican Curia prefers Mother Teresa's line to that of many other sisters and nuns or that Mother Teresa is the one called many times to conferences. In 1990 Mother Teresa was invited to speak, by direct invitation of the Pope, at a synod on Religious Life in Rome attended by 200 bishops. When I was in Rome in April 1996

* Following the 1981 referendum on abortion in Italy, which showed an overwhelming majority in favour of defending the abortion law, the poll was analysed in Northern Italy and revealed that many votes in favour came from neighbourhoods where religious orders were living and working.

the advance publicity for a pro-life conference billed the concluding address by Mother Teresa, then eighty-five, as one of its main attractions. Whether or not she is a living saint, there is no doubt she has been an important spiritual icon for the Vatican which they have not been afraid to make use of.

Most Vaticanisti I spoke to, while agreeing that Mother Teresa will be seen inextricably as part of this Papacy, at the same time insist that she does not stand intellectual comparison to Pope John Paul II. 'The Pope is too great a historical personality, whatever you think of his statements; he is both philosopher and mystic and the only spiritual leader of our age who can speak to the whole world,' was Politi's verdict. A major part of this Pope's vision has been to eradicate what he calls the culture of death and declare unequivocally the supremacy of the culture of life. In fighting this battle, Mother Teresa, as a prophetical woman sharing exactly the same values as him, has been of inestimable value. Her testimony of charity has been completely in sympathy with that of the Pope and they have been valuable collaborators for each other. One high level Vatican Prelate said: 'I think the future will show what a major revolution the Pope with the help of Mother Teresa has introduced. Both the Pope and Mother Teresa have defended the identity and dignity of women in a concentric way, calling on women to assume the function in society for defending life and the family and making sure that the sound values in modern society are a central part of the church, not marginal.'[29] It is precisely this view, according to nuns like Sister Lavinia Byrne, which perpetuates the myth that women are subordinate.

Karen Armstrong, the former nun now an author who has written a history of God, is well aware of how useful Mother Teresa has been to the Vatican. 'The Church has often found its saints too radical and today some Roman Catholics choose to see Mother Teresa as a comforting reminder of older values. Her success, they argue, shows that reform of the Church is unnecessary,' she has said.[30] But when in 1948 Mother Teresa left the Loreto Order her action was a dramatic one, which the Church looked upon with suspicion. 'Similarly, in the last twenty years,' Armstrong pointed out, 'about a quarter of the active Roman Catholic priests throughout the world have left the conventional ministry; unlike her, they have been disowned by the Vatican. Some 60% of them now live and work among the destitute and are regarded by some as heralds of a new Catholicism.'

The evidence appears to indicate that at least from the beginning of the 1990s Mother Teresa wanted to step down but was not allowed to, some say at the Vatican's behest. But also, there are clearly some within her Order who cannot imagine life without her at the helm. In 1990 the 103-strong electoral college of the Missionaries of Charity tried to choose a successor by secret ballot, 'with a lot of support from the Holy Spirit', while Mother Teresa herself went into retreat just outside Calcutta. The power struggle at that time centred around the Indian Sister Agnes Das, Mother Teresa's first disciple who many had assumed would take over by virtue of having been there the longest. The other main contenders were the treasurer, Sister Camilus Pereira, who was a secretary before joining, Sister Priscilla Lewis, an Anglo-Indian from Shillong who handled the media where possible, and two doctors, both graduates of the Calcutta Medical College, Sister Shanti D'Souza, a Bombay-based Goan, and Sister Andrea, a German in her late fifties. The constitution of the Missionaries of Charity stipulates that the Superior General must be at least forty years of age and should have completed ten years of final vows. She is elected for six years and may be re-elected for a second but not a third consecutive term. In Mother Teresa's case, however, the Vatican waived this condition and Mother Teresa held the post of Superior General from the first elections in 1961 until 1997.

The Archbishop of Calcutta's representative, Monsignor Francis Gomes, who presided over the five-hour secret ballot in 1990, announced that in fact, although the Vatican had accepted Mother Teresa's request to retire because of ill health, it was she who had once again been chosen as the leader of the Missionaries of Charity to travel the world on behalf of the poor and lonely. 'It is God's will,' he added. The quiet but spiritual Sister Agnes was not only passed over for the leadership but demoted, as the six-member Council of the Missionaries of Charity was also reduced to four 'by an amendment from the Vatican'; and she was now dropped from this. Apparently, she was deemed not forceful enough to take over Mother Teresa's commanding role on the world stage. From 1990 to 1997 the Council comprised Sister Frederick, the Assistant General and Deputy, Sister Joseph Michael, Sister Priscilla and Sister Monica. One of these four was assumed to be the most likely successor in the next ballot.

In 1996 a constitutional amendment was mooted whereby Mother Teresa could dispense with the democratic set-up and nominate her own successor. Some commentators believed that, shortly before undergoing her heart operation in November 1996, she availed herself of this new privilege and told the Pope whom she wished to succeed her. The name was, however, kept secret.

With Mother Teresa remaining in command, the world was given the clear message that no one else in the Order could handle the top job. Mother Teresa herself told the press: 'I was expecting to be free but God has his own plans.' When asked if her ill health would permit her to continue with her task she side-stepped the question: 'We have sisters who are capable and they will continue God's work.'[31] Nobody doubted the capabilities of the other sisters but why were they held back from assuming a greater role? In fifty years Mother Teresa must have thought about the need for a successor and could have prepared someone to take over from her. Above all, why did Mother Teresa accept a post she had decided to relinquish?

Had she been allowed to spend the last six years quietly (not in obscurity, which admittedly the world's press would never have allowed her to do), working perhaps at Kalighat but still performing God's work, it is unlikely that the controversies that have dogged her final years would even have been aired. As it was, she had journalists begging for interviews to the end and sometimes repented at leisure what she had agreed to in haste. In 1994 she permitted a new film and book about her but, it appears, soon had second thoughts and the project became entangled in a bitter legal battle over rights. According to one account, Random House, the giant US publisher of Pope John Paul's phenomenally successful *Crossing the Threshold of Hope*, which sold well over 200,000 copies worldwide the year before, was hoping to market this book as a companion volume, although Mother Teresa had never been considered an intellectual or deep spiritual thinker in the same category as the Pope. Were the advisers who persuaded her to give her agreement the same ones who, according to Towey, 'had to resort to trickery to persuade their ailing founder into accepting medical care',[32] and if so why did they? The usual answer given in such circumstances is 'if it will help the work'.

For some years Ohmer Ahmed, an Indian-born, London-based film producer, had with a colleague been trying to win Mother Teresa's permission to make a new film. In spite of her initial hesitancy, by the autumn of 1994 she had given her consent to a Canadian religious writer, Lucinda Vardey, starting work on the book. Much of Vardey's research was to have been in the form of listening to Mother Teresa being interviewed for the film as it was intended to be a book by Mother Teresa, written in the first person – 'a spiritual classic from the world-famous champion of the poor'[33] – without the ghost writer's name appearing on the jacket. However, when the book, A Simple Path, appeared in the autumn of 1995 there was no accompanying film as originally planned, and the compiler's name was stated clearly on the jacket. What went wrong? I was told only that it was hoped the film would be completed at a later, as yet unspecified, date.

Yet it was clear the project had not gone according to plan, and not just because of the non-appearance of the film; pasted over the copyright pages of A Simple Path was a blue-bordered white slip which stated 'Introduction © Lucinda Vardey 1995' and 'How this book came about © John Cairns 1995'. Underneath, yet still visible, is the 'Copyright © Mother Teresa' that was originally planned. In the event, there is very little of Mother Teresa herself in this slim volume. Instead, there are thoughts and pieces of advice from Sister Theresina, Sister Katieri and Sister Dolores as well as from Brother Geoff, General Servant of the Missionary Brothers of Charity. There are pages of comments from volunteers, but from Mother Teresa's own lips we hear very little. Perhaps she was too ill or too tired and perhaps she had said it all before. She has certain catchphrases that she has repeated over the years but fresh phraseology is not one of her gifts. Peter Stanford could find nothing memorable written by Mother Teresa when he was putting together an anthology of nuns' writing and Sean Patrick Lovett, of Vatican Radio, trying to produce a book of Mother Teresa's prayers and meditations in the early 1980s, knew it would be impossible to sit down with her and extract the words. Instead he collected what she had already said as 'a synopsis of her thoughts, her philosophy, her way of life, her way of love...'

The most likely explanation for the change of heart was that A Simple Path, never Mother Teresa's own initiative, was being compiled in the immediate aftermath of Christopher Hitchens' documentary, Hell's Angel. Although that film was not officially shown in India, there were a number of privately videoed copies circulating and the Indian press went to town analysing it. Then, in 1995, Hitchens produced a book of the film, The Missionary Position: Mother Teresa in Theory and Practice. Hitchens' title undoubtedly caused considerable offence yet, for different reasons, I am surprised at Mother Teresa's title, reflecting as it does her continuing ability after living in a multi-cultural, pluralistic society like India for nearly seventy years to see life in simple terms. It seems to me unutterably complex. Perhaps therein lies the true miracle of faith.

Mother Teresa had been famously quoted at the time of the documentary polemic as saying she forgave Hitchens, not on behalf of God, but on behalf of herself. Now he was able to respond: 'This was odd, since we had not sought forgiveness from her or from anyone else. Odder still if you have any inclination to ask by what right she assumes the power to forgive. There are even some conscientious Christians who would say that forgiveness, like the astringent of revenge, is reserved to a higher power.'[34]

Forgiveness notwithstanding, there is no doubt that the criticism of Mother Teresa had struck home in Calcutta. The sisters said that their leader was going through the same ordeal as had Jesus Christ and their response was to pray for the souls of those involved in the documentary. Hitchens' continuing attack may have been too ferocious to change the minds of moderate-minded people but the effect was dramatic. Even though a majority of people felt that her reputation as a deeply holy woman was more than strong enough to withstand such an onslaught, it changed the ground rules of reporting on Mother Teresa. Suddenly volunteers wrote long pieces critical of the methods employed by the Missionaries of Charity, while keen young reporters were encouraged to pursue a story that might show Mother Teresa in a negative light, the sort of article for which any editor who cared about his job a decade before would have found a home instantly on the spike.

One of these stories in September 1995 concerned a girl of fifteen, Shahida Kapoor, a pavement dweller who was married, with a child. In cooking a meal on the street she had overturned a fire and, as her sari suddenly engulfed her in flames and she tried to save her child, she was herself badly burned. A local doctor found her some days later lying outside the Calcutta Corporation building with third-degree burns and severe damage to one arm. He managed to get her accepted in an overcrowded government hospital but, without money, it was difficult to obtain the right medication for her. When she complained of ill treatment by the staff her relatives brought her home, to her familiar patch of street. One month later, after she had lain on the pavement unable to visit any doctors, the wound became infected, turned green and was bleeding continually, and she could not keep the flies away. Then a search began to find another place for her and at this point the press got hold of the story.

'A volunteer at Mother Teresa's contacted us and told us Mother Teresa wanted to take the girl in,' explained Meher Murshed, the reporter at the *Calcutta Telegraph* who eventually broke the story. The Missionaries of Charity allowed her the use of one of their ambulances and the girl was taken, with a reporter, to Kalighat, Shishu Bhavan and Prem Dan, but was turned away from the first because she was not dying and from the second because she was not an orphan and moreover was married with a child although only fifteen and a minor and was therefore highly unsuitable. She was told the third was out of the question as well, since she was neither insane nor suffering from tuberculosis. In the end she was deposited back on the pavement. Meher Murshed understood clearly the significance of the story he then wrote. It was the first major anti-Mother Teresa story in India. He had seen Mother Teresa personally at another event and had asked her about the story, but she told him it was neither the time nor the place to discuss the issue. 'Some said the girl was a hospital case and therefore Mother Teresa was not a suitable organisation, but by now all she needed was rest and for her wound to be kept clean and dressed,' Murshed told me. 'But our point was that we never asked Mother Teresa to take her, she stepped in of her own accord and then changed her mind. The story caused considerable disillusionment because Mother Teresa has always said she never refuses anyone.'[35] Eventually the Islamia Hospital, a government hospital essentially for Muslims, heard about the girl and picked her up.

The story of the burnt girl was essentially of Calcutta, but in November 1995 Mother Teresa became embroiled in an even bigger row with international reverberations. This time, as the missionary activity of past centuries came back to haunt her, she found herself facing the most sustained opposition of her career and perhaps for the first time ever was publicly criticised by Church functionaries in India.

On 18 November 1995, the Mother, as Indian newspapers call her, held special prayers at the Sacred Heart Cathedral in Delhi to launch a two-week relay fast and protest campaign demanding scheduled caste (SC) status for Christian Dalits. The Indian state's reservations policy, based on a constitutional provision of 1950, was aimed at reserving a percentage of government jobs for the lower castes within the Hindu spectrum because otherwise opportunities would be denied to them by the upper castes' control of the system. The law was later amended to give the same status to Sikhs and Buddhists. However, reservations were denied to Dalit Christians on the grounds that once a person converts to Christianity his caste becomes irrelevant. It is also argued that Christian SCs have an edge over other SCs because they can study in Christian educational establishments, an argument the Christians object to as it was felt that by giving SCs places in Christian educational establishments they were using up their own limited resources when the country's resources should be made available to them.

Many Dalits have converted to Christianity specifically because it announces itself as an equal brotherhood where untouchability will no longer apply. 'This is the argument that is always offered to prospective converts and to thousands of children in convent schools in India,' wrote one of India's most respected commentators, Vir Sanghvi.[36] 'How can anybody claim that there is a caste of Christians who are so low down the religious ladder that they deserve the same affirmative action as Hinduism's unfortunate harijans? If they are Christians they can't be Dalits. If they are Dalits then they are Hindus and Mother Teresa has nothing to do with them.'

Mother Teresa's unhappy involvement in this highly political issue first aroused the ire of the right-wing Hindu BJP party, whose spokesperson Sushma Swaraj tore into her, saying: 'Christianity does not recognise Chaturbvarna which creates untouchables. Instead of fighting this evil practice, Mother Teresa has sought to introduce this in her own religion. The very basis of Christianity is a casteless society. We believe the demand will do no good to society, the country or her own religion and definitely not to harijans.' Mother Teresa then escalated matters by calling a press conference to rebut the charges and insisted that she had not known what the prayer meeting was all about. 'I realised only later that a demonstration demanding reservations was taking place.'

This statement clearly infuriated the National Co-ordination Committee for Scheduled Caste Christians and its organising secretary, the Rev. Father S. Lourduswamy. He clarified the issue by saying,

> A written invitation was sent to Mother on 1 November by the Most Reverend Alan de Lastic, Archbishop of Delhi. After she accepted the invitation Bishop Vincent Consessao, Auxiliary Bishop of the archdiocese of Delhi, met her and explained to her that the purpose of the meeting was to demand equal justice for Scheduled Caste Christians. Then Brother José Daniel, convenor of the programme, also briefed her.
>
> What's more, the Bishop of Delhi had even sent Mother a background paper on the issue explaining why reservation was necessary even for Christian converts. After all of this, if Mother Teresa had still failed to grasp the nature of the meeting she was attending, then she was even more otherworldly than had been previously believed.

It was a messy affair. In the past, involving Mother Teresa in such agitation would have helped the Christian cause. But this time, after first antagonising non-Christians by her very attendance at the prayer meeting, she then made herself yet more unpopular within the Church. One of the most vocal opponents was the Rev. Somen Das: 'I feel she has been foolish to apologise and backtrack,' he said. 'It is as if she was suffering from serious amnesia. We should take her words with a pinch of salt and forget about it. The fact is that Mother Teresa, with her impractical views on abortion and family planning, is quite obsolete now.'[37] Her presence, far from helping the cause of Dalit Christians, in the event diverted attention from them and created a backlash against them. Even her most loyal press commentators saw her involvement in this issue as ill advised and likely to create new conflicts in a country which already has enough such cleavages to contend with.

Christians in India, both Catholic and Protestant, have in the last few years been putting much greater emphasis on development and social justice and have started to organise agitations on wages, land and basic human rights among the rural poor. There is slowly a recognition that the only way to help Dalits, women, unorganised labour and the rest of the extremely poor and marginalised in society is to play a more active role in working for social justice. Yet nothing of Mother Teresa's work, however valuable it may have been, has ever tried to break the barrier between the rich and poor. She wants to help the poor of the world; but do you ever help them if you fail to break the cycle of poverty and never question why there is poverty in the first place? Picking people up off the street when they are dying is simply one point of entry into the cycle but there are other points, in which Mother Teresa is not interested. Her method may have total inner coherence, as Lavinia Byrne points out: 'But [today] and in her hugely expanded Order isn't it time to develop something more sophisticated which might require of her that she makes better friends with that part of herself which was in the Mary Ward community for so long?'[38]

Mother Teresa has entered the international lexicon now. 'We can't all be Mother Teresas' or 'You'd need to be Mother Teresa to do that' are phrases that need no further explanation anywhere. But they are shallow expressions which do not begin to fathom why a simple Albanian of unprepossessing appearance captured the imagination of the entire world for so long. 'She had a sort of shamelessness' was how one Catholic sister described her to me, a phrase which seems to pinpoint the essence of her very human drive. She disliked intensely those who tried to pull rank but could do so shamelessly herself when it suited her purpose. Secure as she was in God's purpose for her, there was no part of the world she felt was not in need of her message.

EPILOGUE

On 13 March 1997 the Missionaries of Charity finally ended speculation about what would happen when Mother Teresa dies. This was a question she herself had always refused to answer, saying 'Wait until I die, and then see.' The nuns had been deadlocked in their discussions for weeks, unable to elect an outright replacement for the woman who founded their Order forty-seven years before. Eventually, they appealed to the Pope for help and he came up with a compromise. Mother Teresa was to stay as spiritual and titular head while Sister Nirmala, a sixty-three-year-old Hindu convert to Christianity, would become the new Superior General, taking over the arduous administrative chores and generally assisting Mother Teresa. She would hold the post for six years until a further ballot and could then be re-elected for a second, but not a third term.

Within hours, Mother Teresa made it clear she was still very much in the fray with an announcement about her future plans for new homes. Meanwhile Sister Nirmala, a timid personality who had always kept a low profile, declared she would not be taking the title 'Mother'. Elections had been originally scheduled for 1996 but Mother Teresa was critically ill for the last part of the year and the sisters felt it was inappropriate to go ahead at such a time. So they delayed until January, when Mother Teresa was better but still very weak and spending much of her time either in a wheelchair or in bed with back pain. They hoped that she would be able to give her blessing to the new leader, which indeed she has.

Sister Nirmala was an outside candidate, not one of the four councillors among whom the new leader was expected to be chosen. Born in Ranchi, Bihar, in 1934, her Nepalese father was a Brahmin who served in the Indian Army. Of her eight brothers and sisters, six now live in Kathmandu and another sister has joined a different Catholic organisation as a nun. Sister Nirmala became a Missionary of Charity in 1958 at the age of twenty-four and, seven years later, was picked to head the first of Mother Teresa's homes outside India in Venezuela. Ten years after that she was instrumental in founding the contemplative wing, where the sisters do some apostolic works but are not involved in running homes of any sort.

Before the first contemplative house opened, Sister Nirmala had been to stay with Father Bede Griffith, the scholar and friend of C. S. Lewis who lived a highly monastic life in a Benedictine ashram in Tamil Nadu, South India. The intention was that on her return she and Mother Teresa would open a contemplative house at the foot of the Himalayas. However, Mother Teresa alone changed the plans, deciding instead that the first contemplative house should be opened in New York not India, and sent Sister Nirmala to run it. 'In the United States they are ready for it,' she said by way of explanation later, a reference to her conviction that the spiritual poverty of the West was harder to conquer than the material poverty in India, and therefore required a new method to deal with it. She hoped the contemplative branch would provide the answer. At the time of Sister Nirmala's election she was in charge of the contemplatives' twelve convents. It was in this capacity that she became one of Mother Teresa's trusted confidantes as she often accompanied her on trips aboard.

Why did the 226 senior sisters, many of whom had flown into Calcutta from all over the world, remain closeted together for so long before naming a successor for their international organisation? The discernment process, as it is known, involves first an eight-day retreat then a seminar for a little over two weeks followed by a chapter general, which concludes with a vote. The idea is that, through prayer, they will discover God's will, and they obviously wished, therefore, for a unanimous decision on their new leader. In the end they had to settle for Sister Nirmala polling more than 50 per cent of the vote. Her Indian background was a significant factor in her favour, since the vast majority of the Missionaries of Charity are now Indian. Having an

Indian at the top will help deflect criticism that this is a Western-funded organisation ministering to the needs of the third world.

For some time now the Order has been severely top heavy, with many of the most powerful nuns in their eighties or late seventies having served either on the council or having held one of the other top jobs at least once; these positions generally changed hands within a small elite. Yet if there was to be a fresh vision after nearly fifty years it was clearly necessary for the sisters to get to know each other over as long a period as possible in an attempt to discover if somebody younger might be able to take on the demanding role. Part of the problem for the Missionaries of Charity, whose ethos has always been extremely deferential, was convincing themselves that anyone among their number could have the same variety of talents – administrative, spiritual and media – as their foundress. Finding someone with Mother Teresa's charisma and contacts, built on years of personal and historical experience from Skopje and Rathfarnham to Loreto and Darjeeling, was impossible. From the Balkan Wars to the Partition of India, Mother Teresa was shaped by some of the most cataclysmic events of the twentieth century.

In addition, the old concern that, without Mother Teresa to greet would-be donors in person, international donations would drop dramatically refused to lie down. Her persuasiveness in soliciting gifts has been incomparable and the quiet, bespectacled nun from Bihar will have much to learn on this front. Yet failure to elect a successor would have been highly irresponsible given the likelihood of needing to reconvene the sisters, a hugely costly exercise, should Mother Teresa die within a short space of time.

It is impossible now, while Mother Teresa is still alive, to forecast how, if at all, the Missionaries of Charity will change direction in the next century. It could be that many of the sisters at the top lacked the imagination to look for someone in a different mould and therefore plumped, in the end, for a safe bet. 'I expect when Mother Teresa dies there will be bloodletting – with a certain amount of "where are we at?" and "where are we going?" but not now, while she is still alive,' said one priest. The biggest pressure, he believes, which may prove irresistible, is likely to be for a measure of democratisation of the Order, more in line with the pronouncements of the Second Vatican Council.

While Mother Teresa was active, power was very firmly centralised at the top; even details such as whether the door of a house thousands of miles away should be painted blue or white were decided by her alone. But this is scarcely possible any longer, if indeed desirable. At the time of writing Mother Teresa has more than 4,000 sisters and nearly 600 homes in 130 or so countries. The Order could well be divided into four or five more manageable groups in the future with quite marked variations between them. Mother Teresa was typical of her generation and of the corner of Europe whence she came. She was neither sophisticated in her appreciation of technological progress, which she believed had little to offer in any consideration of ethics, nor up to date in her understanding of the rights or needs of women, whether these concerned reproductive rights, including abortion, or less controversial issues such as consultation with her own sisters before moving them to another job or even another country to work.

Mother Teresa based her actions on her unshakeable belief that she was interpreting God's will. There was, in a sense, nothing unusual about this since the whole notion of authority and obedience is at the heart of the Roman Catholic Church and comes directly from Christ asking Peter to follow him and give up his life to do so. In the case of the Missionaries of Charity their charism, to give wholehearted service to the poorest of the poor, is a charism given by God, therefore it is God's will that that should happen, but it is up to the Congregation and its superior to organise their worldly affairs so that it will happen. This is a human will, albeit interpreting a divine will and of course it can be easily abused. 'Even Mother Teresa would agree she had abused it, not deliberately, but at times she would have allowed things to come into her decision-making process ... because she's human,' explained my priestly adviser.[1]

For years the Missionaries of Charity resisted change on the ground that 'the old system worked', but many of the younger women are not ignorant about what goes on in other orders and there will certainly be voices now suggesting either a need to live community life in a different way, or for more help on formation or for more understanding about social structure; above all, for more consultation. Previously, Mother Teresa might have said to one of her nuns, 'You are needed in Africa,' and, on the basis that if Christ is calling you to go, you go without questioning it, the nun obeyed. But today there is an expectation for discussion along the lines of 'How would you feel about working in Africa? Will the climate suit you?' which need not conflict with a command of Christ's.

Becoming a Missionary of Charity has always been a very radical choice. For those who are disillusioned with the values of an increasingly materialistic world, where a welfare state is meant, but often fails, to look after the poorest of the poor and where the individual feels even more alienated by an omnipotent government, joining Mother Teresa appears to offer a real opportunity to do some good. This is especially true in countries like India where the only welfare is often some milk from a street-corner concrete structure. But eventually the realisation dawns on most idealists that providing food and shelter, however necessary it is in an emergency, does little if anything to better the conditions of the people they want so desperately to help. That discovery is very frustrating for intelligent people, and looking at ways the Order can become more involved in developmental work could well be a priority for her successor.

There will also be pressures, which might have been given freer rein had one of the sisters who had qualified as a doctor been elected leader, to allow the sisters to pursue courses in social work and medicine. As a contemplative, however, Sister Nirmala seems more likely to want to follow Mother Teresa's approach in this regard. Many orders do change direction starkly once their founder dies. The FMDMs (Franciscan Missionaries for the Divine Motherhood), for example, would today be unrecognisable to Mother Frances, who died in 1976, having been their Mother Superior since 1937. She oversaw an enormous expansion of the Order in numbers both of vocations and of countries where the sisters ran schools and hospitals. Today, as vocations have dwindled, these sisters no longer run any hospitals or schools nor wear a habit. But then it is unlikely that the situation will be the same, as the FMDMs now believe that the woman they thought was their foundress was not their foundress at all. She joined an existing group of sisters and, thanks to her vision, the Order grew dramatically; when she sought papal recognition it was for a newly named society.

More than 3,000 volunteers turn up in Calcutta each year, most of them searching for a meaningful experience in their own lives. Mother Teresa never lost an opportunity to tell any journalist about the spectacular growth of her organisation, how many people had died with dignity at Kalighat (approximately 30,000 to date), and, not surprisingly as a former geography teacher, illustrated her success on a map with red dots in the parlour of the Mother House. But it dawned on me slowly that in this morass of figures the dying were rarely given a name. All were just numbers. Perhaps this striking lack of individuality, at one level, was because for Mother Teresa we are all, au fond, just souls. Those who criticise Mother Teresa are seeing her as a social worker who should be interested in humanity. She vigorously insisted that that was not her vocation, she was a religious, and yet it was a distinction many felt was untenable once she built up her institutions, and undertook so much social work therein, however much these were underpinned by religion. Should she have been allowed to stand uncriticised because she did something when the rest of us talked?

'Theology is to faith as literary criticism is to poetry,' my Jesuit consultant kept repeating to me. As aphorisms go, it was apposite since I had often justified my own enquiries on these grounds, putting myself in the role of literary critic, not theologian. Many writers have felt justified in examining Shakespeare or Milton while fully recognising their inability to create drama of the same calibre. But Mother Teresa was not simply an embodiment of faith – a faith so secure that theology was viewed as an interference – although her faith was the essence of her. She was also the poem itself. While fully accepting that the poem is more significant than the literary criticism, the latter can create a better understanding of the poem.

Mother Teresa has said time and again: 'We are all called to love, love until it hurts.' Yet the more qualified her helpers the more they were likely to be deflected from this sense of pure love, she believed. Her genius was in understanding how many young people, especially in the successful, post-war economies of the West, yearn for a greater spiritual input in their lives. They have high ideals to help the less fortunate, but how difficult it often is to put those ideals into action. Most voluntary organisations are rigorous about whom they accept and do so only after interviews, and only after the volunteer has committed himself or herself to a minimum length of stay and possibly also has paid a sum for organising the trip. There are sound reasons for this; anything less is seen as disruptive, damaging and patronising to the local populations. Mother Teresa was totally different. Her response was: 'This person wants to give love, he or she will be very welcome.' However clumsy, ill qualified or unattractive, all were accepted on equal terms for a day or a year in one of her homes. She gave people an opportunity to make a difference even if this difference mattered only to their own lives and may even have been at the expense of those they were trying to help.

The Bengali journalist Dharani Ghosh put his finger on it: 'It's easy to dismiss Mother Teresa as a saint, but I'm not sure she represents the tortured man's consciousness because of what she does for the poor. What she does for the poor is absolutely irrelevant, it's infinitesimal. So why will she be a saint? Because she reflects what I'd like to do but I cannot, she also would like to but cannot, and this torment is within her. If you talk to her you see that the torment is slowly being buried under the acclaim, and it's a tragedy ... I'm afraid that one day she'll stop suffering when she looks at the poor and just sees them as one more case; it's inevitable because of her world fame, but I like her too much for that.'[2]

Mother Teresa inspired many people with whom she came into contact not because she preached powerful sermons but because she demonstrated a way, not always effective, of using the power of love as a force of healing and redemption. In spite of all the criticism levelled against her, Mother Teresa gave tens of thousands of people the opportunity to express their love for their fellow human beings.

SOURCE NOTES

PREFACE

1 *New York Times*, 8 February 1995.
2 Malcolm Muggeridge, *Something Beautiful for God* (Collins, 1971).
3 David Porter, *Mother Teresa: The Early Years* (SPCK, 1986).

CHAPTER ONE: ORIGINS

1 Public Record Office, FO 371/1782.
2 Frederick Moore, *The Balkan Trail* (Smith Elder, 1906).
3 Ibid.
4 *Atdheu: The Organ of the Albanian Movement of Legality*, New York, December 1982, based on an interview with La Gente.
5 Anonymous, conversation with author, 29 May 1996.
6 Mary Loudon, *Unveiled, Nuns Talking* (Vintage, 1993).
7 Sister Lavinia Byrne, conversation with author, 24 March 1997.

CHAPTER TWO: MISSIONARIES

1 J. P. Jones, *India's Problem* (1903).
2 Teotonio R. de Souza, *Goa to Me* (Concept Publishing, New Delhi, 1994).
3 Stephen Neill, *Christian Missions* (Hodder & Stoughton, 1965).
4 Matthew 28:19f; cf. Acts 1:8.
5 Navin Chawla, *Mother Teresa* (Sinclair Stevenson, 1992).
6 Address by Cardinal Joseph Ratzinger of the Sacred Congregation for the Doctrine of the Faith to the Presidents of the Asian Bishops Conferences, Hong Kong, March 1995.

7   Ibid.

8   Conversation with author, Missionary Institute, 11 May 1995.

CHAPTER THREE: ARRIVAL

1   Quoted Porter, *Mother Teresa*.

2   Transcript of Everyman Special, *A Candle for Mother Teresa*, BBC Television.

3   Ibid.

4   Denis Kincaid, *British Social Life in India* (Routledge, 1938).

5   Conversation with author, 21 May 1995.

6   India Office Library, London.

7   Tarak Chandra Das, *Bengal Famine 1943* (Calcutta, 1949).

8   Quoted Desmond Doig, *Mother Teresa, Her People and Her Work* (Collins, 1976).

9   Quoted Porter, *Mother Teresa*, based on Lush Gjerji's account.

10 Quoted ibid.

11 Chawla, *Mother Teresa*.

12 Eileen Egan, *Such a Vision of the Street* (Sidgwick & Jackson, 1985).

CHAPTER FOUR: THE EARLY HELPERS

1   Quoted Doig, *Mother Teresa*.

2   Ibid.

3   Porter, *Mother Teresa*.

4   Ibid.

5   *Observer*, 26 August 1990.

6   Frances Meigh, *The Jack Preger Story* (Tabb House, 1988).

7   Letter to Channel 4, 8 November 1994, and interview with author, 7 March 1996.

8   Ibid.

9   Major E. J. Somerset, 'Reminiscences of an Indian Medical Service Officer, 1939–61', India Office Library, January 1979.

10 Ibid.

11 Anonymous, conversation with author, October 1995, Calcutta.

12 Wilfrid Russell, *New Lives for Old: The Story of the Cheshire Homes* (Gollancz, 1980).

13 Dudley Gardiner, *Angel with a Bushy Beard* (St Andrew's Press, Edinburgh, 1980).

14 Conversation with author, November 1995.

CHAPTER FIVE: EXPANSION

1   Conversation with author, 26 March 1996.
2   Muggeridge, *Something Beautiful for God*.
3   Bernard Levin, *The Pendulum Years* (Jonathan Cape, 1970).
4   Conversation with author, 4 March 1996.
5   Muggeridge, *Something Beautiful for God*.
6   Conversation with author, 1 July 1996.
7   Christopher Hitchens, *Right to Reply*, Channel 4, 12 November 1994.
8   *Observer*, 5 March 1972.
9   Safete S. Juka, *Albanian Catholic Bulletin*, 1990.
10 Nicholas Bethell, *The Great Betrayal*, (Hodder & Stoughton, 1984).

CHAPTER SIX: RECOGNITION

1   Co-Workers of Mother Teresa Newsletter No. 8, September 1973.
2   There are no figures available, but Egan (*Such a Vision*) talks about the sisters having received offers of 111.
3   Germaine Greer, *Independent* Magazine, 22 September 1990.
4   Letter to author, 24 March 1995.
5   Although the British outlawed infanticide in 1870, a century later the practice has not died out, poison or neglect being the most frequently used methods. *India Today* reported in June 1986 that 6,000 female babies had been poisoned to death during the preceding decade in one particular area in Tamil Nadu.
6   Egan, *Such a Vision*.
7   *The Templeton Prize* (Christian Journals (Ireland), 1977).
8   Ibid.
9   The English Dominican publication, *New Blackfriars*, March 1974.
10 Clifford Longley, *The Times*, 25 March 1974.
11 Jug Suraiya, 17 July 1996.
12 Conversation with author, 22 October 1995.
13 *Time*, 29 December 1975.
14 Egan, *Such a Vision*.
15 Ibid.
16 Ibid.
17 Ibid.

CHAPTER SEVEN: GLOBETROTTING

1   Co-Workers of Mother Teresa Newsletter No. 8, September 1973.
2   Report on the Works of the Missionaries of Charity in India and Abroad by the M.C. Sisters, 1968.
3   *The Times*, 8 March 1995.
4   *Evening Standard*, 15 February 1980.
5   *The Times*, 16 August 1982.
6   Reuters, 11 December 1984.
7   *Daily Express*, 28 December 1985.
8   *Evening Standard*, 3 January 1992.
9   *Is That It?* (Sidgwick & Jackson, 1986).
10 Conversation with author, 6 March 1997.
11 *Guardian*, 14 April 1988.
12 *Sunday Times*, 15 April 1990.
13 *Sunday Telegraph*, 9 September 1990.
14 Conversation with PLO representative, 26 March 1997.

CHAPTER EIGHT: ATTACK

1   *Hell's Angel*, Channel 4, 8 November 1994.
2   *Daily Mail*, 8 November 1994.
3   *The Times*, 10 November 1994, and letter to author, 4 March 1995.
4   9 November 1994.
5   Letter to Bandung, 24 March 1994.
6   Christopher Hitchens, *Nation*, April 1992.
7   *Right to Reply*, Channel 4, 12 November 1994.

CHAPTER NINE: MEDICINE

1   Conversation with author, 2 March 1996.
2   Ibid.
3   Conversation with author, 28 August 1995.
4   Conversation with author, 19 April 1995.
5   Ibid.
6   *Lancet*, vol. 344, 17 September 1994.
7   *Lancet*, 15 October 1994.
8   Conversation with author, 19 July 1995.
9   Ysenda Maxtone Graham, *Evening Standard*, 22 May 1995.
10 'Information for Volunteers Visiting India', Mary Cox, Co-Workers Letter, June 1993.

11 Mary Loudon, *Spleen*, 1992.

12 Conversation with author, 19 July 1995.

13 Conversation with author, 14 November 1995.

14 Anonymous, conversation with author, 12 May 1997.

15 *Nursing Standard*, vol. 6, 30 October 1991.

16 'Inside Time', Rose Billington, October 1994.

17 Ibid.

18 Damian Furniss, *Poems* ('Tears in the Fence', 1995).

19 Anaya Publishers, 1990.

20 Mother Teresa Letter to Co-Workers, Lent 1996.

21 *Daily Telegraph*, 2 November 1996.

22 Conversation with author, 2 June 1995.

23 Conversation with author, November 1995.

24 Jack Preger to Father Cunnane, quoted Jeremy Josephs, *Dr Jack* (Bloomsbury, 1991).

25 Conversation with author, 5 September 1995.

26 *Irish Sunday Independent*, 22 October 1995.

27 Josephs, *Dr Jack*.

28 Conversation with author, 5 September 1995.

29 Meigh, *The Jack Preger Story*.

30 Conversation with author, 5 September 1995.

31 Josephs, *Dr Jack*.

32 Conversation with author, 12 September 1995.

33 Conversation with author, 20 September 1996.

34 Ibid.

35 *Nature Medicine*, vol. 2, No. 9, September 1996.

36 Conversation with author, 7 October 1995.

37 Conversation with author, 2 October 1995.

38 Anonymous conversation with author, 11 September 1996.

39 Chawla, *Mother Teresa*.

40 S. P. Lovett, conversation with author, 28 March 1996.

CHAPTER TEN: THEOLOGY

1 Conversation with author, 20 September 1995.

2 Lucinda Vardey (compiler), *Mother Teresa: A Simple Path* (Rider Books, 1995).

3 *Daily Telegraph*, 11 November 1994.

4 Quoted Porter, *Mother Teresa*.

5 *A Simple Path.*

6 Ibid.

7 Conversation with author, 28 March 1996.

8 Conversation with author, 20 September 1995.

9 Joan Chittister OSB, *The Fire in These Ashes* (Gracewing, 1995).

10 Anonymous, conversation with author, April 1996.

11 Paul Chetcuti SJ, *Choosing to Serve the Destitute* (Irish Messenger Publications, 1980).

12 Anonymous, conversation with author, April 1996.

13 Sr Gabriel Robin, conversation with author, 20 March 1996.

14 Private information, 28 November 1995.

15 *Spectator*, 28 September 1996.

16 *Mother Teresa*, documentary (1986) by Jan Petrie.

17 Marcelle Bernstein, *Nuns* (Collins, 1976).

18 Conversation with author, 12 April 1995.

19 Conversation with author, 25 March 1996, Rome.

20 Christopher Hitchens, *The Missionary Position* (Verso, 1995).

21 Conversation with author, 28 March 1996.

22 Anonymous International Catholic Aid worker, conversation with author, February 1996.

23 Clifford Longley, *Daily Telegraph*, 11 November 1994.

24 Mother Teresa Letter to Co-Workers, Lent 1996.

25 *The Warmth of a Human Hand*, ITV documentary in series *The Human Factor*, 16 October 1988.

26 Chawla, *Mother Teresa.*

27 Conversation with author, 7 June 1996.

28 Information from St Christopher's Hospice Library.

29 Dame Cicely Saunders, conversation with author, 7 June 1996.

30 Ibid.

31 *Film Transformations*, BBC TV, 23 December 1992.

32 Chawla, *Mother Teresa.*

33 Angelo Devananda, *Mother Teresa: Contemplative at the Heart of the World* (Servant Books, 1985). This has many similar quotations such as 'When we do "our work", visit the families, teach, nurse the sick, help the dying, gather the little children for church, we should do it with one aim in view: "the salvation of the poor". We want to bring them to Jesus and bring Jesus to them.'

34 Anonymous, conversation with author, 18 November 1995.

35 Anonymous, conversation with author, 18 May 1996.
36 Mother Frances Dominica, SRN, FRCN, conversation with author, 11 April 1996.
37 *Palliative Medicine* (Edward Arnold, 1992).
38 David Ariel, *What Do Jews Believe?* (Random House, 1995).
39 Ibid.

CHAPTER ELEVEN: NUMBERS

1 LCM, *Visit to Albania*, 1993 report.
2 Conversation with author, 14 September 1995.
3 Christopher Bagley with L. Young and A. Scully, *International and Transracial Adoption* (Avebury, 1993).
4 *The Times*, 12 September 1996.
5 *Daily Telegraph*, 1 November 1996.
6 Rami Chhabra, *Abortion in India* (a Ford Foundation assisted publication, undated).
7 Letter to author, 1 June 1995.
8 Anonymous, conversation with author, 23 February 1995.
9 *Newsweek*, 18 August 1980.
10 Conversation with author, 5 October 1995, New Delhi.
11 *The Times*, 16 August 1995.
12 Conversation with author, 25 September 1996.
13 Dr Fay Hutchinson, former senior medical adviser to Brook Advisory Centres, conversation with author, 14 June 1995.

CHAPTER TWELVE: POLITICS

1 Dr L. M. Singhvi, conversation with author, 25 May 1995.
2 *Calcutta Telegraph*, 26 August 1994.
3 *Something Understood*, a Unique Broadcasting Production. Interview by Mark Tully, 18 February 1996.
4 *City of Joy*, documentary *Bandung*, 27 August 1991.
5 Amit Chaudhuri, 'Why Calcutta', *London Review of Books*, 4 January 1996.
6 Dharani Ghosh, conversation with author, 10 October 1995.
7 Anonymous former Missionary of Charity, conversation with author, 23 April 1996.
8 Devenanda, *Mother Teresa: Contemplative at the Heart of the World* (Servant Books, 1985).

9   Oxfam Project Report, 18 March 1977.

10   Conversation with author, 2 October 1995.

11   Conversation with author, 6 October 1995.

12   Conversation with author, 10 October 1995.

13   Conversation with author, 21 May 1995.

14   Michael Norton, The Non-Profit Sector in India (CAF International, 1996).

15   Conversation with author, 24 June 1996.

16   Conversation with author, 22 September 1995.

17   Muggeridge, Something Beautiful for God.

18   Conversation with author, 24 June 1996.

19   Irish Times, 7 June 1993.

20   Irish Independent, 5 June 1993.

21   CBS 60 Minutes transcript, 2 September 1994.

22   Newsweek, 18 August 1980.

23   New Albania 1989, official Government publication.

24   Albanian Catholic Bulletin, vol. XI, 1990.

25   Josephs, Dr Jack.

26   Papal Nuncio, conversation with author, July 1995, Tirana.

27   Hitchens, The Missionary Position.

28   Mother Teresa to Hon. Lance Ito, 18 January 1992.

29   Letter to author, 20 November 1996.

30   Hitchens, The Missionary Position.

31   Conversation with author, 22 August 1996.

32   Independent on Sunday, 5 May 1996.

CHAPTER THIRTEEN: EGO

1   Calcutta Telegraph, 26 August 1994.

2   Chawla, Mother Teresa.

3   Quoted Hello!, 1 October 1994.

4   Conversation with author, 2 October 1995, Delhi.

5   Sunday Express, 8 July 1990.

6   Newsweek and the Universe, 24 March 1996.

7   Conversation with author, 15 November 1995.

8   Letter to author, 7 February 1996.

9   Conversation with author, 22 August 1996.

10   Conversation with author, 7 October 1995.

11   Conversation with author, 29 November 1996.

12   Anthony Storr, Feet of Clay: A Study of Gurus (HarperCollins, 1996).

13 Devananda, *Mother Teresa*.

14 *Evening Standard*, 3 January 1992.

15 *Daily Express*, 29 March 1993.

16 Anonymous, conversation with author, 27 February 1996.

17 Conversation with author, 29 March 1996.

18 *The Times*, 29 November 1996.

19 *Independent*, 28 November 1996.

20 James Cameron, *Point of Departure* (Barker, 1967; Oriel Press 1978).

21 Conversation with author, 27 March 1996.

22 Devananda, *Mother Teresa*.

23 Fleur Cowles, *She Made Friends and Kept Them* (HarperCollins, 1996).

24 Kenneth Woodward, *Making Saints* (Chatto & Windus, 1991).

25 Peter Stanford, *Sunday Times*, 1 September 1996.

26 Ibid.

27 Woodward, *Making Saints*.

28 Conversation with author, Rome, 27 March 1996.

29 Conversation with author, Rome, 28 March 1996.

30 *Independent on Sunday*, 26 August 1990.

31 *Savvy*, October 1990.

32 *Independent*, 28 November 1996.

33 Letter to author from Random House, 11 November 1994.

34 Hitchens, *The Missionary Position*.

35 Meher Murshed, conversation with author, 12 October 1995.

36 *Counterpoint*, 3 December 1995.

37 *Sunday*, 10–16 December 1995.

38 Lavinia Byrne, conversation with author, 20 September 1995.

EPILOGUE

1 Anonymous, conversation with author, 8 January 1997.

2 Conversation with author, October 1995, Calcutta.

INDEX